EUROPEAN MONETARY UNION

In 1970 the Werner Committee recommended that the members of the European Economic Community should proceed through ordered stages of monetary integration, finally achieving full union in 1980. In that year the conference whose proceedings are recorded in this book was held at the University of Salford, after a decade in which the objective of European monetary union was first abandoned and apparently forgotten, then dramatically revived in both academic and political circles, and finally translated into limited practice in the European Monetary System.

The contributors to this volume, from Continental Europe, North America and Britain, examine these developments and assess the prospects for continued progress towards complete monetary union from both economic and political perspectives. The reasons for the breakdown of the Werner strategy are first explored, and their implications for the alternative routes towards monetary union that might be pursued in the future are considered. Despite this failure and despite, or because of, the turbulent conditions of the 1970s, the goal of monetary union attracted increasing support both at an intellectual level and among practising politicians; the sources of its revival are traced to developments in economic theory, the interpretation of which remains contentious, and to changes in the political environment.

As the visible manifestation of this revival, the European Monetary System is examined in depth, in terms of the conditions for its survival, its performance to date, its technical operations, its implications for the international monetary system and its potential as a focus for further development. Finally, some of the questions which will arise if those further developments do take place are considered, including the implications for fiscal policy, the adjustment of a monetary union to supply-side disturbances, and the essential reforms of existing political institutions.

M. T. Sumner is Professor of Economics at the University of Salford. He taught in the Universities of Sheffield, Essex, Manchester and Guelph before taking up his present post in 1978. His major research interests and publications are in the fields of macroeconomics and public finance.

G. Zis is Senior Lecturer in Economics at the University of Salford. He also taught at Manchester before moving to Salford in 1978. His research interests and publications are concentrated in the areas of inflation, monetary theory and the balance of payments.

EUROPEAN MONETARY UNION

Progress and Prospects

Edited by

M. T. Sumner and G. Zis

First published 1982 by
THE MACMILLAN PRESS LTD
London and Basingstoke
Companies and representatives
throughout the world

ISBN 0 333 30470 5

Printed in Hong Kong

Contents

Acknowledgements   vii

The Contributors   viii

Introduction   ix

1   EMU: Prospects and Retrospect   *Theo Peeters*   1

2   Experience under the EMS and Prospects for Further
    Progress towards EMU   *Michael Emerson*   18

    Comments on Peeters and Emerson   *David Cobham*   33

3   The EMS: Performance and Prospects   *Norbert Walter*   39

4   Monetary Divergences and Exchange-rate Changes in the
    European Community: the 1970s   *Roland Vaubel*   71

5   Foreign Exchange Market Intervention using an ECU-
    indicator   *Paul de Grauwe and Paul.van den Bergh*   95

    Comments on Walter, Vaubel and de Grauwe and van den
    Bergh   *R. Shone*   120

6   European Monetary Arrangements and the International
    Monetary System   *David T. Llewellyn*   123

    Comments on Llewellyn   *Geoffrey I. Lipscombe*   150

7   The Case for Flexible Exchange Rates in 1980   *David
    Laidler*   152

8   On the Relative Bias of Flexible Exchange Rates
    M. T. Sumner and G. Zis   168

Comments on Laidler and Sumner and Zis   *Geoffrey E. J. Dennis*   191

9 Increased Wage or Productivity Differentials in a Monetary Union   *Polly Reynolds Allen*   195

Comments on Allen   *M. J. Artis*   216

10 Fiscal Policy under EMU   *T. M. Rybczynski*   219

Comments on Rybczynski   *A. M. El-Agraa*   228

11 EMU: the Political Implications   *David Marquand*   232

12 European–American Relations: the Political Context   *William Wallace*   248

Comments on Marquand and Wallace   *Michael Steed*   261

Author Index   265

Acknowledgements

The conference in which this book originated would not have been possible without the generous financial support of Barclays Bank Ltd, the Nuffield Foundation, the University Association for Contemporary European Studies, and the University of Salford. The close link between the University and the City of Salford was demonstrated in the hospitality provided by the Mayor.

Within the University the Registrar's Department, in the person of Mrs L. A. Roberts, ensured that the conference was organised efficiently. Finally, Mrs Susan Mullins, Miss Irene Walsh and Mrs Shirley Woolley prepared the manuscript efficiently and coped admirably with the difficulties created for them by the editors.

The Contributors

Polly Reynolds Allen, University of Connecticut, USA
M. J. Artis, University of Manchester
Paul van den Bergh, Katholieke Universiteit Leuven, Belgium
David Cobham, University of St Andrews
Paul de Grauwe, Katholieke Universiteit Leuven, Belgium
Geoffrey E. J. Dennis, University of Loughborough
A. M. El-Agraa, University of Leeds
Michael Emerson, Commission of the European Communities, Brussels, Belgium
David Laidler, University of Western Ontario, London, Canada
Geoffrey I. Lipscombe, Lloyds Bank, London
David T. Llewellyn, University of Loughborough
David Marquand, University of Salford
Theo Peeters, Katholieke Universiteit Leuven, Belgium
T. M. Rybczynski, Lazard Bros, London
R. Shone, University of Stirling
Michael Steed, University of Manchester
M. T. Sumner, University of Salford
Roland Vaubel, Erasmus Universiteit, Rotterdam, The Netherlands
William Wallace, Royal Institute of International Affairs, London
Norbert Walter, Institut für Weltwirtschaft, Kiel, Germany
G. Zis, University of Salford

Introduction

This volume contains the papers presented at an international conference organised by and held at the University of Salford on the occasion of the tenth anniversary of the Werner Plan for European Monetary Union. When they set 1980 as the year by which European Monetary Union was to be achieved, the government leaders of the then EC member countries were embarking on a path towards a goal with international political and economic implications as profound as those of the Treaty of Rome. The original objectives of establishing a customs union and devising a common agricultural policy had been achieved. The attempt to promote European Monetary Union in the form envisaged and by the processes advocated in the Werner Plan was unsuccessful; but just as European and international politico-economic considerations prompted that first attempt, developments throughout the world during the 1970s ensured that the objective of European Monetary Union survived the failure of the Werner Plan. In October 1977 Roy Jenkins, the President of the Commission, strongly urged the EC member countries to reactivate their efforts to establish a European Monetary Union as a major contribution towards the solution of the economic problems facing not only Europe but the entire world economy. In March 1979 the European Monetary System came into operation. Its principal objective, to create a 'zone of monetary stability', falls far short of the objective set out in the Werner Plan, and of what was advocated by Jenkins. Further, one member, the UK, decided not to participate fully in the system from its inception; though it did not rule out the possibility of becoming a full member at some future date. The limited objectives of the EMS and the UK's reserved position are clear if negative manifestations of how profound the potential politico-economic implications of a European Monetary Union would be for the evolution of the EC and its member states, and for the world economy. But it could further be argued that these hesitations reflect an awareness that a new failure would have far more significant consequences than the collapse of the Werner Plan. It was the importance of the issues to which European Monetary Union gives rise

ix

that prompted the Department of Economics of Salford University to commemorate the tenth anniversary of the Werner Plan by organising this conference, in the hope that it would contribute to stimulating the discussion of a policy field which, in our opinion, has not received the attention which it deserves in the UK. The conference papers touch on a wide range of policy issues which are of interest and concern not only to academic observers but also, and perhaps more importantly, to decision-makers, especially in view of current economic developments in the UK.

The adoption of monetary union as an objective requires the policy-maker to decide on two distinct, but not necessarily independent, sets of issues. First, the nature and principal features of the preferred form of monetary union must be determined. The crucial issue is whether monetary union will involve member countries in adopting a common currency. Second, it is necessary for the eventual participants of the union to decide upon the transitional arrangements which will culminate in the achievement of monetary union. If these arrangements prove to be unworkable, monetary union will not be achieved regardless of the precise form it was envisaged to take. Conversely, the adoption of a parallel currency as the focus of the transitional arrangements would determine the basic form of the ultimate union. In the current context there arises the question of whether the survival and consolidation of the EMS can provide the basis for a future decision by EC member countries to proceed towards a full monetary union. An exchange-rate mechanism is a principal feature of the EMS, and in this respect it is to a limited degree similar to the Werner Plan which had advocated the immediate narrowing of the band of exchange-rate fluctuations as the first step in the process towards monetary union. An analysis of the reasons for the breakdown of the attempt inspired by the Werner Plan is therefore an intrinsic part of an assessment of the potential durability of the EMS. In his paper, Theo Peeters traces how monetary union gradually emerged as a desirable objective towards the end of the 1960s, and suggests that because the Bretton Woods system disintegrated sooner than was expected, the strategy embodied in the Werner Plan turned out to be inappropriate in the post–1971 international monetary conditions; though it is not clear that monetary union would have been achieved by the target date even if the Bretton Woods system had survived for a few more years. Peeters proceeds to consider the alternative but not mutually exclusive strategies of policy co-ordination and policy centralisation, and the conditions that must be met if either is to lead to the desired objective. He expresses the opinion that, though official thinking is still dominated by a preference for the policy co-ordination approach, a greater awareness of the necessity for policy centralisation may be discerned in the EMS provisions. The current situation, however, is characterised by the existence of a multitude of politico-economic forces, pulling in opposite directions, which prevent Peeters from concluding that the EC is now firmly on a path leading inevitably to monetary union.

The decision of the UK to allow sterling to float in June 1972 undermined the strategy of the Werner Plan even before it became properly operational. Many commentators greeted the establishment of the EMS with the prognosis that it, too, would rapidly collapse. By the end of 1980 the EMS was exhibiting sufficient resilience to suggest that these gloomy forecasts of its imminent disintegration were ill-founded. The performance of the EMS during its first eighteen months and its future prospects are the subjects of two papers: one by an academic, Norbert Walter, and the second by a participant in the policy-making process, Michael Emerson. The latter is sufficiently encouraged by what has been achieved during 1979 and 1980 to suggest that the objective of monetary union is not only feasible but also credible. This optimism rests to a large extent on the recognition that the parallel currency approach, with all its implications, has recently become more widely acceptable among policy-makers. Walter is more agnostic in his conclusions. Although he discerns a tendency towards greater convergence of member countries' monetary policies, a necessary condition for the long-run survival of the EMS, the continuing dominant influence of the dollar in international monetary conditions and the unpredictability of US monetary policy lead the author to emphasise that the fate of the EMS is not likely to be determined solely by internal developments.

The degree to which monetary conditions have converged in the EC during the 1970s relative to the 1960s is the subject of more detailed analysis in the paper by Roland Vaubel. He presents evidence to show that the dispersion of inflation rates in the Nine during the last decade was more than twice as large as in the 1960s. The difference, however, is nothing like as sharp if sterling and the lira are excluded from the relevant calculations. Of direct relevance for any assessment of the prospects for the EMS is Vaubel's conclusion that the degree of monetary divergence during the period immediately prior to its establishment was, at best, about the same as that for the years 1969–72. Given the collapse of the Bretton Woods system, however, and its consequences for the post-1973 dispersion of inflation rates, there is no contradiction between Vaubel's and Walter's conclusions on the issue of monetary convergence. Vaubel's study, in presenting evidence of a relationship between changes in nominal and real exchange rates and in demonstrating that the direction of causality in this relationship is ambiguous, is of special relevance to current discussions in the UK of sterling's behaviour in the foreign exchange markets.

Paul de Grauwe and Paul van den Bergh focus on an important technical question concerning the EMS. Recognising that any exchange-rate system which requires the systematic intervention of central monetary authorities in the foreign exchange market is unlikely to survive unless founded on a symmetrical adjustment mechanism, architects of the EMS established the European Currency Unit (ECU) as an 'indicator of divergence'. A member country whose currency's exchange rate *vis-à-vis* the ECU deviates by more than a specified amount is obliged to take corrective measures, which have tended to take the form of foreign exchange market intervention rather than more fundamental actions. De Grauwe and van den Bergh examine the consequences for symmetry when intervention in the foreign exchange market is conducted in alternative currencies and in response to different indicators. It will be recalled that this issue, popularly described as 'grids versus baskets', played a prominent, and probably disproportionate, role in British discussions of the EMS during the period preceding its introduction. De Grauwe and van den Bergh report that the choice of intervention currency is crucial in determining whether a 'snake' type of system operates symmetrically, but that it has little significance when the ECU is used as an indicator of divergence. Use of the dollar, or any other outside currency, to maintain the grid of cross rates produced an asymmetrical response to disturbances, whereas intervention in member countries' currencies produced responses comparable in symmetry to those obtained with the ECU-indicator.

Taken in combination, the papers on the EMS provide some reason to expect the system to survive. Whether it becomes the first stage in a progression towards full monetary union depends on future developments. At the intellectual level one potentially important development, to which Emerson draws attention, is increased familiarity with and acceptance of the concept of a parallel currency. Originally proposed as a route towards European monetary union in 1975 and strongly endorsed by Peeters, the issue of a parallel indexed currency would eventually drive existing national currencies out of circulation. Its exchange rate with the currencies of non-member countries would be market-determined; if that were not the case then foreign monetary policies would be capable of destroying the guaranteed constancy of the new currency's purchasing power. This is one of many examples of how efforts to promote and ultimately achieve European Monetary Union would affect international monetary relations. Indeed, it is generally accepted that the volatility of exchange rates after 1973 was a major reason why Germany, in particular, as well as the other EC member countries decided to establish the EMS. The interdependence of international and European monetary arrangements is considered in the paper by David Llewellyn, who traces in the decline of the Bretton Woods system the emergence of divergent views among the EC member countries on how the international monetary system should be reformed, a divergence which condemned the Werner Plan to failure. Agreement on a new international monetary system did not materialise during the 1970s. The inability to reach such an agreement encouraged the EC to seek a regional and, therefore, partial solution to the exchange-rate problems associated with the 'dirty' floating system. Llewellyn expresses the opinion that the EMS could induce greater exchange-rate stability at a world level. Whether it will do so in fact depends on the degree of convergence between EC and US monetary policies. He argues that, although inflation and the exchange rate are monetary phenomena, it cannot be assumed that governments will not seek to exploit the short-run real effects of changes in monetary policy and, thus, not only delay the creation of a new international monetary system but ultimately undermine the existence of the EMS itself.

Monetary union, with or without the adoption of a common currency by the participating countries, necessarily implies, at least temporarily, fixity of exchange rates. Therefore, the advocacy of monetary union rests to a large extent on the advantages of fixed relative to flexible exchange rates. David Laidler concedes that the economic case for fixed exchange rates cannot be disputed on theoretical grounds. He argues, however, that the case for flexible exchange rates rests on political considerations. Flexibility of exchange rates allows an individual country to pursue its preferred rate of monetary growth independently of the rest of the world and, thus, to determine its own rate of inflation. The discipline of periodically having to face the electorate is considered sufficient to ensure that inflation is kept within acceptable bounds. Laidler goes on to argue that existing political institutions in parliamentary democracies constrain governments to act as if they are monetarily independent. Therefore, flexibility of exchange rates is the only system compatible with current and long established political structures. Michael Sumner and George Zis in their paper reach conclusions which sharply contrast with those of Laidler on the political desirability of flexible exchange rates. Their argument can be summarised in the proposition that flexibility of exchange rates, by increasing the natural rate of unemployment, makes the control and reduction of the inflation rate more costly in terms of unemployment, and therefore a less attractive policy objective.

Two papers are devoted to problems of operating, rather than establishing, a monetary union. Polly Allen analyses the implications for the union and its individual members of supply-side disturbances originating in one of them. She demonstrates that the scope for stabilisation through the fiscal instruments available to individual members is severely limited, and concludes that the effectiveness of fiscal policy would be enhanced if it were conducted by the union, rather than at the level of the individual member. A similar theme is developed by Theo Rybczynski. He outlines the evolution of fiscal policy in Europe, and argues that under a monetary union fiscal policy should be assigned to the elimination of regional disparities. Both these papers touch on areas where the boundary between economics and other disciplines is imprecisely located, and in the process they inevitably raise political issues. These are the explicit focus of the remaining papers.

Whatever their view as to the desirability of monetary union, economists agree that a necessary condition for the success of any strategy aimed at monetary union is that there exists the political commitment to this objective. Such a commitment must rest on a recognition of the international as well as the domestic political implications of a monetary union which encompasses only some of the major countries. The achievement of monetary union inevitably involves the replacement of existing domestic political institutions with new ones. David Marquand devotes his paper to an analysis of the political and institutional implications of monetary union. The current EC structural framework is based on the existence of national institutions which involve a large measure of independence for governments in determining domestic policy. The establishment of a European Monetary Union would require the surrender of national autonomy and, therefore, the substitution of supranational institutions for the current national institutions. Moreover, the existing institutional structure of the EC does not provide an adequate foundation. Marquand concludes that for monetary union to be achieved it is necessary that institutional reform must proceed so as to promote the political commitment to the objective of monetary union. So long as national governments continue to bear responsibility for the consequences of policies determined at a supranational level, their commitment to those policies will remain strictly limited.

The political and institutional implications of a movement towards European Monetary Union would not be confined to Europe itself. Its relations with the USA and the institutional structure of the Western Alliance would both be drastically changed. William Wallace analyses the evolution and current state of 'the atmosphere of Atlantic relations'. It is argued that the Atlantic relationship in 1980 is not that which prevailed in the 1950s. A major reason for this change is that the perception of the 'Soviet threat' in Europe has altered and, as a consequence, there is radically less willingness to accept American leadership unquestioningly. Further, doubts relating to America's military commitment to Europe and the emergence of conflicting interests between the leader and the followers have also contributed to Europe's desire to assert its independence *vis-à-vis* the US. But this shift in European attitudes, Wallace suggests, has been accompanied by a similar change in the US position *vis-à-vis* Europe. America is now much less concerned with European developments, and its stance has become increasingly introverted. Though the atmosphere of Atlantic relations is not such as to prevent progress towards European Monetary Union, existing ambiguities may act as obstacles if, for example, the UK continues to pursue the resurrection of its special relationship with the USA, or if the latter adopts domestic policies which are not compatible with the orderly evolution of the EMS.

All the papers generated lively discussion from the floor as well as the comments contained in this volume. It is our hope that they will be equally fruitful in stimulating the readers of this book.

1 EMU: Prospects and Retrospect

THEO PEETERS

The purpose of this chapter is not to offer a detailed account of the history of European monetary integration. Excellent accounts are available such as the well-documented book by L. Tsoukalis (1977), which was a major source of information in writing the first section of this chapter. We will rather focus on a general reflection about the nature of, and the problems posed by, European Monetary Union (EMU) in the specific context of the European integration process.

The first section of this chapter starts with a retrospect on the background of EMU leading up to the celebrated blueprint of the Werner Committee. This will set the tone for a discussion of alternative strategies for monetary unification. A (modest) look into the future is attempted in a final section on the prospects for EMU.

This chapter by its nature is not an attempt to offer an original contribution to our knowledge about the subject. Its purpose is rather to set a framework that can put other contributions in a broader perspective.

RETROSPECT

The objective of the Treaty of Rome has not only been the creation of a Common Market organising a free movement of goods, services, persons and capital. Article 2 of the Treaty sets the target of 'establishing a Common Market *and* progressively approximating the economic policies of member states . . . '[author's italics]. But the formulation chosen suggests a distinction between two objectives, namely that of '*establishing* a Common Market' and 'progressively *approximating* the economic policies of member states'. The contrast is clearly traceable to

1

the articles devoted respectively to the liberalisation of trade and factor movements and to the economic and monetary policies in the EC. Whereas for the former rather detailed obligations including precise time-tables are set up, nothing comparable can be found on the subject of common economic policies. In the latter case the relevant articles express only a fairly vague agreement about objectives. EMU is not specifically mentioned as an objective in the Treaty of Rome, which contains virtually no obligation that might disturb the freedom for manoeuvre of those member states that remain firmly attached to the principle of national sovereignty in monetary matters.

It is useful to keep this institutional fact in mind when discussing the prospects for further developments towards EMU. It implies indeed that, given the very few and vague provisions relating to economic and monetary policies in the Treaty of Rome, the necessary coalitions for an agreement on steps to be taken in order to move towards EMU have to be built from scratch. Such a coalition, and the specific proposals resulting from it, therefore, depend on a sufficient convergence of interests among the member states. It has been the fate of the rather ambitious plans for EMU launched at the beginning of the seventies that the convergence of interests upon which they were built either did not last very long or was only apparent. This point is stressed heavily and convincingly as one of his main conclusions by Tsoukalis in his study of the history and politics of EMU.

The absence of EMU as an explicit objective in the EC Treaty should not be attributed to a lack of interest in the subject at the time the Treaty was drafted. Monetary unification in the EEC was a topic of discussion and analysis before the signing of the Treaty of Rome, as Peter Oppenheimer (1979) has reminded us. Tibor Scitovsky (1958, ch. 2) wrote an early authoritative contribution on the subject as did James Meade (1957), whose article is still a classic in the field. But it should also be remembered that in 1957 when the EC Treaty was signed, the member states of the Community still adhered to the transitional arrangements under article XIV of the International Monetary Fund. It was only in 1961 that they re-established officially the external convertibility of their currencies and accepted the full obligations under article VIII of the IMF agreement. The cautious and vague approach to the issue of monetary integration and co-operation in the Treaty of Rome can, therefore, hardly be a surprise.

Furthermore, it is difficult to envisage how in the second half of the fifties it would have been easier than at the end of the sixties and the early seventies to reach a consensus on future common economic and monetary policies. The German insistence on the 'social market economy' together with the strong opposition of Mr Erhard, German Minister for Economic Affairs, to extensive government intervention – in contrast with views held in other member states – precluded an agreement on the details which common policies would require.

As a result of both economic feasibility and political acceptability the Treaty focussed on the *integration of markets* through the elimination of artificial barriers to the free flow of goods and services, rather than on the *integration of economic and monetary policies* which EMU requires. The notable exception of the weak emphasis on policy integration is, of course, the Common Agricultural Policy (CAP). But the CAP can be seen as an extension of the process of market integration in the Treaty of Rome. Indeed, given the existing extensive involvement of all national governments in agriculture and this for similar purposes, the obvious strategy to create a common market for agricultural products was to replace separate national policies by a common policy. Already in the early years of the EC various initiatives were taken which attempted to redress the aforementioned imbalance in the Treaty of Rome. Proposals which intended to initiate some co-operation in the monetary field emanated from the economic and financial commission of the European Parliament, the Action Committee for the United States of Europe (the so-called Monnet Committee) guided by the advice of Robert Triffin, and the Commission in its Action Programme for the Second Stage in 1962. But very few concrete results were reached in the field of monetary co-operation before 1969, except for the creation of a set of committees within which co-ordination of monetary, budgetary, conjunctural and medium-term policies, as well as prior consultations on these matters, were supposed to take place.

The fact is that in the period between 1958 and 1969 the Six experienced chronic balance-of-payments surpluses and mounting foreign exchange reserves. Consequently, the internal pressure for greater monetary co-operation inside Europe was lacking. International monetary problems which became the dominant preoccupation of governments during that period were the gradual weakening of the two reserve currencies, the dollar and the pound, and the consequent erosion of the foundations of the existing international monetary system. These external preoccupations could not, however, trigger closer monetary co-operation inside Europe that could result in the creation of a distinct regional monetary bloc. It is symptomatic that in the middle of the sixties the Monetary Committee devoted most of its time to attempting to reach a Community point of view in the international monetary reform talks. But the conflicting views of this matter which often prevailed between France and its other five partners precluded a common position on external monetary policies. This fact alone was a sufficient stumbling-block to any initiative that might try to bring about greater monetary unity.

It was only after 1968 that things changed under external as well as internal pressures. At that time a convergence of widely different interests resulted in a favourable climate in which new initiatives could prosper:

(i) The disintegration of the Bretton Woods system, after the *de facto* end of the gold convertibility of the dollar which followed the creation of the two-tier gold market in March 1968, strengthened the case of those who argued for the creation of a European monetary bloc. They stressed that whereas the member states had become *commercially* integrated with one another, *monetarily* they still communicated mainly with and through the dollar. This could cause sharp conflicts, e.g. when trade cycles diverged on the two sides of the Atlantic. Several factors, including the growth of the Eurodollar market, accentuated monetary interdependence. But given the great disproportion between the US and the fragmented European national markets, interdependence was perceived as being rather lopsided. It was thought that monetary integration would redress the balance and offer Europe a better protection against the instability that resulted from an increasingly weak dollar.

(ii) The parity changes which took place in 1969, in particular the devaluation of the French franc, marked the end of a widespread belief in permanent fixity of intra-EEC exchange rates. And it was thought that this would put at risk '*l' acquis communautaire*', i.e. the customs union and the CAP. The monetary crises of 1968 and 1969 destroyed the illusion of the existence of a *de facto* monetary union which had been nourished by a fairly long period of intra-Community exchange-rate stability under the Bretton Woods rules. The following quotation documents this point.

In its Seventh Report, the Monetary Committee, usually very cautious in these matters, stated: 'progressive integration within the EEC . . . will make devaluation or revaluation increasingly difficult and unlikely. The establishment of a single agricultural market will strengthen this trend'. The Commission hastened to add in its own report that 'the task of the Community institutions is now to render internal devaluation or revaluation impossible or unnecessary instead of merely difficult or unlikely'. It seems that fixity of exchange rates, seen as the core element of monetary union together with the introduction of a common EEC currency, were adopted during the first half of 1965 as the major strategic objectives by the Commission.

(Tsoukalis, 1977, p. 60)

In good neofunctionalist tradition, which dominated thinking on European integration during the sixties, it was thought that the realisation of monetary integration would follow from the logic of European economic integration based on the free movement of goods, services and factors of production among the member states. The neofunctionalist view of the process of integration is that because economic issues and tasks are related functionally, spill-over effects occur which bring about a need for strengthening of general co-operation and integration once co-operation and integration on specific issues have been initiated. The CAP, with its system of common agricultural prices, is a typical example of this approach and way of thinking.

The adoption of a CAP would not only lead to common agricultural prices, but also to fixed intra-EEC exchange rates. This would enforce a closer co-ordination of economic policies on national governments and would ultimately lead to a complete monetary union. Obviously, the other alternative, which was not usually mentioned, would be the collapse of the system of fixed exchange rates together with the CAP.

(Tsoukalis, 1977, p. 62)

Against this background it was logical that initiatives were taken to strengthen intra-European monetary co-operation after the first setback of the monetary crises of 1968 and 1969.

(iii) The end of the transition period left the Community searching for a new mobilising force which could maintain the momentum of European integration after the successful completion of the customs union and the CAP. Initiatives in the monetary field appeared as the logical next step. The objective of monetary union, to be achieved during the seventies, was put forward as the challenge for sustained progress towards the ultimate goal of political union in the same spirit as the creation of the Common Market had fulfilled this role during the sixties.

The rest of the history is well known. In the spring of 1969 the Commission came up with a memorandum – the so-called (first) Barre Plan – which called for tighter consultations between member states concerning economic policy in general and monetary policy in particular. It also included a specific program of short-term monetary support and medium-term financial assistance which would be available to member states in addition to existing international mechanisms. In December 1969 at the Summit in the Hague, the Heads of State formally proclaimed economic and monetary union, to be created in stages, as a long-run aim of the Community. In the months following, a number of actions were taken to implement the resolution adopted at the Hague Summit, including the appointment of a high-level group under the chairmanship of the Prime Minister of Luxembourg, Pierre Werner.

The Werner Committee produced, in October 1970, its celebrated blueprint for EMU, a goal for which a precise date (1980) was set. The Committee itself summarised the major characteristics and most important consequences of EMU as follows:

– the Community currencies will be assured of total irreversible mutual convertibility free from fluctuations in rates and with immutable parity rates, or preferably they will be replaced by a sole Community currency;
– the creation of liquidity throughout the area and monetary and credit policy will be centralised;
– monetary policy in relation to the outside world will be within the jurisdiction of the Community;
– the policies of the Member States as regards the capital market will be unified;
– the essential features of the whole of the public budgets, and in particular variations in their volume, the size of balances and the methods of financing or utilizing them, will be decided at the Community level;
– regional and structural policies will no longer be exclusively within the jurisdiction of the member countries;
– a systematic and continuous consultation between the social partners will be ensured at the Community level.   (Commission of the European Communities, 1970, p.12)

Institutional reform is explicitly envisaged. Two institutions in particular, together with the political implications that go with them, are mentioned in this respect: (i) the creation of a centre of decision for economic policy which will exercise independently, in accordance with the Community interest, a decisive influence over the general economic policy of the Community, and (ii) a Community system for the central banks along the lines of the US Federal Reserve System.

It appears that the members of the Werner Committee had a sufficiently clear view on the implications of the *final* objective to be achieved and that they were in broad agreement on this matter. Disagreement arose with respect to the means and methods to be adopted in order to arrive there. The Werner Report contains detailed proposals for a first stage but remains vague about the intermediate period before the final stage would be reached. In addition, member governments were quick to ignore the implications of the final stage of EMU, and concentrated all their diplomatic skills in shaping up a workable proposal for stage one. The result was a compromise between the antagonistic views of the French and the Germans. The Germans insisted on the prior setting of consistent policy objectives, and on policy co-ordination to meet these objectives, as a necessary condition for EMU. For France, the emphasis was on narrower margins of exchange-rate fluctuations, pooling of reserves and extended credit facilities and financial assistance. Effective co-ordination of economic policies would automatically result under the disciplining force coming in particular from the exchange-rate arrangement.

In practice, the French view prevailed over the German one. Lip service was paid to a better co-ordination of economic and monetary policies, but explicit commitments with clearly defined rules were restricted to the exchange-rate arrangement, the intervention mechanism and the monetary support. Subsequent history has refuted the expectations of a sufficiently strong disciplining force which would follow (automatically) from abiding by the rules of the agreed exchange-rate arrangement.

Experience, therefore, testified to the lack of success of the approach chosen. But did the Werner strategy fail simply because of an unlucky coincidence of unfavourable events, or should the failure rather be attributed to basic deficiencies in the design of the system? It is usually pointed out that the collapse of the Bretton Woods system, the energy crisis and the inflationary explosion during the seventies killed the first attempt to move towards EMU. These factors do suggest that the former explanation carries great weight. But are these arguments really convincing? A careful reading of history, together with arguments put forward initially in support of the objective of EMU, indicate that EMU was considered precisely as a collective European answer to the disintegration of the existing international monetary system. EMU was also expected to be instrumental in achieving greater convergence in economic performance and objectives inside Europe; and one might add that even the energy crisis could have acted as a catalyst, stirring up efforts that would speed up the process of monetary integration rather than acting as a major stumbling-block.

The truth is that arguing along these lines means that the logical sequence of the arguments is turned upside down: the problems towards the solution of which EMU was supposed to contribute are in turn used as an explanation of the failure of the system. This points rather towards basic deficiencies in the design as the major explanation for the failure. Of course, the extent of the problems EMU would have to cope with was undoubtedly amplified as a result of the aforementioned events beyond what could reasonably have been expected at the time the plans were drafted. Nevertheless, the Werner strategy took the Bretton Woods system for granted, while at the same time preparing for a European response to its imminent collapse. It was unable to adjust quickly enough to the changing challenges and to overcome the ambiguities, known as political compromises, that were necessary to build a consensus not only on the objectives of the undertaking but also on the instruments and methods. The convergence of interests out of which EMU was born did not last very long.

This is not to say that the interest, the attitudes and policies of different countries towards EMU have been determined by short-term tactical considerations alone. Real economic motives and long-term objectives did undoubtedly play an important role. Interest in the issue, therefore, has not and will not fade away. This is sufficiently demonstrated by the launching of the European Monetary System (EMS) in the spring of 1979. This chapter does not go into a direct discussion of EMS as there is a separate chapter covering this topic. In the next section we rather focus on a general reflection about possible alternative strategies for moving towards EMU.

THE CHOICE OF STRATEGIES

The experience of the seventies underlined the need for a re-appraisal of the strategy for monetary integration. In his authoritative study on the strategies for currency unification, Roland Vaubel (1978) distinguishes *two major alternatives*, the co-ordination strategy and the centralisation strategy, each with three possible variants. In order to discriminate between the various alternatives Vaubel introduces *two conditions* that have to be met for a strategy to pass the test of a feasible and viable approach towards EMU. These conditions are that the approach should be gradual and at the same time automatic. We will first deal with the conditions before commenting upon the alternative strategies.

Conditions for a viable strategy

A strategy for EMU requires political feasibility as well as economic viability. Both requirements suggests that *gradualism* should rank high in any approach. The political argument is that, except for a major crisis, like war or its aftermath, it would not be feasible to generate at a particular moment in time the political support which brings currency unification all at once. Even the most devoted European among the political leaders of our member states would prefer a transition process that would allow for gradual adjustment of institutional structures and a slow erosion, at least formally, of national sovereignty.

From an economic point of view, a gradual process of monetary unification has the advantage of reducing and spreading the transitory costs which such a move involves. These transition costs are usually linked to the stabilisation-induced unemployment while the high inflation countries adjust to a (lower) Community inflation rate. A gradual process also facilitates the adjustment of expectations of economic agents and, therefore, reduces possible errors when they try to anticipate (or fail to perceive) the trend of the change. *Automaticity*, as opposed to discretionary decision-taking, is also important in the process of monetary integration. Progress towards EMU which depends upon successive negotiations and repeated discretionary policy decisions maximises political friction among member states. EMU is constantly in danger of losing its initial coalition of support built upon a convergence of interests as these interests (or their perception) change over time. Governments always try as much as possible to avoid unconditional commitments. This guarantees the option for accommodation over time of the arrangements agreed upon. In practice, it is usually more than just 'accommodation' to changing circumstances one is interested in when member states want to retain their power of discretion and the instruments to exercise it. In fact they keep open the possibility of either opting out or violating the agreement.

The economic case for automaticity is even more compelling. Automaticity increases predictability in economic decision-making, and hence stability in economic conditions and processes. Reduced uncertainty, in turn, lowers risks and avoids the efficiency losses that result from false expectations about discretionary government measures.

Alternative strategies

Although an old saying tells us that all roads lead to Rome, it appears
that this is not always true of the roads that are built to lead to EMU. Of
course, it is profane to compare the Eternal City with EMU and the
difference, therefore, should not surprise us. But for the roads that may
lead to EMU, it is necessary to remember that some of these roads are
more tortuous than others, as is the case even for Rome. It appears that
the officially preferred approach so far for monetary integration in
Europe is by no means the one which promises the quickest and the
easiest journey. It may be that it is the only one which is politically
acceptable, but that does not ensure that the strategy is at the same time
economically viable. Which strategies then are available? Official
thinking on EMU has been dominated by the so-called *co-ordination
strategy*. It is argued under this approach that through co-ordination of
economic and monetary policies, it is possible to overcome inconsistencies in national economic objectives and policy behaviour that
would otherwise upset balance-of-payments equilibrium under fixed
exchange rates among member states as well as their internal balance.
The approach focusses either on the exchange rates, on domestic
monetary policy co-ordination, or on a mixture of both.

Exchange rate co-ordination has so far attracted most official
support. The objective is to limit intra-European exchange-rate variability through a gradual narrowing of margins of fluctuations and/or
by restricting the scope for parity adjustments. The system is based upon
a set of rules for central bank interventions in exchange markets,
together with a network of monetary support arrangements for deficit
countries. The snake arrangement falls under this approach and it is still
a key element under the present EMS. It is expected that the
commitment to exchange-rate unification together with central bank
interventions will *de facto* achieve the required harmonisation of
domestic monetary policies. The strategy gambles quite heavily on
national self-discipline. It also expects that somehow the interference
with other member states' monetary policies, which foreign exchange
market intervention inevitably entails, will not be neutralised, so that
money supplies consistent with fixed exchange rates will result.

Domestic monetary policy co-ordination, on the contrary, does not
concentrate on the exchange rate as the operational target. The objective
is rather to achieve *ex ante* harmonisation of domestic monetary policies
directly. It is then expected that explicit and pre-announced money
supply targets are set such that they will be consistent with and result in

exchange-rate fixity. A major weakness of this approach is, of course, that the current state of the arts makes this quite a demanding job. Even if member states honoured an agreement to let their money supply grow by the estimated growth of their respective real GNP plus the common target for inflation, it is unlikely that this would lead to exchange-rate constancy. Although relative rates of monetary expansion adjusted for real growth are a very significant factor in explaining exchange-rate movements, the available evidence also shows that their explanatory power is far from complete (on this matter see Vaubel, 1978, pp. 22–30).

The weakness of the two previous strategies automatically suggests a third one, namely a combination of explicit exchange-rate commitments together with *ex ante* monetary policy agreements. The proposal then is for the combination of a price cartel (the exchange-rate union) supported by a quantity cartel (the money supply commitment). A key problem of this approach is, of course, that it requires annually recurrent discussions (negotiations) about money supply targets that might prove to be at least as painful and as divisive as the annual EC farm price review. This is certainly the case if one recalls the purely technical problems involved in estimating money supply targets consistent with exchange-rate constancy.

The most one can expect, therefore, from the co-ordination approach is greater exchange-rate *stability*. It cannot assure permanent exchange-rate *fixity* and it does not lead to the creation of a common currency. *A fortiori*, it is not a strategy, even in its most ambitious form, that will lead to monetary *union*. For a strategy which will bring about EMU, something more, if not something different, is needed. To understand what that might involve we now turn to the *centralisation strategy*, in which three variants are again distinguished.

First of all, one can mention the immediate shift to a European currency. It is an apocalyptic solution which replaces national currencies without any transitional phase. It would call for the immediate centralisation of wide powers in the hands of a European monetary authority, and the subordination to it of each of the national central banks. The political advantages of the merger of the national currencies in one big leap are obvious. It exploits the willingness of the member states to accept monetary union at once. But it is difficult to envisage what under normal circumstances could bring about the shock that is needed to get this solution accepted.

Free currency competition is advocated as a second road to centralisation. It relies on the abolition of all capital controls and the admission of all member currencies for use throughout the Community.

It is expected that only the most useful, i.e. the most stable, currency will survive in the long run. Since the better currency will outdo the others, centralisation of monetary policy is brought about through the market process. The approach does, however, imply a radical departure from the laws and regulations at present in force in the member states. It also means that one national currency will effectively become the common currency. We abstract from even more far-reaching options in the currency competition approach that consider the denationalisation of money through an unrestricted competitive supply of private high-powered money (see, for example, Hayek, 1976).

It is through a process comparable to currency competition that international reserve and transaction currencies impose themselves. However, the fact that national currencies get used for these purposes exacerbates national rivalries and stimulates political frictions. It may be enough to remember in this respect Gaullist complaints during the sixties about the exorbitant privileges of the dollar as a key currency. Such a prospect would be quite damaging in the European context.

A third variant, therefore, suggests that currency competition and substitution be confined to a process where only the prospective Community currency circulates freely alongside each national currency. The approach relies on a European Parallel Currency (EPC) as an instrument of currency unification. It is expected that the EPC will not only compete with, but also outdo eventually, the existing national currencies, thus bringing about currency unification. Whether the EPC will be able to achieve this depends upon its attractiveness and usefulness. For that purpose, it is important for the EPC's value to be more stable than the value of its competitors. Incidentally, this requirement rules out the ECU in its current definition as a possible candidate for the EPC. As an average of the member states' currencies based on a constant basket it can at best successfully compete only with the weaker, not with the stronger, national currencies.

Without going into further details about this most promising approach, it is necessary to clear away at least the most common political objection against the EPC-alternative. The EPC is not a *deus ex machina* designed to circumvent the political process and obstacles. Although it minimises political friction in the long run, it is not and cannot be a substitute for explicit political agreement on the desirability of monetary unification. But it should also be stressed that a decision to move ahead with the EPC-approach is not equivalent to the immediate elimination of the weaker national currencies. Ben Klein (1978) has argued that even an EPC with a purchasing-power guarantee, like the one suggested in the All Saints' Day Manifesto (Basevi *et al.*, 1975), might not succeed in displacing the intrinsically weaker national currencies because it would not be sufficiently attractive.

PROSPECTS

In 1980, the year by which the Werner Committee proclaimed EMU was attainable, I would not dare predict that EMU will ever come about, and even less a possible date for that event. The imminent enlargement will certainly not make things easier. That does not mean that the time has come to write a post-mortem on the subject. The issue is still alive, as well as the real economic motives and long-term objectives behind it.

Some concluding thoughts, therefore, are submitted in an attempt to stimulate discussion and to shed some light on possible future trends.

(i) Official strategy is still strongly oriented towards the co-ordination approach. But a timid attempt has been made in the EMS to extend the exchange-rate commitments in the direction of more automatic policy co-ordination. The introduction of the ECU-divergence indicator is expected to trigger off better policy co-ordination. It is nevertheless symptomatic that in the official statements EMS is not considered as a first stage of an overall plan which is expected to bring about EMU. The focus is rather on short-run exchange stability (a European zone of monetary stability). EMS is not expected to guarantee long-run exchange-rate fixity.

(ii) The next steps currently under discussion concern (a) the creation of a European Monetary Fund (EMF) into which the existing monetary support mechanisms might be consolidated, and (b) the status of the ECU and its uses inside and outside the EMS. Although it was agreed that these matters would be settled two years after the start of the EMS in March 1979, the discussions in the autumn of 1980 are still in the exploratory phase. The initial deadline once more will not be respected.

The design of the EMF raises both questions of internal planning of the relations among member states, and questions concerning the relations between the EMF, other institutions and the world monetary and financial system at large (see for more details the European Monetary Fund, 1980). The Resolution of the European Council in Brussels establishing the EMS states that the credit mechanisms 'will be consolidated into a single fund in the final phase of the EMS'. Currently the financial support mechanisms have a double characteristic: they are largely bilateral credits, the book-keeping of which is entrusted to the EMCF (European Monetary Co-operation Fund); and since the EMCF which issues the ECUs is only a book-keeping agent, the credit mechanisms themselves involve no direct creation of ECUs. Two issues are, therefore, under discussion: the consolidation of the existing credit mechanisms, and the possibility of the EMF creating ECUs against credit. The current arrangements function on the basis of a transfer of liquidity from one country to another. Consolidation only of the various credit facilities into one system would streamline the system, but is not expected to raise major difficulties. But things would be different if the EMF were entrusted with the power to issue ECUs against credits. Granting credits by the EMF would then become a new source of international liquidity creation. The limits and the conditions under which the EMF would exercise this power clearly need to be spelled out.

Under the existing EMS rules the ECU functions as the numeraire in the exchange-rate system, as the basis for the divergence indicator, as the denominator for the intervention operations, and as a means of settlement between monetary authorities of the Community. But the ECU lacks the essential characteristics of money: it is not a means of payment; there is no autonomous creation of ECUs, they are only created as a substitute for other reserve assets; and although they figure as a reserve asset in the balance sheet of central banks they are only the book-keeping counterpart of the gold and dollar reserves against which they are issued under swap arrangements.

If the ECUs are to have a permanent existence of their own, the temporary arrangements have to become permanent. Transfer of gold and dollar reserves to the EMF would solve this problem but it is politically a very sensitive solution. Creation of ECUs against credit would also enhance their perennial character.

The use of the ECU is also to be extended. The full utilisation of the ECU in the Community official circuit requires the abolition of existing limits of acceptability in intra-Community settlements. But this presupposes also a strengthening of the quality of the ECU in terms of its convertibility as well as its yield, if the ECU is to compete successfully with other reserve assets. Another major aspect of an enlarged role for the ECU is whether and how the ECU could be used outside the Community central bank network in private markets and with third countries. The use by the private sector will normally result from spontaneous developments. But official institutions could play a role by stimulating banks to open ECU-denominated accounts, to issue ECU-denominated loans and to accept the ECU as a unit of account in contracts. Different developments can be thought of in the use of the ECU in relations with third countries, including its use as a reserve instrument by third countries, its possible role in the recycling of petro-dollars, and most important perhaps, the ECU could act as a catalyst to bring about at last an effective EMS dollar policy.

The institutional structure of the EMF will depend upon the functions entrusted to it. The various options envisaged include (a) a modest enlargement of the current responsibilities of the EMCF, (b) a regional-IMF-type EMF under a government-dominated authority with central bank participation, (c) a central-bank-type EMF with primary responsi-bility in the monetary, financial support and exchange-rate field, and a governing body organised along the lines of the US Federal Reserve System, and (d) an institution with a mixture of economic and monetary responsibility run by an *ad hoc* mixture of central bankers and government officials. The choices involved are highly political and preferences across member states may diverge widely. It is to be expected that the German Bundesbank, for example, will be very anxious to preserve its constitutional independence against political pressures, a position not enjoyed to the same extent by its colleagues in other member states. Germany may, therefore, favour a monetary consti-tution at the European level that goes against the traditions in other member states. Although they are conceptually different, it will soon become clear that three aspects of the EMF problem will be hard to disentangle, namely the functions of the Fund, the organic structure of the Fund, and the link between the Fund, national monetary authorities (Treasuries and central banks), and Community institutions.

(iii) The specific aspects mentioned under the previous point about the immediate prospects of the EMS are illustrative of a general lesson to be drawn about the future strategy towards EMU. It suggests that the various approaches discussed in the previous section are not necessarily mutually exclusive, but that they may be used in combination. Although this does not necessarily correspond to a theoretically optimal currency unification process, it may be dictated by political realism. The issue then is whether and how the co-ordination strategy can gradually be replaced by centralisation.

Co-ordination alone will not bring about EMU. At some point the centralisation strategy becomes necessary if real progress towards EMU is desired. However, the centralisation strategy, and in particular the EPC-approach, is not an all-or-nothing choice at once. But it should be understood that it incorporates at some stage a monetary reform in the process of monetary integration without which currency unification will not be attained. The President of the Commission, Roy Jenkins (1978, p. 14) in his Jean Monnet Lecture, has used a nice metaphor to describe the process leading to EMU: 'Let us think of a long-jumper. He starts with a rapid succession of steps, lengthens his stride, increases his momentum, and then makes his leap. The creation of a monetary union would be a leap of this kind. . . . We have to look before we leap, and know where we are to land. But leap we eventually must.'

My perhaps over-optimistic understanding of the metaphor would then be as follows. The co-ordination approach is the running start to the centralisation strategy, which will ultimately land us in the Nirvana of currency unification. But let us be constantly aware of the fact that it is easy to stumble along the road if one does not watch one's steps, or if one starts off on the wrong foot. To insist on exchange-rate unification as the first step towards EMU puts the whole approach on the wrong foot.

REFERENCES

Basevi, G., M. Fratianni, H. Giersch, P. Korteweg, D. O' Mahony, M. Parkin, T. Peeters, P. Salin and N. Thygesen (1975), 'The All Saints' Day Manifesto for European monetary union: a Currency for Europe', *The Economist*, 1 November; reprinted in M. Fratianni and T. Peeters (eds), *One Money for Europe* (London: Macmillan, 1978).
Commission of the European Communities (1970), 'Report to the Council and the Commission on the Realization by Stages of Economic and Monetary Union in the Community' (Werner Report), *Bulletin of the European Communities*, vol. 3, no. 11 (supplement).
Hayek, F. A. (1976), *Denationalization of Money* (London: Institute of Economic Affairs).
Jenkins, R. (1978), 'European Monetary Union', *Lloyds Bank Review*, no. 127. (The text of the Jean Monnet Lecture delivered at the European Institute, Florence, on 27 October 1977.)
Klein, B. (1978), 'Competing Monies, European Monetary Union and the Dollar', in M. Fratianni and T. Peeters (eds), *One Money for Europe* (London: Macmillan, 1978).
Meade, J. (1957), 'The Balance of Payments Problems of a European Free Trade Area', *Economic Journal*, vol. 67.
Oppenheimer, P. M. (1979), 'EMS: Origins and Prospects', paper prepared for the SUERF colloquium on Europe and the dollar in world-wide equilibrium (Basle, 10–12 May).
Scitovsky, T. (1958), *Economic Theory and Western European Integration* (London: George Allen & Unwin).
'The European Monetary Fund: Internal Planning and External Relations'

(1980), *Banca Nazionale del Lavoro Quarterly Review*, no. 134.

Tsoukalis, L. (1977), *The Politics and Economics of European Monetary Integration* (London: George Allen & Unwin).

Vaubel, R. (1978), *Strategies for Currency Unification: The Economics of Currency Competition and the Case for a European Parallel Currency* (Tübingen: J. C. B. Mohr).

2 Experience under the EMS and Prospects for Further Progress towards EMU

MICHAEL EMERSON

In the period since President Jenkins (1978) stimulated serious debate again on European monetary integration, the European Monetary System (EMS) has settled into the landscape more comfortably than one might have expected from the debate surrounding the negotiation period. Already in April 1979, only a month after the EMS began its operating, Christopher McMahon (1979), now deputy Governor of the Bank of England observed: 'If the EMS did not exist, it – or something similar – would have to be invented.'

This aphorism seems to imply that the creation of the EMS was fundamentally a sound initiative. But I would not dismiss all the arguments that surrounded its creation, nor overstate its achievements, nor, above all, understate the difficulty of the tasks that lie ahead if one sees the EMS as a step in an evolutionary process leading to more advanced stages of monetary integration.

I propose to examine these issues through attempted answers to questions which are frequently posed about the functioning of the EMS and the prospects for next steps in European monetary integration.

HAS THE EMS ACHIEVED GREATER EXCHANGE-RATE STABILITY AMONG PARTICIPANTS? HAS IT CURBED OVER-SHOOTING?

So far the answer is yes on both accounts. The average variability of Community exchange rates in relation to the ECU (here taking the year-on-year change in the average of daily rates) was lower in 1979 than in years since 1971. The average change in this measure was 1.8 per cent for the EMS currencies (excluding the pound) compared to about 7 per cent in the most unstable intervening years, 1973 and 1976.

Overshooting, meaning substantial exchange-rate movements that prove to be inappropriate for the medium term and are reversed within quite a short period, is virtually excluded for currencies participating in the narrower 2.25 per cent margins agreement. We have seen currencies fluctuate within these bands, and alternate in the role of intervention at their obligatory limits. The expected pattern of persistent intervention in favour of or against certain stray currencies has not materialised. Thus the Deutschemark is currently weak, the French franc strong; the Belgium franc and Danish krone have been weak but have now picked themselves off the floor; the Dutch guilder and Irish pound have been fluctuating within their bands with no clear trend.

By contrast, the UK pound and Japanese yen have shown enormous, and contradictory fluctuations over the past two years. Overshooting is not dead. From the beginning of 1979 the pound against the ECU appreciated 11 per cent to July, then fell back 10 per cent by November, and from there has since appreciated 11 per cent to September 1980. The Japanese yen appreciated 41 per cent against the ECU in the eighteen months to August 1978, depreciated 46 per cent in the next sixteen months to February 1980, and has subsequently recovered 7.2 per cent.

By comparison, the Italian lira operating within its wider 6 per cent margin has had the nearest thing to an overshooting experience. Initially in the EMS the lira appreciated 1.5 per cent above its ECU central rate up to May 1979, and it has since declined to a point 6.5 per cent lower.

This experience should at least disarm the sceptic's view that a greater degree of exchange-rate stability was not feasible, even in difficult circumstances of oil and dollar crises. Sceptics have now to retreat to the position that the exchange rates so defended are too stable, an argument to which we return in a moment.

There are also other ways of assessing exchange-rate stability, for example whether the given degree of stability went with bigger or smaller inflation differentials: i.e. were the underlying conditions better or worse? Did the degree of stability aid a convergence of inflation rates? To these questions also I return later.

HAS THE EMS FOUND A WAY OF MAKING CENTRAL RATE ADJUSTMENTS IN A SATISFACTORY WAY?

There have been two realignments in September and November of 1979. The first realignment, with the Deutschemark revaluing a little, and the

Danish krone devaluing a little, broke the ice: it disabused us of the view that timely exchange-rate negotiations were impracticable in a group of countries larger than the old snake, or in a Community decision-making setting which has implications for agricultural policy.

The second realignment, which involved only a further depreciation of the Danish krone against the remainder, has shown that a substantial effective depreciation of a participating currency can be achieved in ordered conditions.

The revealed behaviour of the EMS on realignments will no doubt tell us more as time passes by. For the time being one can infer that two lessons of the past have been learned: (i) avoid excessive rigidity in defending parities, and (ii) do not try to invent quantitative indicators for triggering automatic changes; we may well recall the Interim Committee's vain search for such formulae after the Smithsonian Agreement.

HAS THERE BEEN A CONVERGENCE OF INFLATION PER-FORMANCE UNDER THE EMS?

Here, performance has been less than brilliant. The average Community inflation rate in 1980 rose as high as it did after the 1973 oil crisis, despite the fact that food and non-oil commodity prices have risen less fast. Consumer and wholesale prices rose 15 per cent on average in the twelve months to mid-1980, and consumer prices are likely to rise 12.5 per cent in the year 1980 as a whole, compared to 13.5 per cent in 1974. The standard deviation of consumer price rises is expected to reach 5.9 per cent in 1980 compared to the previous divergence peak of 5.5 per cent in 1975.

There is some silver lining to this unmistakably large cloud. First, the recent performance has been largely unconstrained by price control in general, or of oil and energy prices in particular, whereas after the first oil shock there were instances of heavy price control, and a more reluctant pass-through of oil prices. These are bonus points for a more healthy resource allocation performance. Second, wage inflation has been more restrained. After 1973, there was a massive and inappropriate attempt by wage-earners to evade the increased oil price, with real per-capita wage compensation in the Community on average rising 3 per cent in 1974 and 4.5 per cent in 1975 at a time when real domestic income was falling. In 1980, we expect real per-capita wage compensation to rise less than 1 per cent.

Thus the EMS has given an exchange-rate stability which has dampened, rather than boosted, vicious circle tendencies in the inflation field.

HAS STABILITY IN THE EMS PROVIDED COVER FOR THE EMERGENCE OF SUBSTANTIAL AUTOMATIC CHANGES IN REAL COMPETITIVE POSITION? HAVE THESE CHANGES BEEN DESIRABLE?

With exchange rates converging more than inflation, there have been changes in real competitive position in the Community since the EMS started.

By far the largest change has of course been outside the EMS, with the case of the UK pound moving 7 points in the effective exchange-rate index (trade weighted against eighteen currencies) from the first quarter of 1979 to the first quarter of 1980, but as much as 20 points when differences in wholesale price inflation are also taken into account. Few people are happy with the excessive appreciation of the UK pound. The difficult question is in what degree full membership of EMS might have abated the upward pressure on sterling, which has in part been due to the oil price rise, but also in part to the markets' knowledge that the government was not seeking to prevent sterling's upward movement. Although the circumstances are not the same, it is worth noting that France and Germany both pursue exchange-rate and money supply objectives, with some flexibility attached to each: exchange rates have margins and can have their central rates changed; money supply objectives usually have margins too, and tend to be rebased periodically. Thus these countries pursue essentially pluralistic monetary policies in which the exchange-rate obligation is absolutely fixed in terms of day-to-day fulfilment, but still adjustable, and in which the monetary target is specified but can be temporarily departed from in practice.

The next largest change has been the 11-point depreciation of the Danish krone (in real effective terms), which was essentially due to the two central rate realignments already mentioned.

Moving on to the essentially automatic changes in competitive position, the next largest moves have concerned the Benelux currencies, where approximate stability of the *nominal* effective exchange rate has gone together with a substantially better than average inflation performance, giving 7-point improvements in real effective competitiveness. There is little doubt about the need for these countries to improve their competitive position: their rate of decline of employment in manufacturing industry has been faster than that of any other Community country, up until recently when they have possibly been overtaken by the UK. The implicit doctrine of the EMS is that if the needed adjustments can be made by internal measures, rather than exchange-rate changes which would threaten price stability, so much the better.

The Irish real, effective, competitive position has improved slightly during the life of the EMS: it is not difficult to understand why the authorities are satisfied with their new monetary environment compared to what the previous status quo would have done in carrying their currency all the way with the UK pound.

To many observers the strength of the French franc against the Deutschemark has been a surprising feature, though the changes in these countries' real effective competitive positions have not been large: -2 per cent and $+3$ per cent respectively from 1979 (first quarter) to 1980 (first quarter). The cyclical weakening of Germany's current account, and France's respectable current account performace and official determination to maintain a stable exchange rate, have no doubt been part of the explanation. Perhaps also France's substantial nuclear energy programme has impressed exchange markets. At any event, this crucial pair of exchange cross-rates is not problematic for the time being. The comparative weakness of the Deutschemark through much of 1980 has in practice explained the relatively calm exchange-rate environment.

HAS THERE BEEN A CONVERGENCE IN THE GENERAL STRATEGY OR PHILOSOPHY OF ECONOMIC POLICY?

Yes, in important respects; not because of the EMS, but rather as part of the general political and economic scenery that gave birth to it.

To start with party politics, the scene is more homogeneous across member states than at most times in the post-war period with liberal/conservative/Christian democrat parties in power in most countries, and present as coalition parties elsewhere. This has come with, and in part created, a greater homogeneity in economic philosophy: a stronger will to arrest the growth of the public sector, to let the price mechanism work, and to pursue internal and/or external monetary targets.

In mid-1980 six out of nine Community countries were applying restrictive programmes of budgetary and monetary policy, and the remainder were pursuing broadly neutral budgetary and restrictive monetary policies. The six countries, Denmark, Belgium, the Netherlands, Ireland, Italy and the UK, all were giving priority to combatting problems of economic inbalance, manifested in various mixes of inflation, public finance and balance-of-payments problems. The other three countries, Germany, France and Luxembourg, were pursuing cautiously neutral budget policies, and cautious or restrictive monetary policies. These three countries' economies are in reasonably good shape: exempt at least from glaring inbalance on any of the three criteria listed, and with good records of productivity growth, investment and flexibility towards structural change.

It may seem unremarkable that this categorisation of countries' policies and conditions fits rather logically; it is more remarkable if one surveys the last decade or so of divergent policy responses to analogous situations.

The policy response in the period ahead, as recessionary tendencies appear to be strengthening and generalising, is a story that remains to be told. The prospects for avoiding the exchange-rate instability of 1974–5 depend on the compatibility of budget and monetary policies. This in turn will require that governments make essentially comparable assessments of their respective room for manoeuvre in the use of economic policy, that international economic constraints are correctly assessed, and that where policy moves have to be made, the necessary collective room for manoeuvre be established at the Community and international level.

Compared to the negotiation period before March 1978, the question of deflationary bias, as a worry or concern, has since become distinctly less topical in reality. The reason is clear enough: some role reversal as between the UK and Germany. The UK outside the EMS has adopted the hardest macroeconomic policy in the Community: the German economy has meanwhile become its most dynamic force. It is one of nature's recurrent little tricks to evaporate in practice issues that had long been laboured by the negotiators as matters of principle. Of course, we must not be trite on this question at a time when the European economy verges on recession. This is a major problem, but one that lies largely outside the present agenda. The EMS is part of a discipline under which countries with unbalanced economies are deciding not to try a delusory 'dash for freedom' out of the oil stagflation. The economies in sounder condition are acting cautiously and not procyclically.

HAS THERE BEEN A STRENGTHENING IN ECONOMIC POLICY CO-ORDINATION?

As a direct result of the setting up of the EMS, the answer is that the procedures of co-ordination have not been much changed. There are three points to be made here.

First, the general procedures of co-ordination in the Community were rather fully equipped in the 1974 Council 'Convergence' Decision, set up incidentally as part of the second stage of the 1972 EMU resolution. Thus, the EMS did not require any new committees of economic policy officials or ministers or central bankers: there were enough already.

Second, and more substantively, on budget policy during the EMS negotiation period in 1978 there was a collective expansionary adjustment of budgetary policies known as the 'concerted action' programme. The operative Council Decision of July 1978, linked to the Bonn and Bremen Summits of that summer, were prepared in detail several months beforehand in the Council's 'Co-ordinating Group' (of high finance ministry officials). This particular operation has come to be recognized as a case-book example of co-ordinated action. At the same time it has also come equally clearly to be recognized that budget policy is not something to be changed fundamentally every six months or even every two years. These are the reason why no general innovation was felt necessary for budget policy co-ordination. But new 'concerted actions' will no doubt be called for in the future.

In monetary policy, the EMS has heightened the correlation of interest-rate adjustments. Over the past year the German Bundesbank had clearly led interest-rate policy in the Community, and other countries in the narrow margins group in the EMS have tended to follow closely, often even on a day-to-day basis. One may look to more co-ordinated interest-rate adjustments as a matter for future agendas of the Committee of Governors of Central Banks.

Third, the pattern of interest-rate changes in 1980 has been consistent with the signals being emitted by the divergence indicator, which is the EMS's principal innovation in the apparatus of co-ordination. The divergence indicator is activated when a currency passes 75 per cent of its intervention margin around ECU denominated central rates. Activation places the country in question under the presumption of the need to adjust its monetary or other economic policies; this is distinguished from the obligation to intervene to defend the margins around the grid of bilateral exchange rates between EMS currencies.

The divergence indicator is addressed to one of the dilemmas of all international monetary systems: how to establish rules conducive to good behaviour, which also leave space for the basic independence of national authorities. The divergence indicator has worked fairly well so far: it has signalled the Belgian and Danish cases which was quite appropriate. However, the technical complications of accommodating a UK pound inside the ECU and outside the EMS intervention system, and of the Italian lira with wider margins than other currencies, has introduced some inertia into the indicator, which impairs its role; movements of the UK pound and the lira outside theoretical 2.25 per cent margins around their ECU central rates are excluded from the calculation of other currencies' divergence.

HOW HAS THE EMS AFFECTED EXCHANGE-RATE RELATIONS WITH OTHER EUROPEAN CURRENCIES, THE US DOLLAR AND YEN?

First, a word on the possibility, provided for in the rules of the EMS, for other European countries to associate with the system. No country has formally asked for association. However, in practice the Swiss authorities have adopted an intervention margin around the Deutschemark, which effectively means a unilateral act of association with the EMS. Meanwhile Norway and Sweden, both ex-snake members, have pegged their currencies to their own tailor-made basket, and seem content with this. Austria seeks to maintain a constant real effective exchange rate, with the Deutschemark and the Swiss franc evidently having important weights here.

Relations between the EMS, the dollar and the yen raise questions about major potential functions of the EMS. While the trade structure of EC countries *vis-à-vis* the principal third countries do still differ fairly substantially, the emergence of organised Community policy towards the dollar and the yen is becoming clearer as a desirable and feasible proposition for the EMS. Europe has interests in both its exchange rates against the dollar and the yen, and in the functions of those currencies as international reserve and transaction media.

The increased use of Community currencies for EMS intervention has helped sharpen the distinction between intra-European and inter-continental exchange-rate policy, and has heightened perception of the Community's potential interest in and capacity for having a dollar policy. All central banks, of course, intervene in dollars, and so the step which would consist of a more explicitly co-ordinated intervention policy is not difficult to imagine.

Vis-à-vis the yen, an additional step would be required: agreement in principle between the Community's central banks and the Bank of Japan to intervene in yen, and thus establish operationally the third side of the dollar – yen – ECU triangle. Improved instruments may not change the fundamentals, but they may help prevent an unreasonable case from going by default. The Community's economic, trading interest in forming a more distinct yen policy is clear enough. For example, the yen's fluctuations in the last two years must be a matter of serious concern. By comparison, it is not obvious that the dollar exchange rate has got out of line; moreover, the dollar still serves as a numeraire for oil prices which complicates the task of identifying the content of Europe's dollar policy. Indeed, life is not simple in the business of intervention: one cannot isolate the effects of intervention policy aimed at a particular bilateral cross-rate. But a more balanced system for the multilateral co-ordination of intervention can be envisaged. Moreover, we see the beginning of this in the fact that the German and Swiss authorities have recently operated for the first time swap lines with the Bank of Japan.

As regards the world's reserve assets, the Community interest is in an orderly diversification away from excessive reliance on the dollar. The Community cohesion represented by the EMS is instrumental in strengthening Europe's powers of negotiation and influence in this process.

HOW HAS THE EMS AFFECTED OTHERS, AND THE INTERNATIONAL INTERESTS?

Two main concerns have been expressed. The first is that a stronger European monetary organisation might weaken international institutions, with the Europeans less motivated to negotiate for world mechanisms. A counter argument is that the Europeans, having created additional facilities for their own internal needs, will leave more funds available for the rest of the world, notably for the developing countries in the IMF. Against highly speculative argument about whether the size of the cake is more or less fixed, it should be recalled that Italy and the UK between them occupied a large share of the IMF's resources in the wake of the first oil shock. This then leads to a secondary concern that the IMF may become a 'developing country institution' like the World

Bank. The developing countries for their part are concerned that the rules of conditionality attaching to IMF credit should not become exclusively targeted at them, with the industrialised countries only prescribing and never taking the medicine in question. There are analogous issues in the domain of reserve-asset diversification, in which some fear that the ECU and SDR would be competing rather than complementary instruments.

In general, these are hypothetical concerns which do not seem to be substantiated. It is understandable that, in the face of a new international development, all interest groups consider seriously how they are affected. The US administration, in particular, examined seriously during the negotiation period whether the emerging EMS was '*for* them' or '*against* them'. After considering such arguments as 'the ECU will weaken the dollar' and 'the EMS will exert a deflationary influence on the world economy', they seem to have concluded that these objections could not be upheld as intrinsic characteristics of the system; and experience has confirmed the view that the EMS and ECU are entirely compatible with the rules of the IMF, and do not distract the Community from world-level problems. A more organised Europe, in its own monetary affairs, means a more coherent negotiating performance over world monetary questions. In fact, the Community has for some time now organised the taking of common positions in IMF negotiations, through preparatory arrangement in the Monetary Committee. In particular, in the recent substitution account negotiations in the IMF the Community adopted a positive, common position, and the negotiations were suspended essentially because the US did not want to share in the cost of provisions to maintain the value of dollar deposits in the substitution account.

HOW HAS THE ROLE OF THE ECU DEVELOPED? HOW CAN WE NOW ENVISAGE ITS GROWTH POTENTIAL IN OFFICIAL USES?

The ECU is still a young plant, whose roots are not yet very strongly established. However, it has now made a qualitative jump from its previous incarnation as the little-known European Unit of Account into the ECU, designated to be at the centre of the EMS and to be a leading instrument of monetary integration.

Its functions are now very numerous, although some of its newer and more important ones are still tenuous. We have completed the application of the ECU in all the Community's internal financial, accounting and statistical functions that require a unit of account. This includes the accounts of the budget, European Investment Bank (EIB), European Coal and Steel Community (ECSC), European Development Fund (EDF); the numeraire role in all money amount tariffs; and for administered prices (agriculture, steel). The transition from the previous, multiple and distorted units of account in fact presented sizeable problems: where the EUA could not overcome the inertial weight of these problems the ECU has now done so.

In its monetary functions the ECU is the formal numeraire of EMS parities; it is the numeraire in Community credit mechanisms and thus defines the exchange risk accepted by creditors and debtors; it is the numeraire for the divergence indicator but only indirectly for the obligatory intervention points which operate on the bilateral grid of exchange rates; it has a large but tenuous foot-hold in the reserve asset function since the 20 per cent of reserves now held in the European Monetary Co-operation Fund (EMCF) in ECU are the counterparts of three-month renewable swaps against gold, dollars and other reserve assets. They are thus neither permanent creations nor even a specific, common exchange risk. Moreover, the use of ECU in settlement between central banks is subject to the limitation that the receiving bank may request that the ECU content of payment may be limited to 50 per cent.

Looking to the future, first steps further forward would seem to be the removal of these last two limitations, which reflect the caution of central banks at the time the EMS was set up. The logic and principles of the EMS require that the ECU be a fully-fledged and permanent asset, whose exchange risk all member states should fully accept; to retain these limitations may be interpreted as a vote of uncertain confidence by others outside Community central banks, notably by the private sector, to which I now turn.

WHAT OF THE USE OF THE ECU AS A PARALLEL CURRENCY IN THE PRIVATE SECTOR?

This has begun, but has not yet taken off in a big way. Many of the major private banks in Europe now accept current account deposits in ECU; the Commission holds ECU accounts, and has placed short-term (three months) paper in ECU to the extent of outstanding balances now typically of the order of 300 million ECU (150 million pounds). There have been some innovations by banks; for example the Credit Lyonnais in France this year introduced medium-term roll-over credits in ECU for some large enterprises in France. In the international banking sector a consortium of European banks has been considering introducing ECU travellers' cheques. A market for ECU denominated bonds, especially in the Eurobond markets, potentially exists. An interesting seminar at Louvain-la-Neuve University in July 1980 explored the potential and obstacles to development along these lines. Two conclusions seemed to emerge at this gathering. First, a potential market for private ECU parallel currency functions exists, although there already exist other ways of assuming a multi-currency exchange cover. Second, there are critical factors of market size, familiarity, and absence of uncertainties about the behaviour of the official sector that have to be respected for the potential market to take off. Here there are tasks for both the Community institutions and national authorities. Until these thresholds are passed the ECU's role will be limited by the unlimited practical availability of ad hoc currency cocktails tailored to the individual users' needs. Private bankers feel that the Community authorities should 'put their money where their mouths are'. Thus some part of Community borrowing, which under the Commission, EIB and ECSC is now on the scale of 3–5 billion ECU per year, and so is not an insignificant fraction of the international bond market, should be placed in ECU, and the market should be supplied with an assured flow of new paper in this denomination. It may be only a matter of time before this takes place: such an initiative is withheld principally for the reason that it must be prepared in conditions that assure its clear success. This in turn means, for example, clarifying future policy with regard to adjustments of the weights of the ECU (provided for at present each five years, or when a currency's actual weight has moved more than 25 per cent from its starting weight in the ECU basket), and with regard to the new or applicant member state (the Greek drachma will be included within five years of accession).

National governments for their part need to remove the restrictions that still remain in some cases against the opening of banking accounts or various types of transactions in ECU. The minimum reasonable commitment to be asked of all member states is that they permit the ECU to be used for 'off-shore' transactions in any way that dollars or other foreign currencies are permitted. National governments could also, of course, support the private role of the ECU by placing part of their own debt in ECU, to which some have in fact already come close, France in the form of exchange-rate risk guarantee, Belgium in statements of intent. But Community bond issues should start the ball rolling.

DO WE NOW SEE MORE CLEARLY THE FUTURE FUNCTIONS AND INSTITUTIONAL FORM OF A EUROPEAN MONETARY FUND?

There is not yet a consensus view, nor the imminence of political negotiation and decision. But ideas are in circulation, and are being worked on. One view starts from the model of the IMF as a manager of credit mechanisms, and of the policy conditionality that goes with it. Another view starts by looking to the Fund as a money-creating institution, having therefore more of a central-bank function, distinct from broader political and economic policy responsibilities. Obvious functions are as agent for the intervention, accounting and short-term credit operations of the EMS: this is broadly what the Bank for International Settlements at present has done under the label of the EMCF.

More ambitious ideas go like this. The European Monetary Fund (EMF) becomes the centre of ECU reserve asset creation; these become definitive and fully usable assets, between Community central banks, and then later outside the Community among other central banking institutions, and in the international private sector. The EMF develops a role in buying and selling ECU assets in international money markets, perhaps to aid the recycling process, perhaps to support a given dollar policy, perhaps supporting Community currencies. The EMF becomes operational in the domain of substitution account activity, i.e. in the mechanics of international reserve asset diversification. As a matter of institutional organisation, one may think of some transposition of the governing structures of the EIB or IMF: a full-time resident executive board, a supranational president, a governing board superstructure representing national authorities.

Technical, exploratory work continues at present at a rather slow speed. One factor justifying due precaution is a wish to see how the international monetary system emerges under the strains of the second oil crisis. What will be the nature of the dollar's role, and of the recycling problem in the next few years? How should the EMF relate to both today's operational needs as well as the day-after-tomorrow's European development?

HOW HAS THE EMS AFFECTED THE INSTITUTIONAL DEVELOPMENT OF THE COMMUNITY?

I would highlight two points. The obvious one is that it has brought a major policy function back into the Community setting, as compared to the snake mechanism that had left it. It has linked together Community monetary and public finance mechanisms, and its economic policy co-ordination procedures. All this represents progress for Community integration.

The less obvious and, in my view, less agreeable point is that Britain's token membership has in practice given support to the concept of two-tier Europe, two-speed Europe, variable geometry Europe – call it what you will. This concept has been struggling to emerge for some time promoted by Mr Brandt and Mr Tindemans and more recently by Mr Barre. The concept has been both abstract, without a major application, and controversial, since it implies an erosion of the unity of the Community and of the institutional equality of status of all member states. The concept still remains controversial but, in informal Community circles, it is now perhaps less so, and is certainly less abstract.

DO WE SEE THE CASE FOR MONETARY UNION, AND THE WAY FORWARD TOWARDS IT DIFFERENTLY TO THREE YEARS AGO, WHEN PRESIDENT JENKINS REACTIVATED INTEREST IN THE QUESTION IN HIS FLORENCE SPEECH?

European monetary affairs have achieved a metamorphosis over the past three years. Before this period European monetary integration seemed to have run into a cul-de-sac. The bold ideas of the early seventies did not weather well as the Bretton Woods system collapsed. The snake preserved only remnants of a broad European project. The EMS has put the show on the open road again. Technically, the EMS is in many respects an out-growth of the snake, but the changes have been sufficiently significant to have created a new growth potential in the institutional organisation of international and European monetary affairs. More precisely, I conclude by listing five respects in which this new potential is manifest.

The idea of a common, hard currency for Europe is a less controversial proposition, and the extent of different national preferences in the conduct of macroeconomic policy has become less. The idea of progressing in monetary integration with the aid of parallel currency techniques has advanced, and could advance much more in the next few years on the basis of the ECU. The idea of Europe having its own reserve asset in a world of diversified international reserves has advanced a lot, and could also advance much more. The idea of giving ourselves the instrument of exchange-rate policy in the setting of a dollar–ECU–yen triangle, and the perceived need for this, has progressed. The idea of having a distinct monetary institution, sponsoring and managing these functions, and designed to host an evolution towards monetary union, has advanced, and could and should, in my view, move ahead to the foundation stage in the not-too-distant future.

NOTE

Views expressed are personal to the author, and should not, unless otherwise indicated, be attributed to the Commission.

REFERENCES

Jenkins, R. (1978), 'European Monetary Union', *Lloyds Bank Review*, no. 127. (The text of the Jean Monnet Lecture delivered at the European Institute, Florence, on 27 October 1977.)
McMahon, C. (1979), 'The Long-run Implications of the European Monetary Sytem', in P. H. Trezise (ed.), *The European Monetary System: its Promise and Prospects* (Washington, D. C.: The Brookings Institution).

Comments on Peeters and Emerson

DAVID COBHAM

Emerson's paper is wide-ranging, interesting and informative but in the end it leaves a feeling of dissatisfaction. I think there are three main reasons for this.

First, Emerson's assessment of the practical economic achievements of the EMS in its first eighteen months is vitiated by a series of inappropriate comparisons. The precise effects of an institutional change such as the EMS can be identified only by comparing what actually occurred with the counterfactual of what would have occurred if the change had not been made but all other determining factors had been the same. This kind of exercise is not always easy in practice but the principle of proceeding in this way is relatively straightforward. However, in the answer to his first question – has the EMS achieved greater exchange-rate stability among participants? – Emerson first compares the degree of exchange-rate stability during the EMS period with that during previous years when other factors were clearly not the same (choosing the two years of greatest instability out of the preceding eight); he then compares the exchange rates of EMS participants with those of the pound sterling – a currency that could have been but was not inside the EMS, but in any case was subject to some quite different forces from those affecting the EMS currencies – and with the Japanese yen, a currency that is definitively outside the EMS. These comparisons are particularly unconvincing in view of Emerson's later emphasis on the weakness of Germany's current account as a factor explaining the relative stability of the French franc/Deutschemark rate.

In his discussion of inflation rates (question 3), on the other hand, Emerson compares the expected response of EMS countries to the 1979–80 rise in the price of oil with the response to the 1973–4 rise. This is certainly a more interesting comparison but the question needs to be asked whether, or rather to what extent, the difference in response is due

33

to the existence of the EMS, and to what extent it is the result of developments in the theory of economic policy on the one hand and 'learning effects' (by both peoples and governments) on the other. The only points at which Emerson seems to me to get near to the right comparisons are in his discussion of Ireland's competitive position (question 4) where the appropriate counterfactual seems relatively obvious, and in his remark (question 5) that 'The EMS is part of a discipline under which countries with unbalanced economies are deciding not to try a delusory "dash for freedom" out of the oil stagflation': if it could be shown that no such discipline, or at least substantially less discipline, would have been exerted over the economic policies of EMS members in the absence of the EMS – and it may well be that this could be shown – then we would indeed have the basis for a positive evaluation of the first eighteen months of the EMS. However Emerson's paper as it stands does not provide such a basis.

Second, the paper fails to make contact with much of the academic debate on EMU of the last few years. A minor example of this is Emerson's discussion of the use of the ECU as a parallel currency in the private sector, which makes no reference to the argument mentioned by Peeters[1] that the ECU would not be able to compete successfully with the stronger national currencies of the EC countries. A more important example is his failure to locate the EMS either in terms of the various strategies for currency unification which have been discussed – and which are lucidly summarised by Peeters – or in terms of the various strategies for integration such as neofunctionalism and federalism. The impression Emerson gives is that the EMS is part of a co-ordination strategy conceived in a neofunctionalist framework. Yet he never discusses or attempts to rebut the critique of co-ordination strategies developed by Vaubel (1978a, 1979), and again summarised by Peeters, or the critique of neofunctionalism developed by various political scientists (e.g. Heathcote, 1975; Harrison, 1978).

Third, Emerson's main reference to Jenkins' 1977 Jean Monnet lecture (Jenkins, 1978) is to contrast attitudes to monetary union then and now. The particular question he poses enables him to give a reply that suggests small but steady progress on a number of fronts – precisely in line with a neofunctionalist co-ordination strategy. But a more interesting question would have been, how does the EMS compare with the scheme put forward by Jenkins in 1977 and why are the two so different? Vaubel has interpreted Jenkins' lecture as advocating the 'big-leap' approach, and remarked acidly that 'Mr Jenkins's subsequent support for the fixed-exchange-rate philosophy of the "New European

Monetary System" must be an enigma to anyone who does not know the difference between an economist and a politician' (1979, pp. 28–9). However, the contrast should not be dismissed as cynically as this, for the history of the origins of the EMS must throw some light on the real political problems involved in implementing the various strategies for currency unification, and Emerson could have made some contribution here. A more detailed point concerns the attitudes to the ECU as an international reserve asset: Jenkins seems to have conceived of a new European-created reserve asset as a rival to the dollar, but Emerson reports with apparent satisfaction and agreement the conclusion of the US administration that the ECU and the EMS were not intrinsically opposed to US interests; however he does not recognise or discuss this apparent shift in attitude.

Peeters has provided a clear and useful introduction to the subject of EMU and I shall therefore confine my remarks to only two (indirectly related) points in his paper.

First, his analysis of the failure of the Werner strategy seems to me not to take account of the reasons why the Werner strategy was what it was, a co-ordination rather than a centralisation strategy. Essentially Peeters argues (i) that an examination of the historical origins of the strategy shows it was designed to meet certain problems connected with the disintegration of the Bretton Woods system (e.g. to protect the CAP from exchange-rate changes such as those of 1969), and (ii) that therefore, even though these problems turned out to be much greater than had been expected at the time the strategy was devised, they cannot be used to explain the strategy's failure, which should be ascribed instead to 'basic deficiencies in the design of the system'. To some extent his analysis complements that of Vaubel (1978a, pp. 215–20; 1978b) who has argued empirically (i) that the *structural* differences and divergences between EC countries during the 1970s were no greater than in the 1960s, in other words the 'unfavourable events' of the early 1970s did not themselves affect the EC economies in very different ways, and (ii) that the failure of the Werner strategy must therefore have been caused by a lack of harmonisation of national monetary policies due to 'the choice of an unworkable strategy' (1978b, p. 330).

In each case it seems to me that the first part of the argument is correct and important but the transition from the first to the second is not valid because it assumes that the EC countries were fully committed to the objective of EMU at the time when the Werner strategy was designed. If that had been the case the latter could legitimately be criticised for its lack of an adequate technical mechanism or discipline capable of enforcing a harmonised response to the dollar and energy crises. However it is arguable that the EC countries were far from fully committed to EMU, even before their limited commitment collapsed under the impact of external events: in this case the Werner strategy should be regarded as a neofunctionalist strategy designed to *develop* the political commitment to EMU. It cannot therefore legitimately be criticised in the same terms, and it is pointless to suggest that some other strategy would have worked better if that strategy is predicated on a complete political commitment of a kind that did not exist.

Second, Peeters' suggestion that what is required for the achievement of EMU is a combination of co-ordination and centralisation strategies seems to me to be extremely useful, and to deserve further discussion. His comment that although such a combination 'does not necessarily correspond to a theoretically optimal currency unification process, it may be dictated by political realism', presumably points to a lack of political realism in the centralisation strategies; it may also indicate that the criteria on which theoretical optimality is being assessed are inadequate. It is probably widely agreed[2] that the 'big-leap' variant of the centralisation strategy would require for its implementation a massive and improbable shock to public opinion, and that free competition between existing national currencies ending in the 'natural selection' of only one currency would generate substantial political frictions. Thus in the academic literature at least the front runner among the centralisation variants is the EPC, particularly in the constant purchasing power form advocated by the All Saints' Day Manifesto (Basevi *et al.*, 1975). However Laidler (1978, p. 58) has argued strongly that the Manifesto 'glosses over the extent of the prior agreement required to implement it', while Peeters emphasises[3] that the EPC 'is not and cannot be a substitute for explicit political agreement on the desirability of monetary unification'. This suggests that the EPC scheme is 'automatic' in Vaubel's sense only because it starts *after* the fundamental political decision has been taken; by the same token it offers no ideas on how that decision might come to be taken. The co-ordination strategies on the other hand are almost entirely concerned with how such a decision can be arrived at, so that they cannot legitimately be criticised for allowing the survival of discretionary political decisions. Thus co-ordination and centralisation strategies are different in kind and cannot usefully be evaluated, as Vaubel evaluates them, with reference to the same criteria.

The problem with the co-ordination strategies is rather that so far they have been situated within a neofunctionalist framework: they have been conceived as strategies designed to lead gradually, via a process of incremental decision-making, towards the final decision to implement EMU, with their attention focussed almost entirely on governments, that is on political and Civil Service élites. Neofunctionalism is now widely discredited in academic circles, for it can be seen to have failed as a strategy and degenerated as a theory.[4] The most important reason for its failure is that 'high politics' issues within the EC have obstinately refused to become 'welfare politics' issues, so that the incremental decision-making process has ceased to extend its scope; and attempts to revise the theory to take account of 'dramatic political actors', such as de Gaulle, have deprived the theory of the ability to make useful predictions (even without the apparently insuperable problems of measurement and testing). Within the context of EMU the influence of neofunctionalism has not only focussed attention on governments rather than electorates, it has also positively discouraged open appeals to the people of the EC countries to support EMU, for fear of increasing the resistance of governments to the next incremental decision. Thus the attempts at co-ordination strategies have been unable to create the political momentum behind EMU which would lead governments to exercise their discretion on this overwhelmingly 'high' political issue in the desired direction.[5]

The conclusion of this argument is that EMU is most likely to be achieved through a process which, as Peeters suggests, starts with a co-ordination strategy and then turns into a centralisation strategy. What is needed, however, is a non-neofunctionalist co-ordination strategy in which co-ordination provides the base for a strong political campaign to persuade the peoples of the EC of the benefits of EMU, for ultimately it is only such persuasion that can bring the EC governments to make the irrevocable centralisation decisions. (There remains, of course, a real problem as to who is going to lead and develop such a campaign.) The EPC scheme can then be used in the centralisation stage. However, in this case it should be seen merely as a convenient technical mechanism for implementing EMU rather than as a fundamental strategy in its own right.[6]

NOTES

1. See also Vaubel (1978a, pp. 154, 407).
2. See Corden (1977, pp. 150–1).

3. See also Vaubel (1978a, pp. 102, 411–12).
4. See for example Heathcote (1975) and Harrison (1978). I am grateful to Mark Imber for discussion on this question.
5. Some of the points made in this paragraph are discussed in greater detail in the paper by David Marquand in this volume.
6. Klein (1978) has disputed whether the EPC would be attractive enough to displace the national currencies, but Zis (1978), O'Mahony (1978) and Vaubel (1978a) have argued persuasively that it would. The issue is important, and I do not feel Peeters helps his own position by citing Klein in the way that he does. For if Klein is right the implication is not that EC member countries' governments should be more willing to give the EPC scheme a chance, but that the scheme should be shelved in favour of some alternative in view of the substantial economic costs involved in setting it up.

REFERENCES

Basevi, G., M. Fratianni, H. Giersch, P. Korteweg, D. O'Mahony, M. Parkin, T. Peeters, P. Salin and N. Thygesen (1975), 'The All Saints' Day Manifesto for European Monetary Union: a Currency for Europe', *The Economist*, 1 November; reprinted in M. Fratianni and T. Peeters (eds), *One Money for Europe* (London: Macmillan, 1978).

Corden, W. M. (1977), *Inflation, Exchange Rates and the World Economy* (Oxford: Oxford University Press).

Fratianni, M. and T. Peeters (eds), (1978) *One Money for Europe* (London: Macmillan).

Harrison, R. J. (1978), 'Neofunctionalism', in P. Taylor and A. J. R. Groom (eds), *International Organisation* (London: Frances Pinter).

Heathcote, N. (1975), 'Neo-functional Theories of Regional Integration', in A. J. R. Groom and P. Taylor (eds), *Functionalism* (London: University Press).

Jenkins, R. (1978), 'European Monetary Union', *Lloyds Bank Review*, no. 127. (The text of the Jean Monnet Lecture delivered at the European Institute, Florence, on 27 October 1977.)

Klein, B. (1978), 'Competing Monies, European Monetary Union and the Dollar', in M. Fratianni and T. Peeters, op. cit.

Laidler, D. (1978) 'Difficulties with European Monetary Union', in M. Fratianni and T. Peeters, op. cit.

O'Mahony, D. (1978), 'Comment on Klein', in M. Fratianni and T. Peeters, op. cit.

Vaubel, R. (1978a), *Strategies for Currency Unification: The Economics of Currency Competition and the Case for a European Parallel Currency* (Tübingen: J. C. B. Mohr).

Vaubel, R. (1978b), 'Real Exchange-rate Changes in the European Community', *Journal of International Economics*, vol. 8.

Vaubel, R. (1979), *Choice in European Monetary Union*, Ninth Wincott Lecture, Institute of Economic Affairs, London, Occasional Paper 55.

Zis, G. (1978), 'Comment on Klein', in M. Fratianni and T. Peeters, op. cit.

3 The EMS: Performance and Prospects

NORBERT WALTER

It is a mistake to try to resist movements in exchange rates rendered inevitable by changes in relative costs and prices or other factors affecting a country's underlying position on current or capital account.

(OECD, 1977, p. 239)

There exist valid reasons why it would be unwise to expect authorities to behave truly in the spirit of systems of fixed rates or of adjustable pegs. . . . Either the countries on the deficit side of the equilibrium must be willing to have considerable unemployment imposed upon them (possibly for periods of appreciable duration), or the countries on the surplus side must give up very much of their resistance against inflationary adjustment, or interest rate differentials must be allowed to develop for the sake of channelling capital movements in directions that may not be in accordance with the relationship between the marginal productivity of capital in different countries.

(Fellner, 1970, p. 24)

A-PRIORI ASSERTIONS FOR THE EMS

Aspirations of the founders of the EMS

While there was almost unanimity among economists, politicians, and practitioners in the middle of the seventies – at least in so-called 'strong' countries – that a flexible exchange-rate regime was an optimal solution for the time being, this consensus discontinued in the course of 1977 and

39

1978, when the US government repeatedly put pressure on European countries and Japan to reflate their economies and at the same time they were badly frustrated in their efforts to successfully do so because of the sustained depreciation of the dollar.

This was the background for European firms and commercial banks to argue for a return to a fixed-exchange-rate regime. (cf. *Frankfurter Allgemeine Zeitung*, 1978; *International Herald Tribune*, 1978; *Financial Times*, 1978a; *Handelsblatt*, 1978; *Finanz und Wirtschaft*, 1978). It was as early as April 1978 that Chancellor Schmidt proposed a new European monetary scheme at the Copenhagen EC summit that rode on the turning tide of the fixed-versus-flexible-exchange-rate debate. This move came as a surprise to almost everybody since Chancellor Schmidt had been one of the most ardent defenders of flexible rates at the previous summit meetings, including the 1977 London summit.

The motives behind the move towards a more rigid exchange-rate regime in a wider Europe are manifold. Some seem to be pretended only, others – less altruistic ones – sound convincing. The EMS was conceived as a 'zone of stability', meaning less volatile intra-EC exchange rates *and* a moderation of inflation rates. These proclaimed goals of the EMS were believed to guarantee some kind of first step toward a full monetary union in Europe with a truly common currency (Roy Jenkins's 'big leap forward'). While such an aspiration seems to be sensible from the standpoint of some French, British or Italian supporters of the new approach, it hardly sounded convincing as an assertion of a German official; this becomes evident, if one learns that Germans apparently appreciated the system because of its effects in relieving some of the upward pressure on the Deutschemark, stemming from the flight out of dollar holdings, a phenomenon observed in 1977–8. There are quite a number of (albeit partly competing) theses on the motives and aims of the different governments. Some of them are mutually consistent, some are not; others are valid only under the special (cyclical) circumstances prevailing in 1978–80.

The years 1977–8 were qualified by a majority of economic observers as years of currency chaos. 'Currency chaos in 1978 precipitated the search for stability in Europe from which the EMS evolved.' (Reading, 1979, p. 35). Effective (nominal) exchange-rate appreciations of the yen, Swiss franc, Deutschemark and similarly other snake currencies of more than 20 per cent endangered the competitive position of the countries concerned. This very fact made it difficult to improve the employment situation and economic activity. In European non-snake countries the strong appreciation of the Deutschemark and the currencies tied to it was looked upon as being a hindrance to more price stability. This assessment holds for France, the UK and to some extent for Italy. Possibly, however, prestige reasons were more important for France than any other argument to aim at fixed exchange rates.

Thus Germany and the snake countries, hoping to achieve full recovery of their economies, and other European countries, desiring to reduce inflation further, brought about an alliance for fixed exchange rates within Europe in 1978.

Another possible explanation for the German government's readiness to take part in a fixed-exchange-rate regime may be seen in the fact that it wanted to pay a price in terms of less internal stability for the sake of gaining more leadership, economically and politically. Since creditor countries have the right to influence heavily conditions for credits (to be given for countries with balance of payment problems) within the EMS, economic policy and political decisions could be influenced by the country dominating economically. Possibly some governments in Europe welcomed such an outside disciplinary force.

Yet another, but maybe over-conspirative, hypothesis for the German government to launch the EMS may be seen in the government fearing the autonomous Bundesbank – with its anti-inflationary bias – would pursue a monetary policy in 1979 not conducive to the re-election of the present SPD–FDP coalition in 1980. The EMS with its fixed exchange rates may have been looked upon as a mechanism that twists arms of the Bundesbank not to pursue an over-restrictive course, or even to force it to become somewhat expansionary in 1979 and 1980 (for a more detailed description of motives and arguments for the EMS, see *Welt am Sonntag*, 1978, or Vaubel, 1979a).

It cannot, however, be ignored that the move towards the EMS was taken to be a political demonstration for a self-conscious Europe in a world with lack of leadership, especially as far as the Western Hemisphere is concerned. Economic disadvantages seemed to be negligible since important and far-reaching political cohesion was expected to be harvested from a big leap towards a united Europe. The EMS was conceived as the first step towards a true monetary union.

Apprehensions of the critics of the EMS

The thrust of most arguments against the EMS is that the agreement on rigid exchange rates is like putting the cart before the horse. Instead of starting with policy co-ordination, which means exchange-rate-oriented monetary, fiscal and wage policy, the countries fixed exchange rates and hoped for disciplinary effects for internal policies (compare, for a judgement of the argument which is almost identical with the assessment of the author, Laidler's contribution to this volume). In contrast to the first attempt to achieve monetary union in the EC, the so-called Werner Plan, no institutional arrangements were made to guarantee policy co-ordination (for an evaluation of various attempts at European monetary union cf. Walter, 1973).

This general argument expresses the conviction that the rigid exchange-rate system has hardly a chance to stay, and thus would not allow the participants to benefit as expected from a principally fixed-rate regime. The reasons underlying this conviction are different for different countries. Most critics, especially those in so-called strong-currency countries, argued that the EMS would develop into an inflation-breeding system. It was advanced that the limitations to a deliberate national decision to revalue a currency and the existence of additional subsidised credit facilities within the system – in addition to the 'threshold-of-divergence-indicator effects' (for a discussion of alternative policy co-ordination strategies see the contribution by Peeters to this volume) – would create a framework of moral hazard for the deficit countries to engage in a lax monetary policy (cf. Vaubel, 1979b). This *ex-ante* judgement was derived from numerous experiences in the Bretton Woods era. But even within the small European snake, with its more homogeneous member countries, its stricter rules for credit creation and its easier procedure for countries to autonomously change the par value, an inflationary bias could not be overlooked; revaluations only took place after massive purchases of foreign currencies in exchange markets and consequently only after excessive monetary expansion (cf. Institut für Weltwirtschaft, 1979).

On the other hand, many observers, especially in so-called weak-currency countries, feared that the new system would lead to a synchronised deflation. It was argued that the question, 'which countries would be forced to adjust their policies to the exchange rate target and which countries would be free to decide on a policy corresponding to their national priorities', would be answered as usual: the hegemonial currency role would be performed by the largest economy of the region, i.e. German monetary policy would dominate. If all EMS countries would try to keep exchange rates constant *vis-à-vis* the Deutschemark, this would imply a rather harsh monetary restriction in most member countries (see the *Financial Times*, 1978b).

The arguments of the critics of the first group dominated the final steps for setting up the structure of the EMS. The German Bundesbank achieved important revisions to the Copenhagen and Bremen concept of the EMS. In particular, their resistance against a par-value system with the ECU as an anchor and in favour of a parity grid (system of bilateral intervention points) served the objective of a less inflation-prone intervention system. The very fact that the threshold-of-divergence indicator became less of an automatic device that enforces specific action, but more of a helpful warning system, made the system more acceptable to the Bundesbank; the same is true of the modifications to the conditions for credit facilities within the EMS, which are almost as tough as the snake regulations were. The hesitancy of potential weak-currency countries to participate was neutralised by a prior-to-entry depreciation of their currencies and a substantial regional transfer (Italy, Ireland).

PERFORMANCE OF THE EMS

The performance of the EMS and its implications for the development of key economic variables in the member countries cannot be measured directly. In order to arrive at some understanding of the consequences and implications of the EMS, a wide sample of indicators will be described and analysed. Not only those variables are included which are in the foreground of the economic–political debate, but also some which are – in the author's judgement – crucial to economic processes, and thus of final relevance for the evaluation of economic policy pursued under the EMS regime. (For the development and analysis of far more sophisticated indicators of the impact of European monetary integration cf. the contribution by Vaubel to this volume.)

The EMS and the development of ultimate targets

It is only fair to say that eighteen months is too short a period properly to assess the performance of a system like the EMS, especially when measured against its ultimate targets. This is due to the fact that the realisation of economic policy after an institutional rearrangement takes a long time, longer if one considers the lagged adjustment of economic variables to changes in economic policy or other exogenous shocks. This statement holds true especially for the development of inflation, a variable which is certainly lagging even more than economic activity and employment.

   Hints for what may be future consequences of the EMS may be

derived from what happened to ultimate targets in those countries belonging to the snake for quite some time (especially from those cases where exchange rates were seldom changed). The argument that the evidence revealed by developments within the snake is proof of the disciplinary effects of such a system is, however, called into question by the different experience of some snake countries (e.g. Denmark), and even more so by very stability-oriented policies in countries having only loose connections with the EMS (the UK in particular).

Inflation rates

If one measures the performance of some ultimate target variables against the aspirations of those in favour of the EMS, the results are poor, to say the least. If the aim of the EMS to develop into a 'zone of stability' is understood as a means to reduce the average inflation rate of the region and to reduce its divergence, the system is a failure (see Fig. 3.1). Not only did average rates of inflation (increase of consumer prices) increase from 7 per cent in 1978 to 8.5 in 1979 and 12 per cent in 1980, but the maximum difference also increased from 10 per cent in 1978 to 15 per cent in 1980. Several observations are noteworthy for the analysis of the price performance of EC countries. First, there is a very strong convergence of inflation rates in Germany, Belgium and the Netherlands. Austria and, to some extent, Switzerland are members of this low and highly cohesive inflation-rate club. This observation should be remembered when exchange-rate developments are analysed later. Second, the inflation levels of Denmark and France move almost in line with the first group's inflation rates, and thus remain persistently higher than the inflation levels of the first group. Third, Italy's inflation performance – together with that of the UK – being worst throughout the seventies among the EC countries diverged from the average even more in 1979 and 1980. This is a rather disappointing assessment for all those who are advocates of the vicious circle argument, since – as will be shown later – the nominal exchange rate of the lira was kept almost constant from late 1978; despite a wider band for the lira. Finally, if one attributes the bad inflation performance in the EMS member countries to the fixing of nominal exchange rates, the case of the UK, where a sustained and vigorous upturn of inflation can be observed, despite the fact that the effective exchange rate of the pound moved upward substantially and despite monetary policy becoming restrictive rather early and rather drastically, is extremely difficult to understand.

The development of inflation rates within the EC thus cannot be

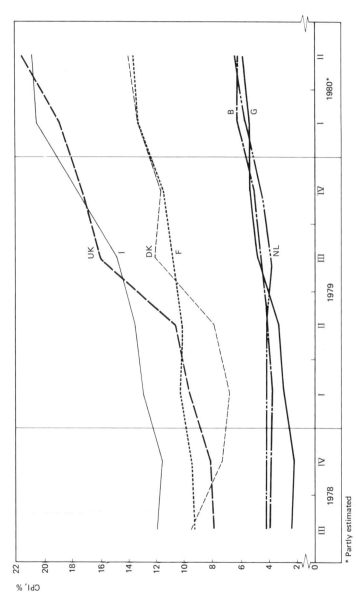

FIG. 3.1 Inflation rates in EC countries (percentage change over corresponding quarter of previous year in consumer price index). (B = Belgium; DK = Denmark; F = France; G = Germany; I = Italy; NL = Netherlands; UK = United Kingdom)

Source: *International Financial Statistics* (Jan 1980) p. 45; (Oct 1980) p. 45.

described either as a case against or in favour of a rigid exchange-rate regime. First, policies possibly induced by the introduction of the system cannot have worked their way into inflation rates since average lags of price effects to policy (especially monetary policy) impulses are as long as six quarters or more. (This may be the best explanation for the higher cohesion of inflation rates in many old snake countries.) Thus the price stabilisation effects of the system – if any are to be expected – are only to be expected for the coming quarters. Second, the sharp increase of oil prices in the period under consideration, affecting different countries differently (degree of energy dependency, degree of oil import dependency, passing-through characteristics of the price system, production structure and flexibility of production structure) makes it difficult to attribute recent price level developments to recent economic and exchange-rate policy. Third, price indices have been affected heavily and differently by tax measures (VAT increases) and by de-regulation of prices in EC countries. These changes distort the measurement of inflation. Short-run changes of the price indices are (incorrectly) identified as changes of inflation rates. The recent reductions of year-over-year inflation rates in the UK and Germany are cases in point.

Employment and output

We need to check possible effects of the EMS on other ultimate targets of economic policy. The dynamics of the underlying economic processes should be analysed properly in order to develop a basis for the judgement of the prospects for the rigid exchange-rate regime. Only if centrifugal forces with respect to other economic variables like output or unemployment are not observed or anticipated can the prospects for the EMS be described as promising.

Again, before evaluating recent developments, it is to be stated that the period since March 1979, when the EMS came into existence, is too short to allow a reliable assessment of its effects on economic variables. However, since the time-lag between changes in economic policy and changes in output and even in employment is shorter as compared to the price level, the performance of these variables may be less misleading. In any case a special analysis of old snake countries' performances may prove to be helpful again.

While economic relevance favours the analysis of employment figures rather than unemployment rates, the fact that unemployment figures are published with a far shorter time-lag and are far more reliable encourages the use of the latter. The most timely output measure, industrial production, is not used since its availability is limited to some countries and its degree of representativeness for the economies concerned differs substantially. Thus, GDP figures are taken as indicators for output developments.

While in the sixties and early seventies unemployment rates almost everywhere exhibited a strong cyclical pattern (compare, for example, Chart 4 in OECD, 1977, p. 46), this tendency could hardly be observed in Europe during the second half of the seventies (Fig. 3.2). It was only Germany that showed a slight improvement of unemployment during recent upswing periods, and there were only very short-lived improvements in the UK and Denmark, the first being caused by special factors like North Sea oil, the second being stimulated by exchange-rate depreciations of the Danish krone. During most of the time and in most countries, however, a trend towards higher unemployment is exhibited. The relative unemployment position in Germany and the Netherlands on one side and practically all other European countries on the other side worsened with respect to the latter. It is, of course, too simple to attribute this divergent development to one single factor. However, supply-side factors like demographic trends and migration explain hardly any part of it. Inappropriateness of combined macroeconomic and wage–price policies is far easier to identify as a 'cause' for the divergent trends.

A factor which I would like to label 'negative money illusion' led to increasing unemployment during recent years in those countries where restrictive policies were pursued as a reaction to the new rigid exchange-rate regime, or induced independently by acceptance of the non-existence of a medium- and long-run trade-off between unemployment and inflation. Negative money illusion exists when and where anti-inflation macroeconomic policy is not credible or not understood, or where institutional hindrances exist to the reduction of inflation and/or inflationary expectations. All of these factors are the more relevant the less reliable are governments and central banks, the more abruptly are policy changes executed and the less informed are individuals and markets.

Given the obviously slow pace of improvement of these structural deficiencies, the performance of employment suggests that strong tensions are emerging within the fixed-exchange-rate regime; thus a realignment of exchange rates is called for.

Similar conclusions can be drawn from the development of GDP (Fig. 3.3). The performance of Germany not only seems to be relatively good (it seems even better if one calculates actual growth rates against

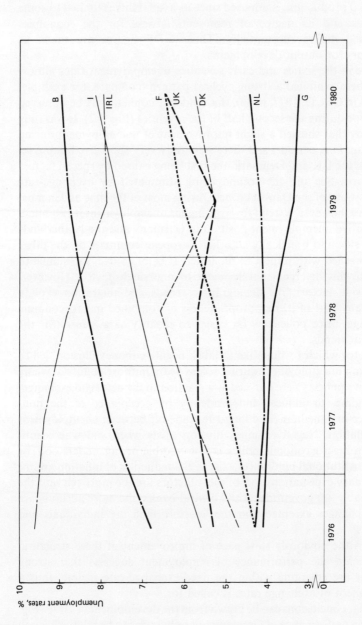

FIG. 3.2 Unemployment rates in EC countries (annual averages). (For key, see Fig. 3.1.)

Source: Kommission der Europäischen Gemeinschaften, *Generaldirektion Wirtschaft und Finanzen, Europäische Wirtschaft,* no. 6 (July 1980) p. 106.

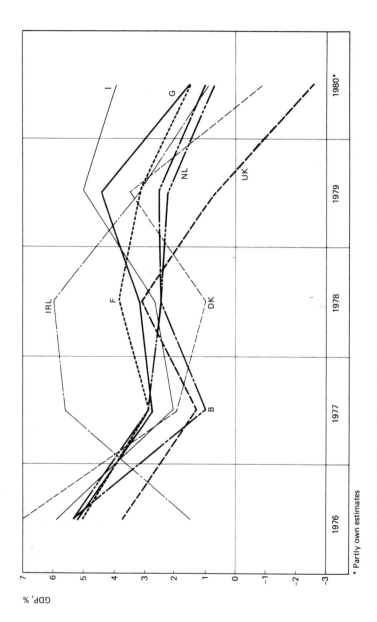

FIG. 3.3 Real GDP in EC countries (change over previous years). (For key, see Fig. 3.1.)

Source: Kommission der Europäischen Gemeinschaften, *Generaldirektion Wirtschaft und Finanzen, Europäische Wirtschaft,* no. 6 (July 1980) p. 106.

potential growth rates) but even more important, the relative weakness of economic activity increased in most of the rigidly-fixed-exchange-rate countries recently. This is the more depressing since even Germany suffers from an impressive worsening of economic activity. Only Italy has apparently obviated any such negative impact of the EMS up to early summer 1980. While in the case of the UK the EMS cannot be blamed for the macroeconomic policies pursued, the very fact that an abrupt restrictive policy and a substantial real appreciation of the pound led to what is possibly the worse post-war downturn in Great Britain, may illustrate a possible economic scenario for those EMS countries sticking for an extended period of time to a nominally fixed exchange rate when simultaneously domestic price and cost developments continuously exceed those of other member countries.

The development of unemployment and output in the EC and within the group of countries belonging to the EMS seems to indicate that the EMS may lead to high costs in terms of output and employment losses. Acknowledging the existence of negative money illusion, less abrupt strategies of macroeconomic policy restraint than those executed in the UK or enforced or induced by the EMS seem to be preferable under those circumstances.

The EMS and the development of intermediate targets

It proved difficult to assess the performance of the EMS in terms of the achievement of ultimate targets. It seems easier to analyse whether the EMS met the expectations for intermediate targets. One difficulty, however, is the fact that, while the ultimate target of price stability is clearly defined and aimed at, it is less clear whether totally rigid nominal exchange rates are aimed at. The EMS explicitly provides for adjustments of exchange rates. So it seems rather arbitrary to evaluate whether a certain exchange-rate development is to qualify as a success according to EMS intentions or as a failure. It is even more difficult to assess other intermediate targets as being in line with the thrust of the EMS. This is true for interest-rate developments as well, and even more so for the development of monetary aggregates.

Exchange rates

It is a declared objective of the EMS 'to stabilise exchange rates between the currencies of the member states of the European Communities' (Deutsche Bundesbank, March 1979, p. 11). Since no further qualification is given, this should be understood as constant bilateral nominal exchange rates. Figure 3.4 shows the development of nominal exchange rates of EC currencies against Deutschemark. It clearly shows that exchange-rate changes have declined since 1976. While EC currencies depreciated at double-digit rates in 1976 against the Deutschemark, depreciation came to an almost complete stop in 1979. Were it not for the Danish krone, the exchange-rate changes would have been practically zero. This certainly can easily be qualified as a 'success' of the EMS: an intermediate target has been almost met.

The reduction of exchange-rate changes would be less clear-cut if a longer period of time were analysed. The year 1976 was one of very pronounced exchange-rate adjustments. For the creation and analysis of the EMS, however, the experience in the second half of the seventies was crucial. Therefore, concentration on that period of time seems to be warranted.

If present (1980) exchange rates can be described as true equilibrium exchange rates (and are not to be attributed to a series of market distortions, such as capital controls, forms of non-tariff trade barriers, hindrances to labour migration, and monetary policies which aim at high short-term interest rates and relatively low long-term rates by selling foreign reserves on money markets and buying bonds, or enforcing commercial banks to buy bonds, thus avoiding a depreciation of domestic currencies by an operation twist) and if the present relative restrictiveness of monetary and fiscal policies in EC countries is there to stay, this would certainly foreshadow a period of price stability for Europe, and thus the achievement of the ultimate aim of EMS. Both conditions, however, are not, or will not be fulfilled.

While intra-EMS exchange-rate relations are of great importance for trade and capital movements in all EC countries, and are crucial in a narrow and technocratic sense for the performance of the EMS, exchange-rate changes against the weighted average of all (important) countries are decisive finally for a particular country's economic performance. Therefore, Table 3.1 exhibits the effective exchange-rate changes of EC countries since 1976. With only a few minor exceptions this table does confirm the impressions derived from the development of bilateral exchange rates: more and more EC countries seem to approach, join, or even overtake the stability-minded German macroeconomic policy. Rates of depreciation narrow or even become rates of appreciation (UK).

While nominal exchange-rate changes are relevant to calculating whether capital movements are profitable, it is necessary to calculate

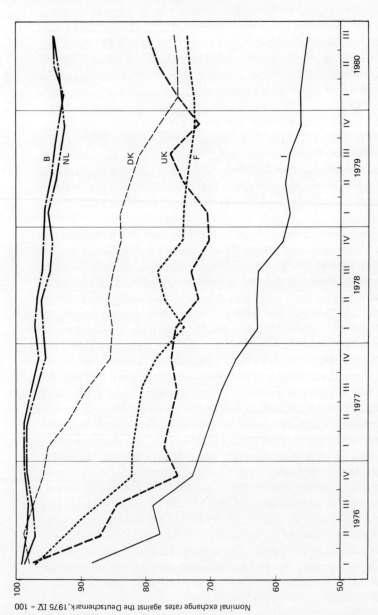

FIG 3.4 Nominal exchange rates of EC currencies against the Deutschemark (1975 IV = 100; quarterly averages). (For key, see Fig. 3.1.)

Source: Based on Deutsche Bundesbank monthly reports (Oct 1980) Table IX, 10, p. 78.

TABLE 3.1 Effective exchange rate changes

	D	F	NL	I	B	DK	UK
1976	3.7	− 5.2	2.1	− 18.0	0.4	2.2	− 15.4
1977	8.1	− 4.9	4.9	− 8.0	4.5	0.2	− 5.0
1978	7.0	0	2.4	− 5.0	2.7	0.9	1.4
1979	5.9	1.8	1.9	− 2.3	1.7	− 0.1	7.6
1980$_{II}$	0.8	1.2	0.5	− 2.6	0.9	− 7.6	8.4

Source: International Financial Statistics (Aug 1980) country tables.

real exchange-rate changes in order to assess the development of the competitive position of a country. (For a more sophisticated analysis, see Vaubel's contribution to this volume.)

As a first step, again bilateral changes are calculated (Fig. 3.5). The bilateral competitive positions show that recent policy moves have led to some correction of worsened positions in the cases of the Netherlands, Belgium and Denmark. However, other EC countries have lost substantially *vis-à-vis* Germany in relative competitiveness since 1978. This is true for France and Italy, and especially true for the UK.

If PPP-adjustments of exchange rates were declared targets within the EMS, the performance so far would have to be assessed as mixed. Should constant real exchange rates be aimed at, though, a more sensible indicator would be multilateral real exchange rates instead of the bilateral ones in Fig. 3.5. It can be deduced from Table 3.2 that the results are not very different.

Whether constant real exchange rates are a sensible target of economic policy is a debatable issue. It is, however, obvious that large and persistent changes of real exchange rates do have an impact on economic activity, employment and inflation. Structural developments between the tradeable and non-tradeable sector are affected. Thus, while reservations about the target of constant real exchange rates are generally valid, arguments against heavily fluctuating and abruptly changing real exchange rates should be taken seriously.

Interest rates

The establishment of a more rigid exchange-rate regime in Europe was understood as a disciplinary factor for the pursuit of a policy conducive to greater stability. Some observers identify such a policy by checking the development of interest rates. To evaluate policy effects by observing nominal interest rates and their development, however, may be

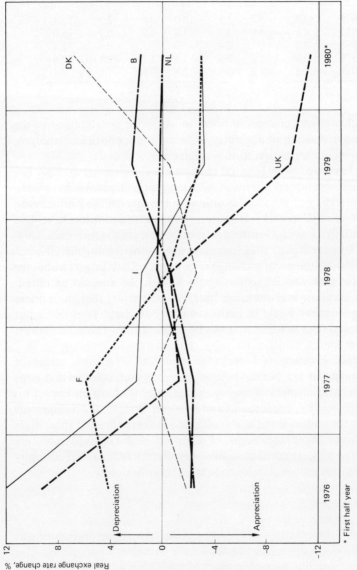

F<small>IG</small>. 3.5 Real exchange rate changes of EC currencies against the Deutschemark (percentage change over previous year, CPI as deflator). (For key, see Fig. 3.1.)

Source: Shadow European Economic Policy Committee, *Policy Statement and Position Papers* (Paris, 1979) p. 51.

TABLE 3.2 Effective real exchange-rate changes (percentage change over previous year, wholesale prices as deflator)

	D	F	NL	I	B	DK	UK
1976	1.6	− 4.2	1.8	− 7.4	1.9	2.1	− 6.1
1977	2.1	− 5.8	3.6	1.0	0.5	− 2.1	7.0
1978	1.4	2.9	− 0.4	− 3.0	− 2.3	− 0.2	4.7
1979	0.9	3.8	− 3.1	2.7	− 1.0	− 2.4	9.9
1980_I	− 1.9	3.4	− 2.5	6.5	− 2.8	− 7.1	8.6

Source: International Financial Statistics (Aug 1980) p. 43.

misleading, when the money demand side is considered and when effects of changing inflation expectations are taken into account. Measured in terms of nominal interest rates, monetary policy has been highly co-ordinated within the EMS since the latter part of 1978, i.e. the period since the EMS came into force (Fig. 3.6). Rates were very different in 1976, moved somewhat more in line in 1977, started to rise in late 1978, and exhibited a strong synchronised increase in spring 1979, when the EMS became effective. The attempts to keep interest-rate developments in the convoy was not limited to EMS countries. If monetary policies are conducive to converging nominal interest rates, this does not automatically imply sensible policy co-ordination. As a rule it leads to reduced exchange-rate changes. The impact of such policies on ultimate targets like inflation, employment and growth may, however, be rather divergent among countries.

Calculating 'real' interest rates may be a device to arrive at some answers. If real rates of interest are increasing, it becomes relatively more attractive to invest in monetary assets. This, as a rule, is conducive to price stability and depresses, in the short term, economic activity (Fig. 3.7). All EC countries have shifted policies towards fighting inflation since early 1979. This is relatively pronounced in Germany, but even more so in Belgium and the Netherlands. If one takes into account how badly output and employment developed in both these countries, this policy bias can be clearly attributed to their exchange rate and/or (low) inflation target, i.e. the Netherlands and Belgium behaved as if living in a fixed exchange rate regime vis-à-vis the Deutschemark. The same evidence cannot be derived from the development of real interest rates for other European countries. This, however, does not mean that they did not pursue an exchange-rate or low-inflation-oriented demand management policy. Some countries' financial systems do not work via a flexible-price (i.e. interest-rate) mechanism, but more via quantitative

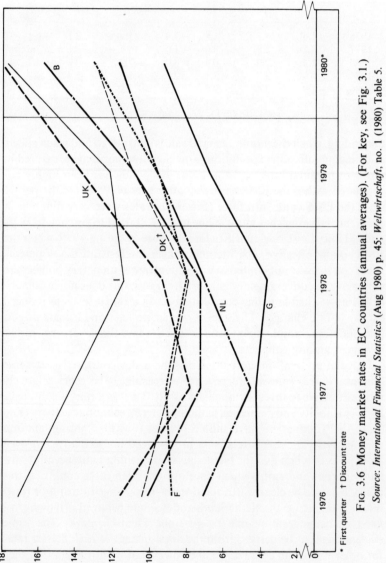

FIG. 3.6 Money market rates in EC countries (annual averages). (For key, see Fig. 3.1.)
Source: International Financial Statistics (Aug 1980) p. 45; *Weltwirtschaft*, no. 1 (1980) Table 5.

* First quarter † Discount rate

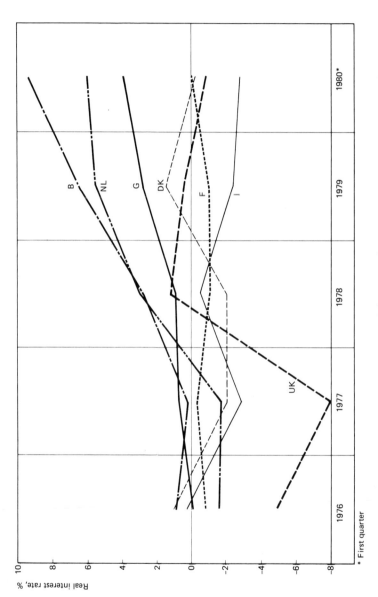

Real interest rate, %

* First quarter

FIG. 3.7 Real interest rates in EC countries (annual averages of three-month money market rates minus rate of CPI. (For key, see Fig. 3.1.)

Source: International Financial Statistics (Aug 1980) p. 45; *Weltwirtschaft*, no. 1 (1980) Table 5.

credit controls. In those cases the observation of Euro-market rates would be preferable. Italy may be a case in point.

In more general terms, the above calculation of 'real' interest rates may not be adequate, since it is only price *expectations* that count for actual economic decisions and not the inflation rate prevailing during the observed period. If these expectations differ from current year-over-year rates, the above calculations are hardly meaningful. If special reasons exist for a divergence of current inflation rates and inflation expectations, as in the case of VAT increases or de-regulation measures for prices (as, for example, in the UK and France), Fig. 3.7 hardly allows us to identify different priority ranking in different EC countries. Some additional information can be derived from the analysis of the term structure of interest rates and their development over time. As a rule the term structure has been perverse since the EMS was founded. This means that short-term rates are higher than medium- and long-term maturities. The negative shape is, as a rule, steeper the higher the real rate of interest (Fig. 3.8). Since investment in longer term maturities generally involves more risk, a higher yield for long term investment is warranted. If, however, monetary policy becomes restrictive, liquidity becomes scarce and interest rates go up. This is especially true for the short-term maturities, since investors expect, as a consequence of restrictive policy, a slow-down of future inflation rates. Since nominal interest rates are moving in line with inflation rates in the longer term, interest rates are expected to decline as well. Thus the term structure of interest rates may be looked upon as a proxy for the market's assessment of the restrictiveness of monetary policy.

Whether the currencies of those countries with a negative real rate are candidates for depreciation, is however, not easy to say because of the above-mentioned objections against the calculation of real rates. It is, however, certainly a relevant indicator in some cases.

Monetary aggregates

Before describing and analysing the development of monetary aggregates, some general remarks seem necessary. Since all participants in the EMS understand the importance of converging economic policy as a precondition for the functioning of the system, and since the theoretical demand management debate shifted emphasis from fiscal to monetary policy, and within that topic from anticyclical interest-rate policy to steady money-supply policy, one should have expected that the policy-makers and the analysts would concentrate on the question of

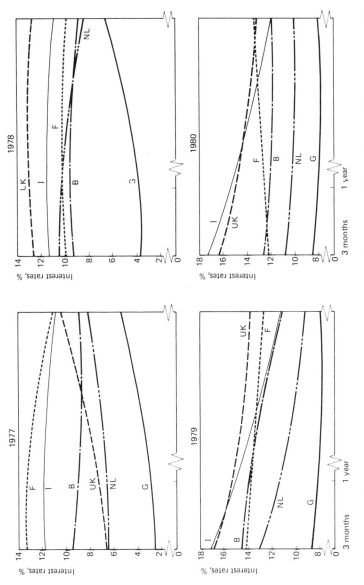

FIG. 3.8 Term structure of interest rates in EC countries: euro-currency deposit rates (3-month maturity, one-year maturity) and government bond yields.

whether money-supply policies should be harmonised or not. There is hardly any indication that this is the case. While most countries do have a money supply target (cf. OECD, 1979), they are taken seriously hardly anywhere. Targets are defined for different aggregates, for different periods, and with different statistical properties (current rates, year-over-year rates, bands, means etc.). However, statistics for a commonly defined monetary aggregate are not supplied to the public by the EC (see, for example, Commission of the *European Community*, 1980, p. 111). Research about the appropriate monetary indicators is not undertaken at the EC level, nor is independent advice welcomed by central banks. The impression is that central banks are determined to restrict the identification of convergence to the discretion of each national central bank (for similar observations see Thygesen, 1978, p. 15).

Another observation seems to be important for a better understanding of monetary developments in Europe. It seems that US monetary policy continues to set the tune for global monetary events. The resulting exchange-rate changes caused by either an expansionary or a restrictive US policy are as a rule unwelcome, since the industrial countries have been in a synchronised cycle since the seventies. Thus, any deviation of US monetary policy from middle of the road is followed by the rest of the world. This does not mean that Europeans and Japanese have no influence on the common course of policy. But this is more via consultations at the BIS or summit meetings of the heads of state or IMF conferences rather than via markets. Since the US shifted from a policy of 'benign neglect' towards a policy of concern for the US dollar in autumn 1978, the period during which Europeans decided to establish the EMS, the possibility cannot be ruled out that the political move towards closer European integration and thus towards more influence in international monetary affairs 'helped' the US government and central bank to embark upon a policy to regain stability of the US dollar. Another 'explanation' of the US shift in policy seems, however, more valid: since Americans felt hurt by high inflation rates (partly stemming from increasing import prices, partly induced by the depreciation of the dollar), they chose to pursue anti-inflation policy and to support the dollar.

Closer convergence of monetary policy, but at the same time continued unsteadiness of monetary policies, is clearly shown in Fig. 3.9. Not only can anti-cyclical efforts not be overlooked, but also an intensified convergence of monetary expansion is to be observed; the standard deviation has become very low since 1977. There is some

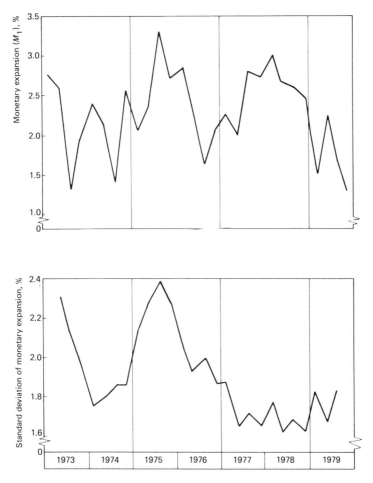

FIG. 3.9 Monetary development in industrial countries: UK, Denmark, France, Germany, Italy, The Netherlands, Norway, Sweden, Switzerland, Canada, Japan, Spain, USA.

indication of a further decline in 1980. Monetary expansion is measured in terms of the narrowly defined money supply (M_1: currency plus sight deposits). This is not done arbitrarily, but because there is evidence from a series of countries that M_1 is the most reliable monetary indicator as well as the indicator with the longest lead with respect to economic activity (see OECD, 1979). The correlation between M_1 and economic activity is higher than with other monetary aggregates (it is even higher with M_1 deflated by the consumer price index). The lag between the monetary impulse and its main impact on economic activity varies between two and four quarters in the observed countries.

Italy's monetary policy exhibits no strong signs of exchange-rate orientation (Figs 3.10 and 3.11). Monetary expansion kept 'Italian levels' throughout the period. Only price developments reduced the expansion of the (real) money supply. In other European countries some kind of cohesion of money-supply developments cannot be overlooked. Again, Germany, Belgium and the Netherlands stick together closer than other countries (in terms of nominal and real monetary expansion), France and Denmark show some loose ties. The UK, the non-participating member of the exchange-rate regulations, performs even more restrictively than Germany. This last case can hardly be qualified as exchange-rate orientation. It seems to be a misconceived anti-inflationary policy, partly explained by the fact that the British government and central bank aim at a $£M_3$ target which possibly is a coincident, if not a lagging, indicator for economic activity (as is the case for Germany). Whether or not ascribed correctly, there is some kind of convergence of monetary growth within the group of EMS countries.

PROSPECTS FOR THE EMS

It was extremely difficult to assess the performance of the EMS, the reasons being the loosely-defined targets of the system, the great ambitions of the founders, and only a very short period of observation. In addition, there are increasing political East–West tensions and a disturbing oil shock. Because of the very vague conclusions about the performance of the EMS, the outline of prospects can be nothing but plausible speculation.

Ambiguous political auspices

The EMS is an arrangement desired by practitioners and established by extremely self-conscious politicians. Thus economic reasoning will be subordinate to political considerations if changes in the EMS are envisaged. Chancellor Schmidt and President Giscard d'Estaing do have strong vested interests in the EMS. Both are facing elections: Chancellor Schmidt in October 1980, President Giscard d'Estaing in Spring 1981. Prestige reasons strongly support the view that fundamental reforms are ruled out before both dates. Most probably exchange-rate changes

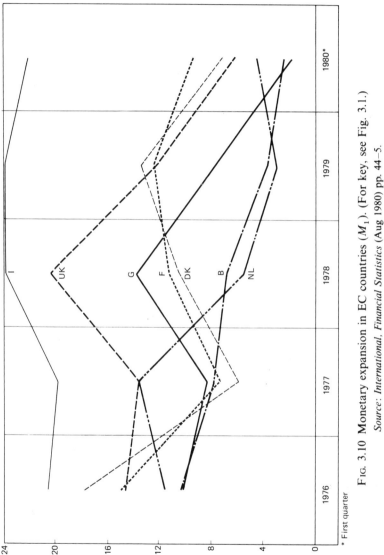

FIG. 3.10 Monetary expansion in EC countries (M_1). (For key, see Fig. 3.1.)

Source: *International, Financial Statistics* (Aug 1980) pp. 44–5.

* First quarter

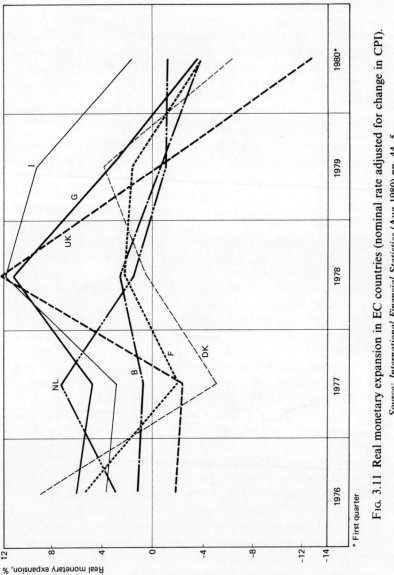

FIG. 3.11 Real monetary expansion in EC countries (nominal rate adjusted for change in CPI).
Source: International Financial Statistics (Aug 1980) pp. 44–5.

* First quarter

between the Deutschemark and the French franc should be avoided as well. Since no EMS member seems ready to depreciate, only a Deutschemark revaluation would be a possible realignment. This seems, in pre-election times however, unwelcome for French politicians. While resistance to any change of exchange rates is the official reading of European governments' policies, mounting requests from entrepreneurs in France and Italy may change governments' attitudes. Whether, therefore, a Deutschemark revaluation will follow a general election in Germany for the fourth time remains doubtful, especially in the light of Germany's persistent current-account deficit.

Shift of emphasis from fighting inflation towards fighting unemployment?

If historical relations hold, the prospects for a world-wide recession are certain: a massive oil price increase, as dramatic in real terms as in 1973/74, an even more marked and sustained monetary deceleration, and a fiscal policy at least as conservative as in 1973/74 on a world-wide level will cool off economic activity severely. Softening factors may be a less aggressive price and wage settling as compared to 1974/75 and the existence of some 'autonomous investment', induced by the belief that the relative oil price has permanently gone up significantly and may continue to do so (investment for energy substitution and energy conservation).

Changes in priority ranking may not come about simultaneously since some countries are in more trouble than others with respect to their competitive position, their output developments and their unemployment situation. Such a scenario is highly likely to emerge during the quarters to come. A less quiet period for the EMS and international (foreign exchange) markets alike will develop.

Since countries with so-called weak currencies have learnt that even the short-run trade-off between unemployment and inflation does not exist, and that a vicious circle may be set in motion if they start to pursue an expansionary policy on their own, they will hesitate to react in such a way. The situation bound to emerge internationally and the accumulated divergences within the EMS will lead to a consideration of the following strategies: implementation of a locomotive approach; realignment within the EMS; increasing use of EMS credit facilities; introduction of protectionist measures for capital and goods markets. The theoretically possible alternative strategy, namely that the European societies agree to shoulder the negative output and employment effects of the 'big bang' strategy to reduce inflation at very short notice to the low levels aimed at in the most stability-minded countries, is considered extremely improbable.

In the following paragraphs the pros and cons of the probable elements of adjustment within the EMS are discussed.

Implementation of a locomotive approach?

In short, the locomotive approach means that 'strong' countries, to be defined as important countries (GNP-weight) with relatively low inflation rates, relatively healthy current-balance positions, and a good credit-worthiness should expand their domestic demand by more than needed for domestic purposes (national employment and growth targets), in order to allow weak countries (to be defined as countries with relatively high inflation rates, relatively bad, i.e. passive, current-balance positions, and difficulties in getting international credit) to rely on an export-led recovery. This implies a relatively restrictive stance of monetary and fiscal policy in weak countries, sometimes complemented by an incomes policy.

The theoretical basis for such a locomotive strategy is to be seen in the diagnosis of economic problems as being caused mainly by a world-wide lack of demand. According to this diagnosis the therapy to be applied is a stimulation of demand. Since, however, not only a lack of demand is to be observed, but also – at existing exchange rates – a disequilibrium in international current balances, the stimulation in countries which are strong should be stronger, in those which are weaker it should be moderate. This advice is based on Keynesian philosophy and the assumption of either rigid exchange rates or ineffective exchange-rate changes (vicious-circle thesis).

In the late seventies it was difficult quickly to persuade Germany and Japan to accept their role as locomotive countries. This time, the very fact that Germany has a current account deficit will add to the resistance. This argument comes in addition to more general and theoretical reasons for rejecting the locomotive approach as a viable strategy to solve international problems. If the problems are attributed not to a lack of demand, but to a lack of structural flexibility, then demand stimulation is only a means to rekindle inflation, but not to stimulate long-term growth. Despite this inevitable reluctance, a policy co-ordination in which Germany and the Benelux countries will take a lead may emerge in the course of 1981, since co-ordination needs will be in line with domestic priorities.

Realignment within the EMS

With few exceptions, exchange rates during history have adhered closely to some purchasing-power-parity path in the medium run (cf. Ahnefeld and Hub, 1979). According to this experience some EMS currencies are out of line, the Italian lira being the most striking case. However, other sets of indicators show that some other currencies may be in trouble as well, i.e. expected changes of exchange rates do not equal forward rates. Extremely high real rates of interest or excessively increasing international borrowing serve as evidence. Cases in point are Belgium and Denmark. The pound, not fixed within the EMS, may be a candidate for a correction of its exchange rate as well.

Up to 1980, hardly any market pressure for an exchange rate adjustment could be observed, and political considerations ruled out a deliberate realignment within the EMS. So the adjustment will only take place after some hefty market speculation that forces central banks to intervene heavily. Thus, exchange-rate adjustments will probably be delayed, especially since a multilateral agreement is necessary, and will be relatively small in size. A special reason for small adjustments is the EC agricultural market rules, which are of hardly-imaginable complexity and which imply highly sensitive vested interests. Whether the difficulties described for realignments within the EMS are a case for opting out for some members, or a case for renegotiation of the system, remains an open question.

Increasing use of EMS credit facilities

The experience during the first six quarters of the EMS is that the new credit facilities have not been used at all. Only the Belgian central bank requested the automatic extension of the very short-term financing (45 days) of intervention balances. However, no debt accumulation took place within the EMS.

Considering the economic outlook, the extent of the socially bearable unemployment burden and the reluctance to realign exchange rates, it should be expected that the existing credit facilities will be used as a first cushion. This sort of cushion is a solution only to temporary difficulties. The therapy has to go further. Since the regulations for credit creation are relatively tough and since conditions for credits imply only mild subsidisation, moral hazard for excessive use of these facilities is not too strong a force (cf. for the opposite view the *Financial Times*, 7 December 1978).

Introduction of protectionist measures for capital and goods markets

It would not be the first time that protectionist measures were introduced to defend a rigid exchange-rate regime. This happened time and again in the Bretton Woods era. It was repeated after the Smithsonian realignment for capital markets in 1972. After the repeated failure of capital controls in the seventies, especially in those countries which are intensely integrated into international financial markets, this device will play hardly any major role in a strategic concept to solve the accumulated problems. In Italy, however, controls for international capital transactions have been tightened recently.

There are, however, distinct signs of a growing protectionist mood with respect to trade. The US and EC propensity to blame Japan for many of the domestic output and employment difficulties is to be mentioned in that context. There is, however, growing concern about negative bilateral trade balances *vis-à-vis* Germany in some European countries. Uneasiness is voiced most often in France, the UK and Italy.

While it is conceivable that non-tariff trade barriers of the very subtle types may be introduced or intensified within Europe – France and Italy are not unexperienced in that respect – an outright protectionist tendency can be qualified as highly improbable.

FINAL REMARKS

Whether the experience with the European snake is a promising guide to the prospects for the EMS is difficult to say. While within the small snake Germany was without any doubt the hegemonial country, this is less clear within the EMS. While the snake allowed unilateral exchange-rate decisions, the EMS necessitates multilateral agreement. Opting out of the system again is probable since adjustments within the system are hardly possible.

Another difficulty in forecasting the EMS performance is the fact that the world seems again to be back to some kind of dollar-standard. Since US monetary policy is hardly predictable, as demonstrated by the wild gyrations of monetary expansion during 1979–80, the tendencies within the EMS are not determined. If the upward movement of US interest rates were to slow down for a sustained period, this would alleviate the situation for the EMS. In that case German interest rates would be allowed to decline.

The background to the author's hesitancy to give an unambiguous forecast of the prospects for the EMS is not only the inconclusive analysis of economic and political factors involved in this question, but also the experience of how unimaginative experts may be with respect to future events in foreign exchange markets. In 1970 a symposium on 'Integration through Monetary Union' was held at the Kiel Institute. It took place in the midst of the break-down of the Bretton Woods system and at the start of the discussion about the first attempt to achieve European monetary integration, the so-called 'Werner Plan'. One participant, a senior member of the OECD, stated at that time: 'We have already got to the stage where it would be legitimate and possible for our governments to sign a piece of paper which said: We agree never to change our exchange rate by more than 2 per cent in any one year' (Marris, 1970, p.32). Between 1970 and 1980 the exchange rate between the Italian lira and the Deutschemark changed by some 10 per cent per annum.

NOTE

Critical comments from my colleague Bodo Risch and Michael Sumner are greatly appreciated. For remaining mistakes the author acknowledges responsibility.

REFERENCES

Ahnefeld, A. and H.-J. Hub (1979), 'Kaum Chancen für Stabile Wecheselkurse', *Die Weltwirtschaft* (Tübingen), no. 2, pp. 44–54.
Commission of the European Community (1980), Statistical Annex, Table 27, *European Economy*, no. 6, p. 111.
Deutsche Bundesbank (ed.) (1979), *Monthly Report* (English version) p.11, March.
Fellner, W. (1970), 'Specific Proposal for Limited Exchange Rate Flexibility', *Weltwirtschaftliches Archiv*, no. 104, p. 24.
Financial Times (1978a), 'Time to Replace Floating Rate', 28 February.
Financial Times (1978b), 'EMS Increase in Bank Drawing Rights has Inflationary Bias', 7 December.
Finanz und Wirtschaft (1978), 'Sehnsucht nach Bretton Woods', 27 May.
Frankfurter Allgemeine Zeitung (1978), 'Engere Bindungen der Europäischen Währungen Untereinander' (Closer ties between European currencies), 1 April.
Handelsblatt (1978), 'Abs Plädiert für Feste Wechselkurse', 12 April.
Institut für Weltwirtschaft (1979), *Internationale Kapitalströme bei flexiblen Wechselkursen* (Kiel: Institut für Weltwirtschaft). (English version: The

Brookings Institution, *International Linkages under Flexible Exchange Rates*, Washington D.C.: The Brookings Institution)

International Herald Tribune (1978), 'Anticlimax for the Dollar', 15 March.

Marris, S. (1970) in H. Giersch (ed.), *Integration through Monetary Union* (Tübingen: J. C. B. Mohr).

OECD (1977), 'Towards Full Employment and Price Stability' (McCracken Report) (Paris: OECD).

OECD (1979), 'Monetary Targets and Inflation Control', *Monetary Study Series* (Paris: OECD).

Reading, B. (1979), 'The Long Road to EMS', *Euromoney*, January.

Thygesen, N. (1978), 'International Coordination of Monetary Policies – with Special Reference to the European Community', in Köbenhavns Universitets Ökonomiske Institut, Memo, no. 62, p. 15.

Vaubel, R. (1979a), 'Die Rückkehr zum Neuen Europäischen Währungssytem', *Wirtschaftsdienst*, no. 1, pp. 25–30.

Vaubel, R. (1979b), *Choice in European Monetary Union*, Ninth Wincott Lecture, Institute of Economic Affairs, London, Occasional Paper 55.

Walter, N. (1973), *Europäische Währungspolitik – Traum oder Trauma* (Tübingen: J.C.B. Mohr).

Welt am Sonntag (1978), 'Scheu vor der Schlange', 11 June.

4 Monetary Divergences and Exchange-rate Changes in the European Community: the 1970s

ROLAND VAUBEL

OUTLINE

This paper gives answers, *inter alia*, to the following questions:

1. In what ways have inflation rates and monetary policies in the EC member countries diverged or converged in the 1970s?
2. To what extent can the difference in inflation rates be explained by differences in monetary policies?
3. To what extent can the exchange-rate changes between the EC currencies be explained by the differences in inflation rates and/or monetary policies and by real exchange-rate trends?
4. To what extent have nominal exchange-rate changes been associated with real exchange-rate changes?

Answers to these questions are important for any appraisal of whether and how the Community may attain more exchange-rate stability in the 1980s. However, the analysis is strictly positive and does not imply that exchange-rate stability and monetary-policy co-ordination are worth their costs for the community.[1]

MONETARY CONVERGENCE?

According to the resolution of the European Council of 5 December 1979, which established the European Monetary System (EMS), 'the

71

most important concern should be to enhance the convergence of economic policies towards greater stability' (B. 1). By stability is meant 'stability at home and abroad' (A.1.3.), which is usually interpreted as price-level stability and exchange-rate stability. While the EMS arrangements contain no provisions designed to attain greater stability of the members' price levels, they do purport to make for more exchange-rate stability.

There is widespread agreement that the convergence relevant for exchange-rate stability is the convergence of inflation rates (adjusted for real exchange-rate changes) and, thus, of their determinants, i.e. of national monetary policies. In a more straightforward way, since an exchange rate is the relative price between two monies, it can be said to be fully determined by the relative supplies of, and demand for, the two monies.[2]

The CPI inflation rates of the EC member countries in the 1960s and 1970s and two measures of their dispersion are given in Table 4.1. Unlike previous studies,[3] this one reports standard deviations that are weighted;[4] it uses the weights which the various member currencies occupied in the European Unit of Account on the day it was introduced into the operations of the Community institutions (10 March 1975).[5] (The European Unit of Account is now called European Currency Unit and is used as a 'divergence indicator' in the European Monetary System.)

The ranges give the difference between the highest and the lowest inflation rate for various groups of member currencies. While the ranges for 1960–8 and 1970–9 refer to the compound average inflation rates indicated above, the weighted standard deviations reported for these periods are arithmetic averages of the annual weighted standard deviations and therefore capture the year-to-year variations of inflation-rate dispersion.

Both the standard deviations and the ranges reveal that the dispersion of inflation rates in the Community as a whole has been more than twice as large in the seventies as in the sixties. However, the increase has been much smaller for the permanent member currencies of the 'snake' (DM, BF, DKr, HFL).[6] The increase in the standard deviations is also considerably reduced if sterling and the lira are excluded.[7] Dispersion did not increase markedly before 1974, i.e. one year after the transition to widespread floating had made widely divergent monetary policies possible and at a time when the first oil-price hike became effective. Dispersion peaked in 1975 but stayed at relatively high levels thereafter. Even the exceptionally low standard deviation for 1978, the year in which the EMS was established, was still about twice as large as what had been

TABLE 4.1 Inflation rates (consumer prices, per cent per annum)

	1960–8	1969	1970	1971	1972	1973	1974	1975	1976	1977	1978	1979	1980	1970–9
Belgium	2.9	3.9	3.9	4.3	5.4	6.9	12.7	12.7	9.2	7.1	4.5	4.4	6.5	7.1
Denmark	5.5	3.6	6.5	5.8	6.6	9.4	15.2	9.6	9.0	11.1	10.1	9.6	14.3	9.3
France	3.6	6.2	5.8	5.5	6.2	7.4	13.7	11.7	9.2	9.5	9.2	10.7	13.8	8.9
W. Germany	2.5	1.8	3.3	5.4	5.5	6.9	7.0	5.9	4.5	3.9	2.6	4.1	6.0	4.9
Ireland	3.6	7.4	8.3	8.8	8.7	11.3	17.0	20.9	18.0	13.6	7.6	13.2	15.6	12.7
Italy	3.8	2.6	4.8	5.0	5.7	10.8	19.1	17.0	16.8	17.0	12.2	14.7	20.5	12.2
The Netherlands	3.5	7.3	3.8	7.4	7.9	8.0	9.6	10.5	8.8	6.4	4.1	4.2	6.6	7.0
UK	3.2	5.4	6.3	9.4	7.3	9.1	16.0	24.2	16.5	15.9	8.3	13.4	21.9	12.5
Weighted standard deviation														
Excluding L, F	0.52	0.79	0.52	0.63	0.37	0.57	1.65	2.39	1.86	1.90	1.31	1.65	2.44	1.29
Excluding L, F, UK	0.51	0.91	0.57	0.41	0.40	0.67	1.86	1.83	1.87	1.91	1.52	1.74	2.25	1.28
Excluding L, F, UK, I	0.65	1.05	0.68	0.48	0.47	0.55	1.68	1.80	1.58	1.45	1.39	1.51	1.79	1.16
Six excluding L, F	0.62	1.08	0.51	0.39	0.39	0.70	2.18	2.02	2.12	2.27	1.85	2.10	2.74	1.45
Snake core	0.82	1.30	0.59	0.56	0.59	0.51	1.97	1.81	1.53	1.53	1.42	0.98	1.48	1.15
Range														
Excluding L, F	3.0	5.6	5.0	5.1	3.3	4.4	12.1	18.3	13.5	13.1	9.6	10.6	15.9	7.8
Excluding L, F, UK	3.0	5.6	5.0	4.5	3.3	4.4	12.1	15.0	13.5	13.1	9.6	10.6	14.5	7.8
Excluding L, F, UK, I	3.0	5.6	5.0	4.5	3.3	4.4	10.0	15.0	13.5	9.7	7.5	9.1	9.6	7.8
Six excluding L, F	1.3	5.5	2.5	3.1	2.5	3.9	12.1	11.1	12.3	13.1	9.6	10.6	14.5	7.3
Snake core	3.0	5.5	3.2	3.1	2.5	2.5	8.2	6.8	4.7	7.2	7.5	5.5	8.3	4.4

For all tables: L = Luxembourg; F = France; UK = United Kingdom; I = Italy.

typical (also of 'the six') in the years 1969–72, the period in which various plans for European Monetary Union were drafted and adopted. In other words: the chances of the EMS leading to exchange-rate stability between the member currencies have been incomparably smaller than the chances of European Monetary Union at the beginning of the seventies.

From 1978 onwards, the dispersion of inflation rates has again been increasing. However, since price levels tend to react with a longer lag to monetary policies than exchange markets, which are not only pure asset markets but also auction markets, the underlying policy divergence is likely to be of less recent origin. For this reason and for an appraisal of those current policies which have not yet had their full effect on national inflation rates, it may be helpful to look at national money supplies and money demand as 'early divergence indicators'.

Table 4.2 reports the equilibrium inflation rates that are implied by the simplest version of the quantity theory, which assumes a constant velocity of circulation. Hence, these equilibrium inflation rates are simply equal to the rate of expansion of money supply (M_1) minus the rate of growth of real GDP (or GNP) as a proxy for money demand.[8] Except for 1980,[9] the rates of change are computed from annual averages and are listed according to the year in which the monetary policy was pursued (not according to the year in which the equilibrium inflation rate is likely to prevail).

The results of Table 4.2 confirm the findings from Table 4.1 that the policy differences were much larger in the seventies than in the sixties. The increase of the differences was much smaller for the permanent members of the snake and, with respect to the weighted standard deviations, for the group excluding sterling and lira. The policy differences in 1978–9 were larger than those typical of the period 1969–72 (although the change is now less pronounced). The main change is that the time profile of the divergencies has shifted; they are now more volatile and increase earlier: in 1973 instead of 1974, and in 1978 instead of 1979. It is worth noting that the most recent figures (1979, 1980) signal only very feeble convergence.

The equilibrium inflation rates calculated in Table 4.2 do not allow for changes in velocity due to changes in interest rates. To avoid this omission, fully-fledged money-demand functions were estimated for each EC member country; these include a long-term or a short-term interest rate, the difference between the long-term and the short-term interest rate (to allow for term-structure effects)[10], and the difference between the domestic short-term interest rate and the Eurodollar

TABLE 4.2 Equilibrium inflation rates (p.a.) implied by simple quantity theory $\hat{M}_1 - \hat{Y}$

	1960–8	1969	1970	1971	1972	1973	1974	1975	1976	1977	1978	1979	1980	1970–9
Belgium	0.8	−3.0	−10.0	5.8	8.7	4.0	2.0	13.6	4.4	6.8	5.8	0.6	−5.8	4.0
Denmark	5.6	7.0	1.6	1.7	5.3	6.9	5.9	17.0	10.8	4.1	9.6	10.2	4.3	7.2
France	5.7	−0.7	−4.1	8.4	7.2	4.5	9.4	9.7	9.9	4.6	7.6	8.3	5.9	6.5
W. Germany	3.1	2.1	0.5	9.1	10.1	0.4	5.5	16.0	5.1	5.7	10.4	3.6	−2.8	6.5
Ireland	3.1	0.3	1.3	0.4	8.3	13.4	4.9	15.3	15.5	12.2	18.1	18.2	1.7	10.6
Italy	8.2	9.2	16.8	21.2	14.4	14.2	12.4	11.8	14.6	17.8	21.6	18.2	8.7	16.3
The Netherlands	2.5	2.8	4.2	12.5	14.1	1.3	−0.5	20.6	6.8	11.1	3.3	0.8	2.9	7.2
UK	0.6	−2.1	4.8	10.7	14.9	2.0	5.1	16.8	11.0	12.1	17.0	9.9	9.6	10.3
Weighted standard deviation														
Excluding L, F	1.21	1.42	2.71	1.92	1.19	1.82	1.40	1.27	1.37	1.72	2.13	2.14	2.04	1.97
Excluding L, F, UK	1.24	1.50	3.14	2.27	1.16	2.10	1.64	1.44	1.57	1.93	2.26	2.50	2.04	2.00
Excluding L, F, UK, I	1.18	1.05	1.86	1.48	1.05	1.56	1.52	1.66	1.37	1.12	1.32	1.88	1.96	1.48
Six excluding L, F	1.48	1.83	3.96	2.44	1.38	2.40	2.06	1.75	1.78	2.41	2.80	2.92	2.55	2.39
Snake core	1.24	1.45	2.65	1.78	1.34	1.41	1.45	1.28	1.10	1.25	1.76	1.43	2.00	1.55
Range														
Excluding L, F	7.6	12.2	26.8	20.8	9.6	13.8	12.9	10.9	11.1	13.7	18.3	17.6	15.4	12.3
Excluding L, F, UK	7.4	12.2	26.8	20.8	9.1	13.8	12.9	10.9	11.1	13.7	18.3	17.6	14.5	12.3
Excluding L, F, UK, I	4.9	10.0	14.2	12.1	8.8	13.0	9.9	10.9	11.1	8.1	14.8	17.6	11.7	6.6
Six excluding L, F	7.4	12.2	26.8	15.4	7.2	13.8	12.9	10.9	10.2	13.2	18.3	17.6	14.5	12.3
Snake core	4.8	10.0	14.2	10.8	8.8	6.5	6.4	7.0	6.4	7.0	7.1	9.6	10.1	3.2

interest rate (to take account of currency substitution in demand)[11]:

$$\hat{M} - \hat{P} = K + \eta\hat{Y} - \varepsilon\Delta i^{l,s} + \varepsilon^t(\Delta i^l - \Delta i^s) - \varepsilon^e(\Delta i^s - \Delta i^{e\$}) + u \quad (1)$$

where

M = money supply (M_1),
P = the consumer price index,
Y = real income (GDP or GNP),
i^s = the short-term interest rate (three months),
i^l = the long-term interest rate (long-term government bonds),
    and
$i^{e\$}$ = the Eurodollar interest rate (three months);
    a circumflex $(\hat{})$ indicates rates of change.

It has been assumed that the actual change of the inflation rate in any one year is only a fraction (λ) of the change of the equilibrium inflation rate $(\hat{P}^*)$:

$$(\hat{M} - \hat{P}) - (\hat{M} - \hat{P})_{-1} = \lambda[(\hat{M} - \hat{P})^* - (\hat{M} - \hat{P})_{-1}] + v. \quad (2)$$

Substituting the equilibrium relationship (1) for $(\hat{M} - \hat{P})^*$ in (2), we obtain the familiar partial-adjustment model with the lagged value of the dependent variable on the right-hand side:[12]

$$\hat{M} - \hat{P} = (\lambda K) + (\lambda\eta)\hat{y} - (\lambda\varepsilon)\Delta i^{l,s} + (\lambda\varepsilon^t)(\Delta i^l - \Delta i^s)$$
$$- (\lambda\varepsilon^e)(\Delta i^s - \Delta i^{e\$}) + (1 - \lambda)(\hat{M} - \hat{P})_{-1} + (\lambda u + v). \quad (3)$$

The OLS estimates of this equation are presented in Table 4.3, the implicit long-run equilibrium elasticities in Table 4.4. The results are most satisfactory for Denmark and Germany. For most other countries, the intercepts are implausibly large in absolute terms. The same is true for the Belgian interest semi-elasticity.[13] With the exception of the Netherlands, all income elasticities are consistent with the unity postulate. In the case of Italy, the Durbin h test is marginally significant; for the UK the Durbin h test breaks down, but there does not seem to be a disturbing degree of first-order autocorrelation of the residuals. Since we are dealing with first differences, the (adjusted) coefficients of determination are not disappointing. The interest-rate differentials were not included unless they raised $\overline{R}^2$. While the coefficient of the currency-substitution parameter is close to significance only for Denmark, it also enters the money-demand functions for Belgium and Germany with t-values between 0.5 and 1.0. The term-structure variable takes a significant coefficient in the Dutch equation. The speed of adjustment

TABLE 4.3 Money demand in eight EC countries, 1960–79, partial-adjustment model

$\hat{M}_1 - \hat{P}$	K	$\hat{v}$	Δi^l	Δi^s	$\Delta i^l - \Delta i^s$	$\Delta i^s - \Delta r^{s\xi}$	$(\hat{M}_1 - \hat{P})_{-1}$	$\bar{R}^2$	Durbin h	DW
Belgium	1.35 (1.00)	0.22 (0.76)	−5.42 (4.61)				0.42 (2.25)	0.51	−1.02	2.26
Denmark	0.48 (0.32)	0.94 (2.79)	−2.05 (2.30)			−0.67 (2.02)	0.01 (0.05)	0.57	−0.99	2.21
France	−5.43 (2.00)	1.64 (2.94)		−1.09 (2.55)			0.45 (2.60)	0.51	1.35	2.38
W. Germany	0.70 (0.56)	0.81 (3.04)	−2.02 (3.40)				0.25 (1.27)	0.56	−0.81	2.16
Ireland	−3.07 (0.95)	1.35 (1.83)	−1.26 (1.29)				0.41 (1.37)	0.37	0.53	1.79
Italy	−0.42 (0.18)	1.38 (2.77)		−0.84 (1.75)			0.37 (2.06)	0.48	1.75	1.54
The Netherlands	3.06 (2.82)	0.12 (0.46)	−2.59 (2.73)		1.06 (2.49)		0.22 (1.23)	0.69	−0.12	2.03
UK	−3.96 (2.13)	1.62 (2.80)		−1.21 (1.50)			0.16 (0.61)	0.29	n.a.	2.12

Note: t-values in parentheses; n.a. indicates that h statistic not calculable.

TABLE 4.4 Money demand in eight EC countries, 1960–79: long-run equilibrium elasticities

$\hat{M}_1 - \hat{p}$	Intercept $\bar{K}$	Income elasticity $\bar{\eta}$	Long-run interest semi-elasticity $\bar{\varepsilon}^l$	Short-run interest semi-elasticity $\bar{\varepsilon}^s$	Term-structure semi-elasticity $\bar{\varepsilon}^t$	Exchange rate expectation elasticity $\bar{\varepsilon}^e$	Adjustment coefficient	Adjustment lag (years)
Belgium	2.32	0.38	−9.32*					0.58	1.72
Denmark	0.49	0.95†	−2.07†				−0.68	0.99	1.01
France	−9.88	2.98*		−1.98†				0.55	1.82
W. Germany	0.93	1.08*	−2.69*					0.75	1.33
Ireland	5.19	2.28	−2.13					0.59	1.69
Italy	−0.67	2.19†		−1.34				0.63	1.59
The Netherlands	3.92†	0.47	−3.32†			1.36†		0.78	1.28
UK	−4.71†	1.93†		−1.44				0.84	1.19
Mean		1.53						0.71	1.45

Note: * significant at 1 per cent level; † significant at 5 per cent level.

implied by the coefficient of the lagged dependent variable ranges between one year and twenty-two months, with an average of a little less than one and a half years (see Table 4.4). Table 4.5 gives the long-run equilibrium inflation rates implied by the coefficients of Table 4.4, and the weighted standard deviations and ranges of these inflation rates. Since several of the coefficients reported in Tables 4.3 and 4.4 take implausible values, these money-demand functions have been adjusted in several respects. The income elasticities which are consistent with a value of unity at the 5 per cent level were set equal to one; otherwise (i.e. in the case of the Netherlands) the income elasticity was set equal to the highest value that fell within the 5 per cent confidence interval. The long-term interest semi-elasticity for Belgium was set up at the lowest absolute value compatible with the 5 per cent confidence interval. Finally all intercepts were set equal to zero. The equilibrium inflation rates implicit in these adjusted money-demand functions and their dispersion are reported in Table 4.6.

To compare the predictive quality of the long-run money-demand functions underlying the equilibrium inflation rates of Tables 4.2, 4.5 and 4.6, the compound average inflation rates predicted by each function for 1970–9 were regressed on the actual compound average inflation rates on a cross-section basis. The correlation coefficients were 0.749 for the simple quantity theory, 0.428 for the estimated money-demand functions and 0.786 for the adjusted money-demand functions. The adjusted money-demand function also fared best in a time-series analysis, in which the standard deviations of the predicted inflation rates were regressed on the standard deviations of the actual inflation rates a year later (1969–79, standard deviation of all eight countries). The correlation coefficients were now very low, thus confirming the view that the (lagged) association between monetary policy and inflation is fairly loose in the short term, but very powerful in the longer term.

As has already been noted, the existence of sizable real exchange-rate changes (with respect to the CPI) implies that the dispersion of actual or long-run equilibrium inflation rates (as measured by the CPI) is not an accurate indicator of the need for nominal exchange-rate adjustment. Thus, the inflation rates have to be adjusted for the compound average rate of real exchange-rate change which the country in question experienced *vis-à-vis* the weighted Community average in 1959–70 and in 1970–9. As Table 4.7 shows,[14] the structure and size of long-term real exchange-rate changes altered substantially around 1970 so that different adjustments seemed advisable for the two sub-periods. The largest real exchange-rate changes were the real appreciation of the Danish

TABLE 4.5 Equilibrium inflation rates implicit in long-run money demand estimated from partial-adjustment model

	1960–8	1969	1970	1971	1972	1973	1974	1975	1976	1977	1978	1979	1980	1970–9
Belgium	3.3	4.8	−2.6	1.8	7.2	9.4	14.3	8.4	10.9	2.9	1.8	10.3	25.3	6.3
Denmark	5.9	8.0	5.1	2.0	5.0	6.1	14.9	11.6	14.4	6.6	10.3	8.4	5.6	8.4
France	5.1	0.9	−6.1	2.0	3.6	11.5	20.9	9.3	11.1	9.9	7.8	12.4	21.1	8.0
W. Germany	1.9	1.4	3.1	7.1	8.6	2.8	7.4	10.1	1.9	0.3	8.1	6.6	−1.1	5.6
Ireland	−7.1	−9.4	−6.6	−9.5	−4.1	6.9	7.3	8.4	8.8	−5.4	6.1	13.4	2.8	2.2
Italy	2.1	4.1	15.8	17.9	10.0	8.8	18.3	11.4	15.0	13.9	15.8	13.4	−1.8	14.0
The Netherlands	2.3	7.9	5.3	4.9	7.2	8.5	5.0	6.1	10.0	1.9	3.5	3.8	13.1	5.6
UK	2.4	1.9	6.5	10.9	17.7	4.7	14.2	21.4	13.7	10.6	19.8	18.6	24.6	13.7
Weighted standard deviation														
Excluding L, F	1.14	1.02	2.55	2.28	1.90	1.26	2.14	1.75	1.92	2.05	2.17	1.73	4.36	1.98
Excluding L, F, UK	1.31	1.21	2.93	2.57	1.29	1.42	2.52	0.61	2.15	2.25	1.64	1.37	4.44	1.88
Excluding L, F, UK, I	1.50	1.41	2.06	1.84	1.40	1.67	2.81	0.62	2.23	2.00	1.12	1.40	4.79	1.72
Six excluding L, F	1.30	1.26	3.65	2.73	1.16	1.81	3.13	0.76	2.59	2.68	2.07	1.69	5.67	2.23
Snake core	1.52	1.95	1.50	1.52	0.76	1.86	2.19	0.96	3.34	1.31	1.65	1.19	6.32	1.63
Range														
Excluding L, F	13.0	17.4	22.4	27.4	21.8	8.7	15.9	15.3	13.1	19.3	18.0	14.8	27.1	11.8
Excluding L, F, UK	13.0	17.4	22.4	27.4	14.1	8.7	15.9	5.5	13.1	19.3	14.0	9.6	27.1	11.8
Excluding L, F, UK, I	13.0	17.4	11.9	16.6	12.7	8.7	15.9	5.5	12.5	15.3	8.5	9.6	26.4	6.2
Six excluding L, F	3.2	7.0	21.9	16.1	6.4	8.7	15.9	5.3	13.1	13.6	14.0	9.6	27.1	8.4
Snake core	4.0	6.6	7.9	5.3	3.6	6.6	9.9	5.5	12.5	6.3	8.5	6.5	26.4	2.8

TABLE 4.6 Equilibrium inflation rates implicit in preferred long-run money-demand functions

	1960–8	1969	1970	1971	1972	1973	1974	1975	1976	1977	1978	1979	1980	1970–9
Belgium	1.6	0.3	−6.9	3.5	7.1	6.0	8.2	12.7	7.2	5.5	4.0	5.9	9.4	5.2
Denmark	6.2	8.1	5.5	2.3	5.2	6.3	15.4	12.1	14.6	7.0	10.8	8.8	5.9	8.7
France	6.2	4.9	−4.7	2.8	5.4	12.3	17.3	−0.2	11.2	5.6	5.4	10.4	16.8	6.4
W. Germany	3.2	2.9	4.5	8.3	9.8	4.2	8.5	10.9	3.2	1.4	9.3	7.9	0.2	6.8
Ireland	3.6	3.5	2.8	0.7	8.1	17.6	14.3	14.1	17.7	6.9	19.1	27.3	7.5	12.6
Italy	8.2	10.2	21.1	19.1	13.6	16.3	22.6	6.5	21.4	15.6	18.2	18.7	15.3	17.2
The Netherlands	4.0	9.2	6.8	7.2	9.7	10.1	7.5	10.8	12.1	4.9	6.5	7.0	16.3	8.2
UK	0.7	−1.3	3.9	8.6	14.9	7.5	8.0	15.1	12.4	7.1	18.2	16.3	16.6	11.1
Weighted standard deviation														
Excluding L, F	1.21	1.45	3.05	1.97	1.29	1.67	2.09	2.05	2.30	1.64	2.07	1.89	2.69	2.00
Excluding L, F, UK	1.22	1.31	3.60	2.32	1.14	1.95	2.31	2.14	2.72	1.93	1.98	2.05	2.97	2.21
Excluding L, F, UK, I	1.24	1.17	2.34	1.34	0.92	1.81	1.90	2.56	2.32	1.09	1.44	1.76	3.35	1.75
Six excluding L, F	1.45	1.62	4.54	2.74	1.38	2.31	2.90	2.47	3.18	2.43	2.28	2.06	3.80	2.63
Snake core	1.33	1.88	2.71	1.51	1.02	1.39	1.26	0.46	2.88	1.50	1.26	0.48	4.03	1.45
Range														
Excluding L, F	7.5	11.5	28.0	18.4	9.7	13.4	15.1	14.3	18.2	14.2	15.1	21.4	16.6	12.0
Excluding L, F, UK	6.6	9.9	28.0	18.4	8.4	13.4	15.1	14.3	18.2	14.2	15.1	21.4	16.6	12.0
Excluding L, F, UK, I	4.6	8.9	13.7	7.6	4.6	13.4	9.8	14.3	14.5	5.6	15.1	21.4	16.6	7.4
Six excluding L, F	6.6	9.9	28.0	16.3	8.2	12.1	15.1	12.9	18.2	14.2	14.2	12.8	16.6	12.0
Snake core	4.6	8.9	13.7	6.0	4.6	5.9	7.9	1.8	11.4	5.6	6.8	2.9	16.1	3.5

TABLE 4.7 Compound annual average rates of
real exchange-rate change *vis-à-vis* the weighted
EC average

	1959–70	1970–9
Belgium	− 0.5	+ 1.2
Denmark	+ 1.3	+ 1.3
France	− 0.4	− 0.1
W. Germany	+ 0.4	+ 0.7
Ireland	− 0.4	− 1.2
Italy	+ 0.4	− 2.7
The Netherlands	+ 1.0	+ 1.9
UK	− 1.1	− 0.8

krone *vis-à-vis* the pound sterling (2.4 per cent p.a.) in the 1960s, and the real appreciation of the Dutch guilder *vis-à-vis* the Italian lira (4.7 per cent p.a.) in the 1970s.

The inflation rates adjusted for real exchange-rate 'trend' are reported in Tables 4.8–4.11 which otherwise exactly mirror Tables 4.1, 4.2, 4.5 and 4.6. To check which of the inflation-rate dispersions is most relevant for predictions of nominal exchange-rate changes, each of the four compound average inflation rates for 1970–9 was regressed on the 1970–9 compound average rate of nominal exchange-rate change *vis-à-vis* the US dollar (Table 4.12, last column) on a cross-section basis. The simple correlation coefficients were − 0.857 for the adjusted inflation rates predicted by the simple quantity theory (Table 4.9), − 0.672 for the adjusted inflation rates from the estimated money-demand functions (Table 4.10) and − 0.869 for the adjusted inflation rates from the preferred money-demand functions (Table 4.11), but − 0.975 for the actual inflation rates (Table 4.1) and, not surprisingly,[15] − 0.994 for the actual inflation rates adjusted for real exchange-rate 'trend' (Table 4.8). Once more, a time-series analysis of the overall standard deviations yielded the same results as to *relative* performance, but much lower *absolute* correlation coefficients. To summarise, the dispersion of actual inflation rates (especially if adjusted for real exchange-rate 'trend') is the best indicator of the need for nominal exchange-rate adjustment, but it is an *ex post* or lagging indicator; the best early indicator is the dispersion of the adjusted inflation rates predicted by our preferred money-demand function which contains constrained coefficients for both real income and interest rates.

A closer look at Table 4.8 reveals that the monetary divergences were even larger in the 1970s than is indicated by Table 4.1. This holds both

TABLE 4.8 Inflation rates adjusted for compound average rate of real exchange-rate change

	1960–8	1969	1970	1971	1972	1973	1974	1975	1976	1977	1978	1979	1980	1970–9
Belgium	3.4	4.4	4.4	3.1	4.2	5.7	11.5	11.5	8.0	5.9	3.3	3.2	5.3	5.9
Denmark	4.2	2.3	5.2	4.5	5.3	8.1	13.9	8.3	7.7	9.8	8.8	8.3	13.0	8.0
France	4.0	6.6	6.2	5.6	6.3	7.5	13.8	11.8	9.3	9.6	9.3	10.8	13.9	9.0
W. Germany	2.1	1.4	2.9	4.7	4.8	6.2	6.3	5.2	3.8	3.2	1.9	3.4	5.3	4.2
Ireland	4.0	7.8	8.7	10.0	9.9	12.5	18.2	22.1	19.2	14.8	8.8	14.4	16.8	13.9
Italy	3.4	2.2	4.4	7.7	8.4	13.5	21.8	19.7	19.5	19.7	14.9	17.4	23.2	15.2
The Netherlands	2.5	6.3	2.8	5.5	6.0	6.1	7.7	8.6	6.9	4.5	2.2	2.3	4.7	5.1
UK	4.3	6.5	7.4	10.2	8.1	9.9	16.8	25.0	17.3	16.7	9.1	14.2	22.7	13.3
Weighted standard deviation														
Excluding L, F	0.56	0.90	0.69	0.83	0.59	0.99	2.05	2.71	2.25	2.32	1.72	2.09	2.86	1.62
Excluding L, F, UK	0.60	0.98	0.66	0.60	0.61	1.13	2.30	2.22	2.31	2.39	1.99	2.24	2.76	1.65
Excluding L, F, UK, I	0.66	1.12	0.79	0.54	0.53	0.65	1.82	1.90	1.68	1.60	1.57	1.75	2.01	1.28
Six excluding L, F	0.66	1.16	0.69	0.64	0.67	1.34	2.76	2.53	2.69	2.90	2.47	2.75	3.40	1.94
Snake core	0.72	1.21	0.54	0.43	0.34	0.35	1.79	1.58	1.28	1.33	1.27	0.90	1.37	0.98
Range														
Excluding L, F	2.2	6.4	5.9	7.1	5.7	7.8	15.5	19.8	15.7	16.5	13.0	15.1	18.5	11.0
Excluding L, F, UK	2.1	6.4	5.9	6.9	5.7	7.8	15.5	16.9	15.7	16.5	13.0	15.1	18.5	11.0
Excluding L, F, UK, I	2.1	6.4	5.9	6.9	5.7	6.8	11.9	16.9	15.4	11.6	7.4	12.1	12.1	9.7
Six excluding L, F	1.9	5.2	3.4	4.6	4.2	7.8	15.5	14.5	15.7	16.5	13.0	15.1	18.5	11.0
Snake core	2.1	4.9	2.4	2.4	1.8	2.4	7.6	6.3	4.2	6.6	6.9	6.0	8.3	3.8

TABLE 4.9 Equilibrium inflation rates of Table 4.2 adjusted for compound average rate of real exchange-rate change

	1960–8	1969	1970	1971	1972	1973	1974	1975	1976	1977	1978	1979	1980	1970–9
Belgium	1.3	−2.5	−9.5	4.6	7.5	2.8	0.8	12.4	3.2	5.6	4.6	−0.6	−7.0	2.8
Denmark	4.3	5.7	0.3	0.4	4.0	5.6	4.6	15.7	9.5	2.8	8.3	8.9	3.0	5.9
France	6.1	−0.3	−3.7	8.5	7.3	4.6	9.5	9.8	10.0	4.7	7.7	8.4	6.0	6.6
W. Germany	2.7	1.7	0.1	8.4	9.4	−0.3	4.8	15.3	4.4	5.0	9.7	2.9	−3.5	5.8
Ireland	3.5	0.7	1.7	1.6	9.5	14.6	6.1	16.5	16.7	13.4	19.3	19.4	2.9	11.8
Italy	7.8	8.8	16.4	23.9	17.1	16.9	15.1	14.5	17.3	20.5	24.3	20.9	11.4	19.0
The Netherlands	1.5	1.8	3.2	10.6	12.1	−0.6	−2.4	18.7	4.9	9.2	1.4	−1.1	1.0	5.3
UK	1.7	−1.0	5.9	11.5	15.7	2.8	5.9	17.6	11.8	12.9	17.8	10.7	10.4	11.1
Weighted standard deviation														
Excluding L, F	1.15	1.24	2.65	2.28	1.47	2.20	1.82	1.12	1.79	2.10	2.58	2.60	2.41	2.06
Excluding L, F, UK	1.25	1.37	3.02	2.69	1.44	2.59	2.15	1.19	2.05	2.35	2.78	3.02	2.45	2.33
Excluding L, F, UK, I	1.21	0.81	1.64	1.42	0.85	1.71	1.79	1.43	1.56	1.00	1.52	2.12	2.11	1.50
Six excluding L, F	1.50	1.68	3.81	3.01	1.72	3.04	2.71	1.43	2.43	2.90	3.45	3.62	3.09	2.81
Snake core	1.16	1.17	2.39	1.79	1.28	1.28	1.72	1.11	0.95	1.03	2.04	1.51	1.80	1.51
Range														
Excluding L, F	6.5	11.3	25.9	23.5	13.1	17.5	17.5	8.9	14.1	17.7	22.9	22.0	18.4	16.2
Excluding L, F, UK	6.5	11.3	25.9	23.5	13.1	17.5	17.5	8.9	14.1	17.7	22.9	22.0	18.4	16.2
Excluding L, F, UK, I	4.8	8.2	12.7	10.2	8.2	15.2	11.9	8.9	13.5	10.6	17.9	20.5	13.0	9.0
Six excluding L, F	6.5	11.3	25.9	6.0	13.1	17.5	17.5	8.9	14.1	17.7	22.9	22.0	18.4	16.2
Snake Core	3.0	8.2	12.7	6.0	8.2	6.2	7.2	6.3	6.3	6.4	8.3	10.0	10.0	3.1

TABLE 4.10 Equilibrium inflation rates of Table 4.5 adjusted for compound average rate of real exchange-rate change

	1960–8	1969	1970	1971	1972	1973	1974	1975	1976	1977	1978	1979	1980	1970–9
Belgium	3.8	5.3	−2.1	0.6	6.0	8.2	13.1	7.2	9.7	1.7	0.6	9.1	24.1	5.1
Denmark	4.6	6.7	3.8	0.7	3.7	4.8	13.6	10.3	13.1	5.3	9.0	7.1	4.3	7.1
France	5.5	1.3	−5.7	2.1	3.7	11.6	21.0	9.4	1.2	10.0	7.9	12.5	21.2	8.1
W. Germany	1.5	0.9	2.7	6.4	7.9	2.1	6.8	9.4	1.2	−0.4	7.4	5.9	−1.8	4.9
Ireland	−6.7	−9.0	−6.2	−8.2	−2.9	8.1	8.5	9.6	10.0	−4.2	7.3	14.6	4.0	3.4
Italy	1.7	3.7	15.4	20.6	12.7	11.5	21.0	14.1	17.7	16.6	18.5	16.1	0.9	16.7
The Netherlands	1.3	6.9	4.3	3.0	5.3	6.6	3.1	4.2	8.1	0.0	1.6	1.9	11.2	3.7
UK	3.5	3.0	7.6	11.7	18.5	5.5	15.0	22.2	14.5	11.4	20.6	19.4	25.4	14.5
Weighted standard deviation														
Excluding L, F	1.19	0.93	2.49	2.64	2.10	1.43	2.47	2.02	2.22	2.45	2.56	2.11	4.32	2.25
Excluding L, F, UK	1.35	1.11	2.80	2.95	1.48	1.66	2.89	1.07	2.47	2.70	2.15	1.83	4.29	2.20
Excluding L, F, UK, I	1.44	1.29	1.83	1.75	1.25	1.78	3.02	0.82	2.27	2.15	1.31	1.66	4.85	1.78
Six excluding L, F	1.41	1.16	3.48	3.29	1.50	2.10	3.61	1.37	3.02	3.29	2.73	2.27	5.48	2.67
Snake core	1.49	1.83	1.22	1.73	1.01	1.61	2.17	1.21	3.10	1.13	1.86	1.29	6.11	1.63
Range														
Excluding L, F	12.2	15.9	21.6	28.8	21.4	9.5	17.9	18.0	15.5	20.8	20.0	17.5	27.2	13.3
Excluding L, F, UK	12.2	15.9	21.6	28.8	15.6	9.5	17.9	9.9	15.5	20.8	17.9	14.2	25.9	13.3
Excluding L, F, UK, I	12.2	15.9	10.5	14.6	10.8	9.5	17.9	6.1	11.9	14.2	8.4	12.7	25.9	4.7
Six excluding L, F	4.2	6.0	21.1	20.0	9.0	9.5	17.9	9.9	16.5	20.8	17.9	14.2	25.9	4.4
Snake core	3.3	6.0	6.4	5.8	4.2	6.1	10.5	6.1	11.9	5.7	8.4	7.2	25.9	3.4

TABLE 4.11 Equilibrium inflation rates of Table 4.6 adjusted for compound average rate of real exchange-rate change

	1960–8	1969	1970	1971	1972	1973	1974	1975	1976	1977	1978	1979	1980	1970–9
Belgium	2.1	0.8	−6.4	2.3	5.9	4.8	7.0	11.5	6.0	4.3	2.8	4.7	8.2	4.0
Denmark	4.9	6.8	4.2	1.0	3.9	5.0	14.1	10.8	13.3	5.7	9.5	7.5	4.6	7.4
France	6.6	5.3	−4.3	2.9	5.5	12.4	17.4	−0.1	11.3	5.7	5.5	10.5	16.9	6.5
W. Germany	2.8	2.5	4.1	7.6	9.1	3.5	7.8	10.2	2.5	0.7	8.6	7.2	−0.5	6.1
Ireland	4.0	3.9	3.2	1.9	9.3	18.8	15.5	15.3	18.9	8.1	20.3	28.5	8.7	13.8
Italy	7.8	9.8	20.7	21.8	16.3	19.0	25.3	9.2	24.1	18.3	20.9	21.4	18.0	19.9
The Netherlands	3.0	8.2	5.6	5.3	7.8	8.2	5.6	8.9	10.2	3.0	4.6	5.1	14.4	6.3
UK	1.8	−0.2	5.0	9.4	15.7	8.3	8.8	15.9	13.2	7.9	19.0	17.1	17.4	11.9
Weighted standard deviaton														
Excluding L, F	1.16	1.27	2.95	2.33	1.61	2.02	2.46	2.01	2.67	2.07	2.46	2.32	2.92	2.29
Excluding L, F, UK	1.23	1.21	3.47	2.73	1.50	2.39	2.82	1.99	3.13	2.42	2.43	2.54	3.21	2.54
Excluding L, F, UK, I	1.28	1.05	2.11	1.23	0.80	1.98	2.15	2.38	2.38	1.18	1.52	1.96	3.41	1.77
Six excluding L, F	1.48	1.51	4.38	3.28	1.82	2.86	3.55	2.26	3.73	3.03	2.88	2.75	4.08	3.06
Snake core	1.24	1.61	2.46	1.69	1.18	1.10	1.23	0.47	2.61	1.26	1.45	0.67	3.74	1.41
Range														
Excluding L, F	6.0	10.0	27.1	20.8	12.4	15.5	19.7	16.0	21.6	17.6	18.1	23.8	18.5	15.9
Excluding L, F, UK	5.7	9.0	27.1	20.8	12.4	15.5	19.7	15.4	21.6	17.6	18.1	23.8	18.5	15.9
Excluding L, F, UK, I	4.5	7.4	12.0	6.6	5.4	15.3	11.8	15.4	16.4	7.4	17.5	23.8	17.4	9.8
Six excluding L, F	5.7	9.0	27.1	19.5	10.8	15.5	19.7	11.6	21.6	17.6	18.1	16.7	18.5	15.9
Snake core	2.8	7.4	12.0	6.6	5.2	4.7	8.5	2.6	10.8	5.0	6.7	2.8	14.9	3.4

absolutely and in comparison with the 1960s. Again the dispersion of inflation rates is much smaller for the snake countries and the group excluding sterling and the lira, and much larger in 1978–9 (even if sterling and lira are excluded) than in 1969–72 (even if only the Six are considered). There are signs of divergence from 1978 onwards. Surprisingly, these findings with regard to the most recent years are not supported by our early indicator of Table 4.11. It indicates some convergence from 1978 to 1979 (but not if sterling is excluded), and although the estimated dispersion for 1980 is dramatically large, this may be misleading because those rates of change do not relate to annual averages. Moreover, while the dispersion for the whole Community is still larger for 1978–9 than for 1969–72, the standard deviations are now somewhat smaller for the Community (with or without Italy and the UK) in 1978–9 than for the Six in 1969–72. However, this is not because Table 4.11 gives lower standard deviations for 1978–9 than Table 4.8, but because it reports much higher standard deviations for 1969–72. Thus, one may at best conclude that the prospects for nominal exchange-rate stability in the Community were about as bad at the end of the seventies as at their beginning.

These results stand in marked contrast to the information about nominal intra-Community exchange-rate changes as conveyed by Table 4.12. Nominal exchange-rate changes in 1978–9 and even in 1980_1 (especially between the EMS currencies) have been remarkably small compared with those in 1973–7, and hardly larger than the small changes of 1969–72.

There seem to be two possible explanations of why the large measured monetary divergences of 1978–9 (even after allowing for real exchange-rate trend) have not (yet) fed through into nominal exchange-rate changes; one refers to monetary, the other to real causes.

The monetary explanation is that, say, German monetary policy has been less restrictive than is indicated by the preferred money-demand function, because money demand has shifted back from the Deutschemark to the dollar and because our preferred money-demand function, having been estimated for 1959–79 rather than for the floating-rate period only, does not capture currency substitution in demand.

The non-monetary explanation is that there have been offsetting temporary real exchange-rate changes, due either to the recent oil-price rise or to the current desynchronisation of trade cycles, notably the familiar Keynesian hypothesis that, say, a boom in Germany lowers the German terms of trade and real exchange rate; for a case with opposite signs take the UK. This hypothesis is plausible if the marginal propensity

TABLE 4.12 Rates of nominal exchange-rate appreciation *vis-à-vis* US dollar

	1960–8	1969	1970	1971	1972	1973	1974	1975	1976	1977	1978	1979	1980	1970–9
Belgium	0.0	−0.4	+1.0	+2.3	+10.3	+13.4	−0.2	+6.0	−4.9	+7.7	+14.1	+7.1	+1.7	+5.5
Denmark	−0.9	−0.5	+0.3	+1.3	+6.5	+15.4	−1.0	+6.0	−5.1	+0.7	+8.9	+4.8	−6.9	+3.6
France	−0.1	−4.4	−6.4	+0.3	+9.2	+13.7	−7.7	+12.2	−10.3	−2.7	+8.9	+6.1	+2.9	+2.0
W. Germany	+0.5	+1.8	+7.6	+4.9	+9.0	+20.4	+2.6	+5.2	−2.4	+8.5	+15.6	+9.6	+4.6	+7.9
Ireland	−1.8	−0.1	+0.2	+2.0	+2.3	−2.0	−4.5	−5.1	−18.8	−3.4	+10.0	+6.7	+3.7	−1.5
Italy	0.0	−0.6	0.0	+1.4	+5.9	+0.4	−10.6	−0.3	−21.4	−5.7	+4.0	+2.1	+1.7	−2.8
The Netherlands	+0.5	−0.1	+0.2	+3.6	+8.8	+15.5	+3.6	+6.4	−4.5	+7.7	+13.4	+7.8	+2.5	+6.1
UK	−1.8	−0.1	+0.2	+2.0	+2.3	−2.0	−4.5	−5.1	−18.8	−3.4	+10.0	+10.5	+11.8	−1.2
Weighted standard deviation														
Excluding L, F	0.38	0.82	1.85	0.66	1.05	3.31	1.93	2.20	2.76	2.25	1.47	1.04	1.58	1.85
Excluding L, F, UK	0.31	0.96	2.18	0.77	0.76	3.03	2.25	1.89	2.78	2.46	1.72	1.06	1.04	1.89
Excluding L, F, UK, I	0.36	1.15	2.60	0.89	0.77	2.40	2.07	1.86	1.89	2.36	1.38	0.79	1.25	1.70
Six excluding L, F	0.21	1.21	2.74	0.95	0.65	3.43	2.83	2.07	3.35	3.03	2.13	1.30	0.62	2.25
Snake core	0.37	0.72	2.42	0.88	0.53	1.97	0.96	0.33	0.82	1.40	1.31	1.07	2.17	1.17
Range														
Excluding L, F	2.3	6.5	15.0	4.6	7.8	22.9	15.9	18.2	24.2	15.1	11.2	8.2	20.1	11.0
Excluding L, F, UK	2.3	6.5	15.0	4.6	7.8	22.9	15.9	18.2	24.2	15.1	11.2	7.3	12.4	11.0
Excluding L, F, UK, I	2.3	6.5	15.0	4.6	7.8	22.9	12.2	18.2	20.2	12.3	6.2	4.6	12.4	9.5
Six excluding L, F	0.6	6.5	15.0	4.6	4.2	19.9	15.9	12.5	24.2	15.1	11.2	7.3	2.9	11.0
Snake core	1.4	2.3	7.4	3.6	3.6	6.2	4.6	1.1	2.8	7.7	6.2	4.6	12.4	4.2

Note: the range indicates the maximum annual rate of exchange-rate change between any pair of member currencies.

to import exceeds the average propensity, or if, owing to some degree of exchange-rate flexibility, price adjustment is faster for importables than for home goods.

In either case, there is no reason to expect that these special factors will offset the fundamental monetary divergences for very long.

REAL EXCHANGE-RATE CONVERGENCE?

According to Vaubel (1976), the size of real exchange-rate changes within groups of countries or regions can be viewed as a comprehensive criterion of the desirability of their monetary unification. The main rationale of this suggestion is that, in the presence of large real exchange-rate changes, nominal exchange-rate fixity or currency union prevents the member countries from all attaining price-level stability. As can be seen from Table 4.7, for example, exchange-rate fixity between the guilder and the lira combined with price-level stability in the Netherlands would have implied a rate of *decrease* of about 5 per cent per annum for the Italian price level (as measured in lire).

Table 4.13 reports two measures of real exchange-rate changes in the European Community: the weighted standard deviations and the ranges of the inflation rates of a US dollar spent on the local CPI basket of the various member countries. The formula for the standard deviations is

$$SD_w^{S/P} = \sqrt{\left\{ \frac{\sum_i^n w_i [\Delta \ln(S_i/P_i) - \Delta \ln(\overline{S/P})]^2}{n-1} \right\}}$$

where

S_i is the spot nominal exchange rate of currency i per US dollar,
$\overline{S/P}$ is the (unweighted) average EC purchasing power of one US dollar.

Both the averages of the annual standard deviations and the ranges of the annual compound average rates of change indicate a substantial increase in real exchange-rate changes from the sixties to the seventies, both for the whole Community and for the original Six. However, if we look only at the long-term trends, i.e. at (the ranges of) the compound average rates of change, we find that for some subgroups (the snake core and even the seven 'normal' EMS members without Luxembourg), the seventies exhibit less real exchange-rate change than the sixties. Since for

TABLE 4.13 Real exchange-rate changes in the EC (as measured by the cross-country dispersion of the annual inflation rates of a US dollar spent in various member countries)

	1960–8	1969	1970	1971	1972	1973	1974	1975	1976	1977	1978	1979	1980	1970–9
Weighted Standard Deviation														
Excluding L, F	0.67	0.71	1.66	0.91	0.94	3.07	1.22	1.83	1.56	1.09	0.30	1.85	3.25	1.44
Excluding L, F, UK	0.64	0.81	1.96	0.93	0.69	2.64	1.43	2.16	1.72	1.27	0.36	0.96	1.85	1.41
Excluding L, F, UK, I	0.71	0.91	2.34	1.02	0.56	2.11	1.64	2.58	1.13	1.50	0.18	1.06	1.67	1.41
Six excluding L, F	0.64	0.94	2.48	1.15	0.77	3.03	1.57	2.73	2.13	1.62	0.42	1.14	2.16	1.70
Snake core	0.76	0.78	2.30	1.10	0.59	1.79	1.27	2.28	0.63	0.68	0.30	0.50	1.00	1.14
Range														
Excluding L, F	2.8	5.7	12.6	5.4	6.9	20.3	8.9	12.5	13.6	8.3	2.7	13.5	26.2	4.1
Excluding L, F, UK	2.8	5.7	12.6	5.2	5.4	17.7	8.9	12.5	13.6	8.3	2.7	8.0	13.6	4.1
Excluding L, F, UK, I	2.8	5.7	12.6	5.2	5.4	17.7	8.9	12.5	8.6	8.3	1.4	8.0	13.6	2.4
Six excluding L, F	1.5	5.7	12.6	5.2	4.6	15.7	8.3	12.5	13.6	8.3	1.0	5.1	13.5	4.1
Snake core	1.5	4.1	7.6	4.4	3.3	6.1	4.1	7.2	2.0	3.0	1.4	2.7	4.5	0.5

Note: the range indicates the maximum annual rate of real exchange-rate change between any pair of member countries.

Germany, Belgium, Denmark and the Netherlands, the range fell to a third of its 1960–8 level, this group has become a decidedly more desirable currency area than it used to be in the sixties. Within the seventies, a trend is hard to discover. There were peaks in 1970 and 1973 and a pronounced trough in 1978, but no sustained convergence or divergence. Since the peaks are likely to reflect the large nominal exchange-rate adjustments in the second half of 1969 and in 1973, it seems tempting to conclude that most of the year-to-year real exchange-rate changes were due to nominal exchange-rate changes. Consistent with this hypothesis is the fact that a time-series correlation between the nominal (Table 4.12) and the real (Table 4.13) standard deviations in 1969–79 yields a correlation coefficient of 0.686. Moreover, a cross-section correlation of 0.889 between the nominal and the real compound average rates of change (1970–9) for the eight main member countries demonstrates an even closer association between nominal and real exchange-rate changes in the long run. Does this mean that nominal exchange-rate changes had a lasting effect on real exchange rates and 'competitiveness'? Not necessarily, for the causation may also work the other way round: autonomous real exchange-rate trends may have forced the member countries to adjust their nominal exchange rates in order to attain more price-level stability. The nominal appreciation of the Deutschemark, for example, to some extent merely served to prevent Germany from being forced by an autonomous long-term real appreciation to experience higher inflation rates than most of her partners.

SUMMARY

The results of our analysis can be summarised as follows:

1. Differences in inflation rates, especially if adjusted for real exchange-rate trend, were a reliable but lagging long-term indicator of the need for nominal exchange-rate adjustment in the EC in the 1970s. The best early indicator is the difference between the long-run equilibrium inflation rates predicted by constrained money-demand functions with income and interest variables and adjusted for real exchange-rate trend.

2. Monetary divergences as measured by these indicators were two or three times larger in the seventies than in the sixties, if the weighted standard deviations for the whole Community are taken. However, the increase was much smaller if sterling and the lira are excluded,

and very small indeed for the permanent member currencies of the snake.

3. The weighted standard deviations for the whole Community in 1978–9 (the period in which the EMS was contemplated and established) were two or three times larger than the weighted standard deviations for the whole Community or the Six in 1969–72 (the period in which various plans for European Monetary Union were drafted and adopted), if the inflation rates adjusted for real exchange-rate trend are taken as a standard of reference, and about the same if the adjusted inflation rates predicted by the preferred money-demand functions are used.

4. Since 1978 monetary divergences have been increasing, at least for the countries participating in the EMS exchange-rate arrangement. The fact that these divergences have not yet led to sizable nominal exchange-rate adjustments may be due to currency substitution (e.g. from the Deutschemark into the US dollar), or to offsetting temporary real exchange-rate changes caused by the oil price increase and/or desynchronised trade cycles.

5. Year-to-year real exchange-rate changes within the Community have been about twice as large in the seventies as in the sixties (somewhat less for the snake core). Long-term real exchange-rate change has also increased for the Community as a whole (also excluding sterling) and for the Six, but it has fallen to a third for the snake core. Thus, the snake core has become a more desirable currency area, while the Community as a whole has become a less desirable currency area.

6. Real exchange-rate changes are closedly associated with nominal exchange-rate changes, both on a year-to-year basis and for the seventies as a whole. However, it is not clear whether and to what extent the long-term correlation reflects a line of causation from nominal exchange-rate change to real exchange-rate change or vice versa.

NOTES

I am indebted to Jan Ooms for his generous help in executing the extensive computations.

1. For an appraisal of the normative policy issues see Vaubel (1976, 1978, 1979).
2. It should be emphasised that this central tenet of the monetary approach to

exchange rates is perfectly compatible with the existence of real exchange-rate changes; for as long as the price of money in terms of goods is measured in terms of different commodity baskets consumed in different parts of the world, both temporary and permanent deviations from purchasing power parity should be expected. For applications of the monetary approach which incorporate real exchange-rate changes see Vaubel (1980b) and Bomhoff and Korteweg (1980).

3. Cf. de Grauwe and Peeters (1979, p. 40) and Vaubel (1980a, c).

4. The formula for the computation of the weighted standard deviations (SD_w) is

$$ SD_w^P = \sqrt{ \left\{ \frac{\sum\limits_i^n w_i (\hat{P} - \bar{\hat{P}})^2}{n - 1} \right\} } $$

where w_i is the weight of currency i ($\Sigma w_i = 1$), $\hat{P}_i$ the inflation rate of currency i, $\bar{\hat{P}}$ the mean inflation rate in the Community, and n the number of independent currencies ($n = 8$).

5. The percentage weights were: BF: 8.2; DKr: 3; DM: 27.4; FF: 20.9; HFL: 9.2; Irish Punt: 1.4; Lit: 13.2; Lux. Fr.: 0.3; Sterling: 16.4. In this study, the Lux. Fr. is ignored and its weight allocated to the BF.

6. Of course, this does not imply that the snake reduced monetary divergences, for it could also have been the case that the Benelux countries and Denmark (as, for example, Austria) would have adjusted their monetary policies to German monetary policy even in the absence of the snake. In that case, it would be more appropriate to say that willingness to harmonise monetary policies was the cause of the snake's survival.

7. When currencies are excluded from the standard deviations, their weights are allocated proportionally to the remaining currencies.

8. For unweighted standard deviations of these rates see Vaubel (1980a,c). Throughout this study the data used are taken from the International Monetary Fund's *International Financial Statistics*. Where available, real GDP was preferred to real GNP.

9. The rates of change for 1980 relate to the last month for which data were available and compare it with the same month in the previous year.

10. See notably Heller and Khan (1979). The coefficient of the long-short interest differential should take a positive sign because a large differential implies expectations of an increase in short-term interest rates, and thus a reduced willingness to substitute short-term financial assets for money holdings.

11. See notably Vaubel (1980b) who presents evidence of currency substitution in demand for the Deutschemark, the Swiss franc and sterling. The interest differential *vis-a-vis* Eurodollar deposits should take a negative sign because, with covered interest arbitrage, a higher interest rate at home tends to signal expectations of a depreciation of the home currency.

12. Note, however, that the partial-adjustment model allows only for the lag of adjustment of real money balances to (unexpected) changes in the determinants of the demand for money, but not to (unexpected) changes in the supply of money. For a discussion of this point see, for example, Laidler (1980).

13. With an average long-term interest rate of 6.25 per cent (five countries), the average long-run interest semi-elasticity of 3.91 is equivalent to a long-run interest elasticity of 0.088. The implict short-run interest elasticity (3 countries) is 0.042.

14. For measures of dispersion see Table 4.13 and, in more detail but without weighting, Vaubel (1976).

15. Since in this case the inflation rates and nominal exchange-rate changes relate to almost the same long-term period as the real exchange-rate average, the equivalence of real-exchange-rate-adjusted inflation differences and nominal exchange-rate changes reflects a near-identity.

REFERENCES

Bomhoff, J. and P. Korteweg (1980), 'Exchange Rate Variability and Monetary Policy under Rational Expectations: Some Euro-American Evidence', paper presented at the Konstanzer Seminar on Monetary Theory and Monetary Policy, June.

Grauwe, P. de and T. Peeters (1979), 'The EMS, Europe and the Dollar', *The Banker*, April.

Heller, H. R. and M. S. Khan (1979), 'The Demand for Money and the Term Structure of Interest Rates', *Journal of Political Economy*, vol. 87.

Laidler, D. (1980) 'The Demand for Money in the United States – Yet Again', in K. Brunner and A. H. Meltzer (eds), *On The State of Macroeconomics*, Carnegie-Rochester Conference Series on Public Policy, vol. 12 (Amsterdam: North-Holland).

Vaubel, R. (1976), 'Real Exchange-rate Changes in the European Community', *Weltwirtschaftliches Archiv*, vol. 3; reprinted in revised form in *Journal of International Economics* (1978), vol. 8.

——(1978), *Strategies for Currency Unification: The Economics of Currency Competition and the Case for a European Parallel Currency* (Tübingen: J. C. B. Mohr).

——(1979), *Choice in European Monetary Union*, Ninth Wincott Lecture, Institute of Economic Affairs, London, Occasional Paper 55.

——(1980a), 'Why the EMS may have to be Dismantled', *Euromoney*, January.

——(1980b), 'International Shifts in the Demand for Money, their Effects on Exchange Rates and Price Levels, and their Implications for the Preannouncement of Monetary Expansion', *Weltwirtschaftliches Archiv*, vol. 116, no. 1.

——(1980c), 'The Return to the New European Monetary System: Objectives, Incentives, Perspectives', in K. Brunner and A. H. Meltzer (eds), *Monetary Institutions and the Policy Process*, Carnegie-Rochester Conference Series on Public Policy, vol. 13 (Amsterdam: North-Holland).

5 Foreign Exchange Market Intervention using an ECU-indicator

PAUL DE GRAUWE and PAUL VAN DEN BERGH

INTRODUCTION

One feature of the European Monetary System (EMS) is the introduction and the use of the European Currency Unit (ECU). As is well known, the ECU is defined as a basket of currencies in much the same way as the SDR. The objective of the introduction of the ECU was to contribute to a fully-fledged European Monetary Union. Whether or not this objective will be attained is uncertain. The question remains outside the scope of this article.

At this moment (1980) the ECU has acquired some limited functions within the EMS. One of these is its use as an 'indicator of divergence'. This implies that a country participating in the EMS should take action whenever the ECU rate of its currency deviates by a certain amount from the ECU parity.[1] In the EMS agreement it was left unspecified what actions should be taken. However, in practice these actions tend to take the form of foreign exchange market intervention.

In this chapter we analyse how the use of the ECU as the trigger for foreign exchange market intervention affects the money markets and the intercountry transmission of monetary shocks. We will assume that interventions are carried out using national currencies (either the dollar or EC currencies). The only role of the ECU is to function as an indicator triggering off interventions in the foreign exchange markets.

One of the issues which will be analysed is whether the use of the ECU as an indicator for intervention allows more symmetry in the adjustment mechanism than the snake intervention mechanism. In the latter, central

banks use the bilateral exchange rates as indicator for their interventions.

In order to analyse these issues we use an econometric model of the
money markets in the EC countries.[2] This model is simulated under
different exogenous shocks, and the simulations in the ECU-
intervention system are compared to those of the snake intervention
system.

GRAPHICAL REPRESENTATION OF THE MODEL

In this section a simple two-country model is developed graphically. The
purpose is to highlight the main characteristics of the econometric model
which is used for simulation purposes in the next section.

Assume there are two countries in the monetary system and call these
countries France and Germany. Their respective monetary sectors are
represented in Fig. 5.1. In the right-hand quadrant we have the money
demand function in Germany represented by the downward-sloping
L_G-line. German money demand is negatively related to the German
nominal interest rate, r_G. In the left-hand quadrant the French money
demand is represented as a negative function of the French interest rate,
r_F.

The French and German interest rates are linked through the interest

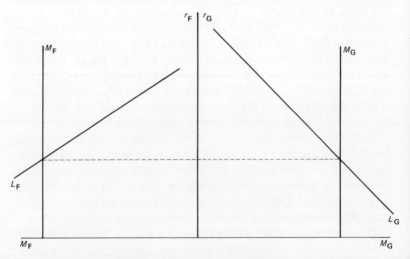

FIG. 5.1 Monetary equilibrium.

parity condition,

$$r_F - r_G = \frac{F - S}{S}$$

where

F = the forward price of the Deutschemark (DM) expressed in units of the French franc (FF), and

S = the spot price of the DM expressed in units of FF.

In an efficient market F expresses the state of expectations about the future spot rate (S_{+1}), i.e.

$$F = E(S_{+1}).$$

For the sake of simplicity it is assumed here that the money supply in both countries is independent of the interest rate. It is represented by the vertical lines M_F and M_G.

In Fig. 5.1 monetary equilibrium is obtained when the interest rates are equalised in both countries. This implies that the forward premium of the DM $\left(\dfrac{F - S}{S}\right)$ is equal to zero. In other words, there is strong confidence that the future spot rate will be the same as the observed present spot rate $[F = E(S_{+1}) = S]$. Suppose now new information reaches the market which leads speculators to change their expectations about the future spot rate. Let us assume that the DM is expected to appreciate in the future. Since both countries keep a fixed spot rate with each other $(S = \overline{S})$ this implies that the DM now must show a premium, i.e.

$$\frac{F - \overline{S}}{\overline{S}} > 0.$$

The result of this change in expectations is that the interest rates in the two countries must diverge. More specifically we must have that

$$\frac{F - \overline{S}}{\overline{S}} = r_F - r_G > 0,$$

i.e. the French interest rate must increase relative to the German interest rate. How this divergence is brought about is indeterminate. It can be obtained by an increase of the French interest rate, by a decline of the German interest rate, or by a combination of both. The outcome depends on how these countries intervene in the exchange markets and whether or not they attempt to offset (sterilise) these interventions. Here we consider three cases, a symmetrical intervention system, an asymmetrical intervention system and an ECU system.

Symmetrical intervention

In a symmetrical intervention system the expectation of a depreciation of the French franc must lead to a decline in the money stock in France and an increase of the money stock in Germany. This then produces an increase in the French interest rate and a decline of the German interest rate such that interest parity can be maintained.

Such a symmetrical adjustment is represented in Fig. 5.2. It will automatically occur in a 'snake-type' intervention arrangement. In order to avoid an increase in the spot price of the Deutschemark relative to the French franc, the French (or German) authorities sell Deutschemarks in exchange for francs in the exchange market. This intervention behaviour increases the money stock in Germany and reduces the money stock in France. The amount of intervention must be such that the combination of monetary contraction in France and expansion in Germany produces an interest differential exactly matching the forward premium of the Deutschemark. In Fig. 5.2 this is obtained when the interest differential is equal to p.

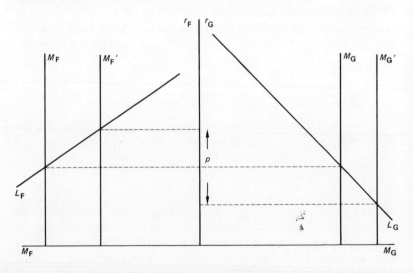

Fig. 5.2 Symmetrical adjustment.

Asymmetrical intervention

The same expectational shock leads to asymmetrical effects on the money markets of the two countries if one country sterilises the effects of the intervention; or if the intervention is performed using a third currency (say the dollar), and one country takes an attitude of 'benign neglect' *vis-à-vis* its dollar exchange rate.

Suppose Germany fully sterilises the effect of its intervention. We then have the situation shown in Fig. 5.3. The German money supply is unaffected by the sales of Deutschemarks in the exchange market. As a result, the interest differential between the French and German interest rates must come about by an increase in the French interest rate (and a constant German interest rate). The contraction of the money stock will have to be more pronounced in France than in the previous symmetrical system. As a result, the money stock in the 'European' monetary system will decline. This was not the case in the symmetrical system where the contraction in France and the expansion in Germany left the 'European' money stock unchanged. The same result will obtain if the French authorities support their currency by buying francs in exchange for dollars. In that case the French money stock declines without affecting the German money stock.[3] Note, however, that the French sale of dollars will tend to reduce the price of dollars in terms of francs, thereby also reducing the price of the dollar in terms of Deutschemarks.[4] If the

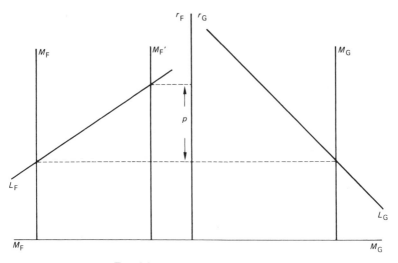

F ig. 5.3 Asymmetrical adjustment.

German authorities view the dollar–Deutschemark rate with benign neglect, and so abstain from intervention in the dollar–Deutschemark exchange market, the German money market will be unaffected by the French interventions.

The ECU intervention system

In the ECU intervention system we assume that France and Germany intervene when the ECU price of their respective currencies deviates from the ECU parities by more than a certain margin.

One aspect of the ECU system is that if one currency appreciates (depreciates) *vis-à-vis* all the other currencies in the ECU basket, this currency will reach its upper (lower) limit *vis-à-vis* the ECU parity before any other currency reaches the lower (upper) limit. As a result, the appreciating (depreciation) currency will be forced to do most of the intervention, i.e. sell (buy) its own currency. In the scenario developed here, Germany would be forced to expand its money stock, at least if the appreciation of the Deutschemark is expected to occur *vis-à-vis* all the other currencies in the system.

THE ECONOMETRIC MODEL

The econometric model consists of demand and supply equations for money in six EC countries, and interest parity conditions linking the national interest rates. In addition, reaction functions describing the intervention behaviour in the exchange market are added. Here we concentrate on the intervention behaviour when the ECU is the indicator. In the appendix the other equations of the model are described.

The ECU is defined as follows

$$E_i = \sum_{j=1}^{n} a_j S_{ji} \qquad \text{for } i = 1, \ldots, n \qquad (1)$$

where

E_i = the price of the ECU in terms of currency i,
a_j = the amount of currency j in the ECU basket, and
S_{ji} = the price of currency j in terms of currency i.

Note that E_i and S_{ji} relate to observed market prices. The official ECU price of currency i (the ECU parity) can be written as

$$E_i^* = \sum_{j=1}^{n} a_j S_{ji}^* \qquad \text{for } i = 1, \ldots, n \qquad (2)$$

where

E_i^* = the official price of the ECU in terms of currency i, and
S_{ji}^* = the official price of currency j in terms of currency i.

The matrix of S_{ji}^* forms the so-called parity grid. It is clear that the following conditions must hold:

$$S_{ji}^* = \frac{1}{S_{ij}^*} \qquad \text{and} \qquad S_{ji} = \frac{1}{S_{ij}}$$

$$S_{ii}^* = 1 \qquad \text{and} \qquad S_{ii} = 1.$$

In the ECU intervention system considered here the monetary authorities buy and sell foreign exchange (dollars or European currencies) so as to maintain the ECU rate of their currency within a predetermined margin.

This can be formalised as follows

$$\Delta R_{it} = \gamma_i (E_{it} - E_{it}^*) \qquad (3)$$

where

R_{it} = the stock of international reserves of country i in period t, and
γ_i = the intervention parameter of country i. In the simulations of the model the numerical values of γ_i are chosen such that the ECU rate cannot diverge from the ECU parity by more than the prescribed margin.[5]

The EMS agreement provides that intervention in the exchange market should be carried out using European currencies. In practice, however, EMS participants have also used dollars. Therefore, in the following, intervention in both dollars and in European currencies will be analysed.

If the authorities choose to intervene in dollars it is convenient to rewrite equation (3) as follows

$$\Delta R_{it}^{\$} = \gamma_i E_{\$t} \left(S_{\$it} - \frac{E_{it}^*}{E_{\$t}} \right) \qquad (4)$$

where

$E_{\$t} = \dfrac{E_{it}}{S_{it}}$, the price of the ECU in terms of dollars in period t,

$S_{\$it}$ = the price of the dollar in terms of currency i in period t, and

$R_{it}^{\$}$ = the dollar holdings of country i (expressed in domestic currency) in period t.

Note that equation (4) is an equivalent expression to equation (3) where we have made use of the triangular arbitrage condition $E_i = E_{\$} S_{\$i}$ and $E_i = E_{\$} S_{\$i}^{*}$. There is no official price of the ECU in terms of dollars, so that $E_{\$}^{*} = E_{\$}$. The intervention function (4) will be used when the authorities intervene in dollars.

In a similar way we can rewrite equation (3) so as to obtain the cross rates in the intervention function

$$\Delta R_{it}^{j} = \gamma_i (E_{jt} S_{jit} - E_{jt}^{*} S_{jit}^{*}) \tag{5}$$

where

E_{jt} = the market price of the ECU in terms of currency j in period t,

E_j^{*} = the official price of the ECU in terms of j in period t, and

R_i^{j} = the holdings of currency j by country i in period t.[6]

Note that we have used the triangular arbitrage conditions $E_i = E_j S_{ji}$ and $E_i^{*} = E_j^{*} S_{ji}^{*}$, and that in contrast to the intervention function (4) we have to introduce E_j and E_j^{*} separately.

In the simulations of the model the ECU intervention system will be compared to the snake intervention system. In order to do so we specify the intervention system as follows. Assume first that snake intervention is carried out using European currencies. We then have

$$\Delta R_{it}^{j} = v_i (S_{jit} - S_{jit}^{*}) \tag{6}$$

i.e. country i sells (buys) currency j whenever S_{jit} tends to increase (decrease) beyond a certain limit.

Similarly, when country i intervenes in dollars to keep the bilateral rate S_{jit} within the margins we obtain

$$\Delta R_{it}^{\$} = v_i \left(\frac{S_{\$it}}{S_{\$jt}} - \frac{S_{\$it}^{*}}{S_{\$jt}^{*}} \right) \tag{7}$$

where use has been made of the triangular arbitrage conditions

$$S_{jit} = \frac{S_{\$it}}{S_{\$jt}} \quad \text{and} \quad S_{jit}^{*} = \frac{S_{\$it}^{*}}{S_{\$jt}^{*}}.$$

Note, however, that in this intervention system at least one country should abstain from rigidly pegging its dollar rate. For if all countries were to follow an intervention rule like equation (7) the currencies of the system would *de facto* be on a fixed rate with the dollar. In the simulations it is assumed that one reference country (Germany) abstains from intervention in the dollar–Deutschemark market.[7] As a result, the dollar–Deutschemark rate floats freely. We thus have for the other countries the following intervention rule

$$\Delta R_{it}^{\$} = v_i \frac{1}{S_{\$Dt}} (S_{\$it} - S_{\$it}^{*}) \tag{8}$$

where

$S_{\$Dt}$ = the price of the dollar in terms of the Deutschemark
$S_{\$it}^{*} = S_{Dit}^{*} S_{\$Dt}$.

Note that $S_{\$Dt} = S_{\$Dt}^{*}$ because by assumption the German central bank does not have a target for the dollar–Deutschemark rate.

SIMULATION RESULTS: DOMESTIC MONETARY SHOCKS

In this section the results of the simulation of the ECU intervention system are reported. These are then compared to the same simulations under a snake intervention system.[8]

We first analyse the results of domestic monetary shocks. These take the form of a 10 per cent increase of the domestic component of the money base above its observed values in Germany, France and the UK. Table 5.1 reports the effects of a German monetary expansion on interest rates, exchange rates and reserve flows in the EMS. Tables 5.2 and 5.3 report similar results when the monetary shock originates in France and the UK respectively. In these simulations we assume the UK to be part of the EMS.[9]

The tabulated results suggest the following conclusions. First, in a ECU intervention system the choice of the intervention currency seems to matter little. Whether intervention is executed in dollars or Deutschemarks, the results are very similar. Second, the ECU system allows a certain degree of symmetry in that the expansionary country will have to sell foreign exchange in the foreign exchange market, whereas all the other countries buy foreign exchange. This then tends to contract the money supply in the expansionary country and to expand it in the other

TABLE 5.1 Effect of a 10 per cent domestic credit expansion in Germany

	ECU spot rate	DM spot rate	Interest rate	Reserves (in billions of national currencies)
A. ECU AS INDICATOR				
Intervention in dollars				
Belgium	0.002	− 0.034	− 0.006	0.58
Germany	0.036	—	− 0.145	− 0.169
France	0.001	− 0.035	− 0.003	0.30
The Netherlands	0.002	− 0.034	− 0.008	0.011
UK	0.001	− 0.035	− 0.002	0.004
ECU-$	− 0.012	—	—	—
Intervention in DM				
Belgium	0.002	− 0.033	− 0.007	0.63
Germany	0.035	—	− 0.145	− 0.47
France	0.001	− 0.034	− 0.004	0.33
The Netherlands	0.003	− 0.032	− 0.009	0.012
UK	0.001	− 0.034	− 0.002	0.005
ECU-$	− 0.016			
B. CROSS RATES AS INDICATORS (SNAKE MECHANISM)				
Intervention in dollars				
Belgium	0.020	− 0.031	− 0.085	8.6
Germany	0.051	—	− 0.186	0.0
France	0.017	− 0.034	− 0.057	5.3
The Netherlands	0.040	− 0.011	− 0.156	0.208
UK	0.069	0.018	− 0.115	0.442
Intervention in DM				
Belgium	0.004	− 0.033	− 0.015	1.4
Germany	0.037	—	− 0.135	− 0.93
France	0.002	− 0.035	− 0.009	0.75
The Netherlands	0.005	− 0.032	− 0.021	0.037
UK	0.009	− 0.028	− 0.022	0.056

Note: the shock occurs in the first quarter of 1973; the changes are those occurring between the first and second quarters.

countries. This expansionary effect in the other EMS countries remains relatively small because in the simulation run the authorities use sterilisation policies,[10] and the cross rates move within the permissible margin of fluctuation.

The results of the ECU intervention system should be compared with the results obtained when the snake mechanism is operative.[11] The latter are shown in the bottom halves of the tables. The comparison of these results allows us to draw the conclusion that a snake mechanism can be made to operate under similar symmetry conditions as an ECU system. In order to obtain symmetry in the snake mechanism it is sufficient that the central banks participating in the arrangement intervene in each other's currency. Asymmetries in the adjustment mechanism will be obtained in the snake mechanism if the intervention is in dollars and if one country follows a 'benign neglect' policy as far as its dollar exchange rate is

TABLE 5.2 Effect of a 10 per cent domestic credit expansion in France

	ECU spot rate	FF spot rate	Interest rate	Reserves (in billions of national currencies)
A. ECU AS INDICATOR				
Intervention in dollars				
Belgium	0.002	− 0.033	− 0.005	0.48
Germany	0.001	− 0.034	− 0.005	0.06
France	0.035	—	− 0.139	− 0.70
The Netherlands	0.002	− 0.033	− 0.007	0.009
UK	0.001	− 0.034	− 0.002	0.004
ECU-$	− 0.010	—	—	—
Intervention in DM				
Belgium	0.002	− 0.033	− 0.006	0.55
Germany	0.010	− 0.025	− 0.034	0.37
France	0.035	—	− 0.140	− 0.668
The Netherlands	0.002	− 0.033	− 0.008	0.011
UK	0.001	− 0.034	− 0.002	0.004
B. CROSS RATES AS INDICATORS (SNAKE MECHANISM)				
Intervention in dollars				
Belgium	—	− 0.046	0	—
Germany	—	− 0.046	0	—
France	0.046	—	− 0.137	− 0.558
The Netherlands	—	− 0.046	0	—
UK	—	− 0.046	0	0.0
Intervention in DM				
Belgium	0.014	− 0.021	− 0.003	0.323
Germany	0.007	− 0.028	− 0.043	0.350
France	0.035	—	− 0.139	− 0.786
The Netherlands	0.002	− 0.033	− 0.005	0.006
UK	0.002	− 0.033	− 0.005	0.014

Note: the shock occurs in the first quarter of 1973; the changes are those occurring between the first and second quarters.

TABLE 5.3 Effects of a 10 per cent domestic credit expansion in the UK

	ECU spot rate	£ spot rate	Interest rate	Reserves (in billions of national currencies)
A. ECU AS INDICATOR				
Intervention in dollars				
Belgium	0.006	− 0.114	− 0.019	1.85
Germany	0.006	− 0.114	− 0.019	0.24
France	0.004	− 0.116	− 0.011	0.97
The Netherlands	0.009	− 0.111	− 0.027	0.037
UK	0.120	—	− 0.489	− 0.042
ECU-$	− 0.032			
Intervention in DM				
Belgium	0.006	− 0.112	− 0.018	1.76
Germany	− 0.006	− 0.126	0.015	− 0.16
France	0.004	− 0.116	− 0.011	0.93
The Netherlands	0.009	− 0.111	− 0.026	0.035
UK	0.120		− 0.490	− 0.043
B. CROSS RATES AS INDICATORS (SNAKE MECHANISM)				
Intervention in dollars				
Belgium	—	− 0.217	—	—
Germany	—	− 0.217	—	—
France	—	− 0.277	—	—
The Netherlands	—	− 0.217	—	—
UK	0.217	—	− 0.291	− 0.236
Intervention in DM				
Belgium	0.006	− 0.091	− 0.012	1.17
Germany	0.018	− 0.079	− 0.141	1.15
France	0.003	− 0.094	− 0.007	0.628
The Netherlands	0.008	− 0.089	− 0.018	0.23
UK	0.097	—	0.353	− 0.248

Note: the shock occurs in the first quarter of 1973; the changes are those occurring between the first and second quarters.

concerned. In the simulations reported here we assumed that Germany was this country. In that particular set-up Germany will determine the monetary conditions in other countries. This means, for example, that if it expands the domestic money base and reduces the interest rate, the other countries will have to follow suit. The opposite will be true if there is a contraction in Germany.

We conclude that both intervention systems have similar (and symmetric) effects on the adjustment mechanism in the money markets, provided intervention is conducted in EMS currencies under the snake system.

SIMULATION RESULTS: CHANGES IN EXPECTATIONS

In this section the simulations of expectational changes are reported. First, we assume a speculative cycle involving the Deutschemark. Second, a similar speculative cycle is assumed for the Belgian franc.

Expected appreciation of the Deutschemark

In the simulation runs reported here we assume that the Deutschemark is expected to appreciate against all currencies during three quarters, and then return to its initial value. The forward rate increases by 1 per cent each quarter during three quarters, and returns to this observed value afterwards.

The results are shown in Figs 5.4 and 5.5. Figure 5.4 represents the time path of the endogenous variables under a snake system, Fig. 5.5 under an ECU system. In both cases the authorities buy and sell dollars. In the snake system all EMS countries have to adjust by increasing their domestic interest rate (because they sell dollars so as to raise their currency value *vis-à-vis* the dollar). Germany can insulate its domestic money market from the effects of the expectational change by letting the dollar–Deutschemark ($S_{\$D}$) rate decline.

The ECU system changes this picture considerably. The expected appreciation of the Deutschemark reduces the ECU–Deutschemark rate, thereby forcing the German authorities to buy dollars. This leads to reductions in the German interest rate.[12] As a result the effects on the other countries' money markets are substantially reduced. Thus, the ECU adds substantial symmetry forcing Germany, in this case, to do much of the adjustment by letting its domestic interest rate drop. This reduces the burden of the adjustment for all countries.

In a second set of simulations we assumed that the intervention takes place using Deutschemarks instead of dollars. The format of the simulations is identical to the previous case. Two results of these simulations stand out. First, in the snake system (Fig. 5.6) Germany is doing most of the adjustment, i.e. the German interest rate declines substantially.[13] This limits the increase in other countries' interest rates. Second, in the ECU system (Fig. 5.7) the adjustment burden imposed on Germany is somewhat reduced. At the same time the upward pressure on

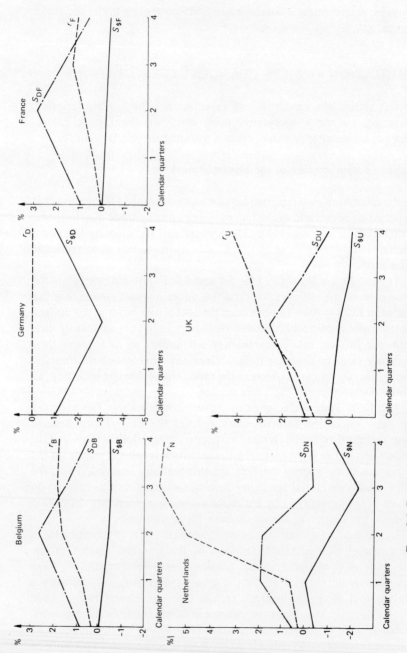

Fig. 5.4 Response to Deutschemark appreciation: dollar intervention under a snake system.

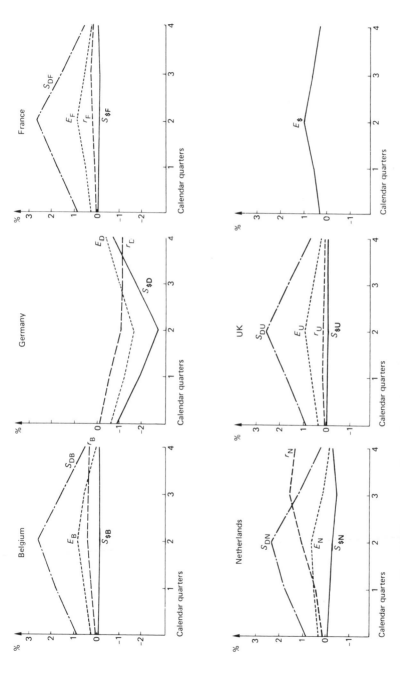

FIG. 5.5 Response to Deutschemark appreciation: dollar intervention under an ECU system.

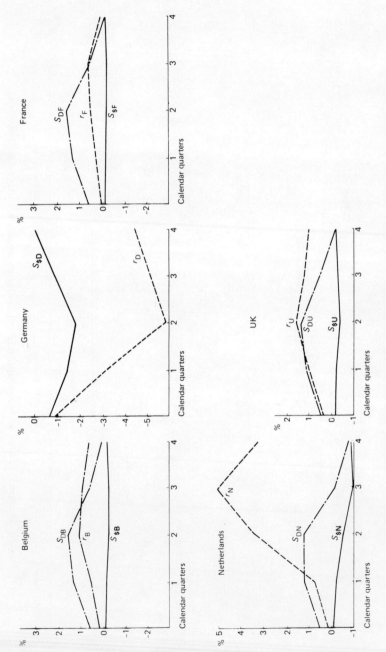

Fig. 5.6 **Response to Deutschemark appreciation: Deutschemark intervention under a snake system.**

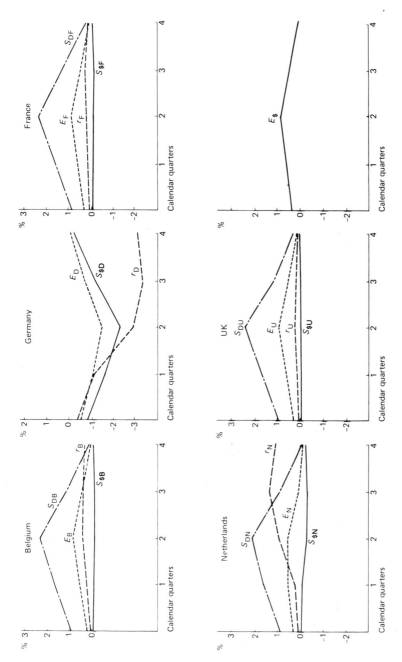

FIG. 5.7 Response to Deutschemark appreciation: Deutschemark intervention under an ECU system.

the other countries' interest rates is reduced even further. This may seem paradoxical. The rationale for this result is that in an ECU system the other countries intervene very little, because their ECU rates move very little. The Deutschemark accounts for 'only' 30 per cent in the ECU basket. As a result, most of the adjustment is taken care of by movements of the cross exchange rates within the EMS. As can be seen the cross rates (S_{DB}, S_{DF}, S_{DN} and S_{DU}) increase substantially more in the ECU system than in the snake system. This then reduces the need to adjust interest rates.

This brings us to a problem of the ECU system as simulated here. When intra-EMS exchange rates move in opposite directions (e.g. the Deutschemark appreciates *vis-à-vis* the French franc and the latter appreciates *vis-à-vis* the Belgian franc) third countries' ECU rates may move very little. As a result, little or no intervention will occur even if the cross rates move substantially. Put differently, setting fixed margins around ECU parities is compatible with a great number of variations of cross rates.[14] If one wants to avoid large variations of intra-EMS exchange rates, fixed ECU margins must be supplemented by fixed margins on bilateral exchange rates. One then returns, *de facto*, to a snake-type arrangement.

Expected depreciation of the Belgian franc

In a final set of simulations the effects of an expected change in the exchange rate of a small country, Belgium, were investigated. We assumed that the Belgian franc was expected to depreciate continuously by 1 per cent during three quarters, after which it would return to its control value, and that intervention is in Deutschemarks.

Here we found that there is practically no difference between the snake and the ECU system. In both cases Belgium bears most of the burden of the adjustment through an increase in the Belgian interest rate. There is also a limited decline of the German interest rate, in both systems, as the Belgian authorities sell Deutschemarks to maintain the cross-rates (or the ECU rate) within the margins. The other countries are mostly unaffected.

The reason why the ECU system is little different from the snake system is that the small size of Belgium (and the small weight of the Belgian franc in the ECU basket) leaves the other currencies' ECU rates very little affected. Thus most of the intervention has to be done by the Belgian monetary authorities to keep its ECU rate within the margin. This leads to the conclusion that asymmetries in the adjustment mechanism due to differences in size cannot be remedied by an ECU system. These asymmetries will continue to exist with or without ECUs.

CONCLUSION

In this paper the use of the ECU as an indicator for foreign exchange market intervention within the EMS was analysed. It was shown that such a system introduces some symmetry in the monetary adjustment mechanism, compared to a snake intervention system in which countries buy and sell dollars to maintain their cross exchange rates within the margins. The ECU, however, does not augment the symmetry of the adjustment mechanism when the EMS participants intervene in European currencies. Other simulations reported in this paper suggest that, without being harmful, the ECU does not stand out as a particularly attractive indicator for the intervention mechanism within the EMS.

NOTES

1. This has been set at 75 per cent of the official margin around the ECU parities.
2. The detail of the model is explained in de Grauwe and van den Bergh (1980).
3. Note that the US money stock is affected if the Federal Reserve does not sterilise the effects of this sale of dollars by the French monetary authorities.
4. The reason is that the DM–FF rate is fixed. Triangular arbitrage then also reduces the DM price of the dollar.
5. It should be noted that if the bilateral (snake) margins are the same for all currencies (2.25 per cent above and below parity in the present EMS), the margins around the ECU parity will be different because the weights of the individual currencies in the ECU differ. In general, currencies with a low weight have a larger maximum margin of fluctuation around the ECU rate, than the currencies with a high weight.
6. Typically country i holds little of currency j in the present EMS. However, through a swap with country j, country i can obtain any amount of currency j in the short run.
7. Another possibility would be to assume that the reference country follows a 'leaning-against-the-wind strategy' in the dollar exchange market.
8. More detail on these simulations can be found in de Grauwe and van den Bergh (1980).
9. Italy was omitted from these simulations.
10. These were assumed to be partial (50 per cent).
11. Note that we again assume sterilisation policies to be 'partial', i.e. 50 per cent.
12. Elsewhere we showed that with an extension of the currency union to more

members, the currency which is expected to depreciate or appreciate is forced to do more of the adjustment (see de Grauwe and van den Bergh, 1980).
13. This is essentially due to the under-determinacy of the ECU system.
14. Here also we assume partial sterilisation policies of 50 per cent.

REFERENCE

Grauwe, P. de and van den Bergh, P. (1980), 'Monetary Policies and Exchange Rates in the EC', *European Economic Review*, vol. 13.

APPENDIX

In this appendix the econometric model used for the simulations is outlined.

The theoretical model: money market block

The money demand equation

$$\ln M_{it}^d = a_{1i} + a_{2i} \ln Y_{it} + a_{3i} \ln r_{it} + \ln P_{it} \tag{A1}$$

where

M_{it}^d = the money demand in country i in quarter t,
Y_{it} = real GNP in country i in quarter t,
r_{it} = the nominal (short term) interest rate in country i in quarter t, and
P_{it} = the price level in country i in quarter t.

The money supply equation

$$M_{it}^S = m_{it} B_{it} \tag{A2}$$

where

M_{it}^S = the money supply in country i in quarter t,
m_{it} = the money base multiplier in country i in quarter t, and
B_{it} = the money base in country i in quarter t.

The money base

This is defined in first-difference form as

$$\Delta B_{it} = \Delta R_{it} + \Delta D_{it} \tag{A3}$$

where

R_{it} = the foreign component of the money base in country i in period t, and

D_{it} = the domestic component of the money base in country i in period t.

The interest parity relationship

$$r_{it} - r_{Et} = x_{it} \qquad (A4)$$

where

r_{Et} = the Eurodollar interest rate,

x_{it} = the forward discount on currency i, i.e. $x_{it} = \dfrac{F_{\$it} - S_{\$it}}{S_{\$it}} \times 400,$

$F_{\$it}$ = the (three-month) forward exchange rate of currency i in quarter t, and

$S_{\$it}$ = the spot exchange rate of currency i in period t.

All exchange rates are defined as prices of the *dollar* in terms of domestic currency.

The use of the interest parity equation implies that transaction costs are absent. The existence of capital controls and of political risk, however, leads to deviations from the interest parity condition.

Equilibrium condition

$$M_{it}^d = M_{it}^S. \qquad (A5)$$

The theoretical model: wage price block

The price and wage equations are specified as follows:

$$\ln P_{it} = b_{1i} + b_{2i} \ln PM_{it} + b_{3i} \ln W_{it} + b_{4i} \ln P_{it-1} \qquad (A6)$$

and

$$\ln W_{it} = c_{1i} + c_{2i} \ln PR_{it} + c_{3i} \ln U_{it} + c_{4i} \ln P_{it} + c_{5i} \ln W_{it-1} \qquad (A7)$$

where

PM_{it} = the import price index, in domestic currency i,

W_{it} = the index of the wage rate in country i,

PR_{it} = the index of average labour productivity in country i, and

U_{it} = the unemployment rate in country i.

The import price index PM_{it} is defined as:

$$PM_{it} = \frac{S_{\$it}}{S_{\$i0}} \sum \gamma_j^i \left[PX_{jt} / \left(\frac{S_{\$jt}}{S_{\$j0}} \right) \right] \tag{A8}$$

where

$PX_{jt\cdot}=$ the export price index of country j expressed in currency j,

$\gamma_j^i =$ the share of imports from country j in country i's total imports, and

$PX_{jt} / \left(\dfrac{S_{\$jt}}{S_{\$j0}} \right) =$ the export price index of country j expressed in dollars.

From the preceding calculations it follows that by affecting the import price index, exchange-rate changes have an influence on the wage–price mechanism. This feeds back into the demand for money.

The estimated equations

The results are summarised in the following tables. Standard errors are shown in parentheses. The estimation period is 1966_I–1977_{IV}.

TABLE 5.A1 Money demand functions

Country	Dependent variable	Constant	P	Y	r	Lagged dependent variable	R^2	DW	Average lag
Belgium	M_1	−0.419 (0.43)	0.566 (0.12)	0.203 (0.09)	−0.057 (0.02)	0.433 (0.12)	0.98	2.6	1.76
Germany	M_1*	7.954 (0.29)	1.00	1.224 (0.04)	−0.077 (0.01)	—	0.94	2.24	—
France	M_1	−0.279 (0.29)	1.182 (0.04)	0.120 (0.06)	−0.03 (0.02)	—	0.98	1.02	—
Italy	M_2	−12.79 (1.9)	1.193 (0.07)	1.625 (0.18)	−0.048 (0.04)	—	0.98	1.28	—
The Netherlands	M_1	−4.89 (0.31)	1.09 (0.06)	0.719 (0.11)	−0.918 (0.01)	—	0.99	1.99	—
UK	M_1	3.52 (0.31)	0.785 (0.028)	0.818 (0.13)	−0.044 (0.02)	—	0.99	0.73	—

* Estimated in real terms.

TABLE 5.A2 Price equations

Country	Constant	Wages	Import prices	Lagged dependent variable	R^2	DW	Average lag (in quarters)	Long-run import price elasticity
Belgium	0.0936 (0.0699)	0.057 (0.015)	0.0569 (0.0126)	0.87 (0.025)	0.99	1.8365	7.69	0.437
Germany	0.319 (0.085)	0.089 (0.019)	0.039 (0.018)	0.80 (0.0517)	0.99	1.6575	5.0	0.195
France	0.425 (0.069)	0.1378 (0.0198)	0.052 (0.0084)	0.72 (0.0386)	0.99	1.579	3.57	0.186
Italy	0.278 (0.059)	0.0621 (0.0128)	0.0718 (0.0113)	0.81 (0.03)	0.99	2.007	5.26	0.378
The Netherlands	0.27 (0.076)	0.1205 (0.0286)	0.0147 (0.016)	0.81 (0.048)	0.99	2.519	5.26	0.077
UK	0.076 (0.039)	0.0898 (0.0407)	0.0533 (0.031)	0.84 (0.036)	0.99	1.5615	6.25	0.333

TABLE 5.A3 Wage equations

Country	Constant	Prices	Productivity	Unemployment rate	Lagged dependent variable	R^2	DW
Belgium	-1.747 (0.498)	0.5915 (0.183)	0.1107 (0.064)	-0.014 (0.003)	0.70 (0.10)	0.99	2.92
Germany	-0.599 (0.262)	0.169 (0.114)	0.0603 (0.0641)	-0.0091 (0.0027)	0.911 (0.05)	0.99	1.98
France	-1.069 (0.499)	0.401 (0.20)	0.094 (0.0629)	-0.00108 (0.0063)	0.743 (0.141)	0.99	1.76
Italy	-1.158 (0.39)	0.106 (0.085)	0.264 (0.089)	0.0005 (0.004)	0.888 (0.064)	0.99	1.63
The Netherlands	-0.519 (0.34)	0.156 (0.176)	0.187 (0.065)	0.0083 (0.0064)	0.763 (0.123)	0.99	2.29
UK	-0.773 (0.388)	0.146 (0.131)	0.165 (0.0879)	-0.00965 (0.0047)	0.87 (0.126)	0.99	1.81

Comments on Walter, Vaubel and de Grauwe and van den Bergh

R. SHONE

These three chapters address themselves to some very important issues. From the wide range of specific questions considered there emerge four critical concepts which are in urgent need of clarification, and which form the focus of this discussion. These concepts are stability, convergence, symmetry and balance, both internal and external.

Roland Vaubel takes it that stability is desired and asks whether it is feasible; and if feasible, how it can be attained. There is agreement that stability refers to inflation and exchange rates, but there the agreement ends. Neither the chapter by Vaubel nor that by Walter refers to stability of inflation rates but rather to their *variability* (along with the average level of changes). Are instability and variability being used synonymously? Can we not have a variable economic series within a stable system?

Even though concerned with variability, Norbert Walter points out that it is difficult to apply this concept to the exchange rate, since the EMS allows realignments. Furthermore, there is more than one measure of exchange-rate variance. The distinctions between bilateral and multilateral rates, and between real and nominal rates, mean that when we are assessing performance or success we have a variety of possible indicators. The evidence presented in these papers suggests that they do not tell the same story!

I find convergence an even more slippery concept. Both Vaubel and Walter are concerned about convergent inflation rates. This seems to mean bringing the level of members 'close' together by reducing the standard deviation about the European average. Both begin by looking at actual levels of inflation. Vaubel then considers a variety of other measures based on 'equilibrium inflation rates' derived from a simple money market equilibrium condition. I find this analysis dubious. I can only list some of my reservations. The use of such a simple money market model is notorious for giving poor results outside the sample period. What does he mean by the statement that 'policy differences were much larger in the seventies than in the sixties', other than that $\hat{P} = \hat{M}_1 - \hat{Y}$ was larger – an argument which is circular. Why use $\hat{M}_1 - \hat{P}$ as a dependent variable? Imposing a zero intercept is always misleading in econometric work since it is a 'catch-all' term. To conclude, as Vaubel does with regard to Table 4.8, that monetary divergences were even larger than the raw inflation rates would indicate, is unjustified, unless one believes that an increase in the money supply is the sole cause of inflation. At best Vaubel's analysis gives information about variations in inflation, actual and 'equilibrium'. Strictly, it gives little information about monetary policy. Although Walter mentions interest rates and monetary aggregates (as intermediate targets) he is not precise about the pattern that would indicate divergence or convergence.

It has been well documented that the Bretton Woods system contained two asymmetries: one concerning the burden of adjustment, and secondly the *n*th country problem. The paper by Paul de Grauwe and Paul van den Bergh takes up this point, amongst others, in relation to an ECU-based intervention system.

Their concept of symmetry is a very special one. In their stylised model of France and Germany, it refers simply to the effects of a disturbance on the money supply, which changes in each country in such a way that the uncovered interest differential equals the forward premium on the foreign currency. Asymmetry then arises whenever one country sterilises (or they both sterilise to different degrees). The symmetrical system has the effect of leaving the 'European' monetary stock unchanged, while the asymmetrical system decreases it. Symmetry is here a purely monetary concept.

Given their usage, however, is the ECU system symmetrical? The authors say that in an ECU system there is a 'certain degree of symmetry'. This must mean a degree of asymmetry; but more importantly, the conclusion depends on the assumption of 50 per cent sterilisation. In line with their introduction, what should be established is whether, in the absence of sterilisation, the ECU system is symmetrical. To conclude that symmetry is absent in the presence of sterilisation does not make it logically true that it must be present in the absence of sterilisation.

They go on and say that asymmetry will result if intervention is carried out in dollars and if *one* country follows 'benign neglect'. But it is not the dollar intervention which is relevant, it could equally well be yen; what is crucial is the benign neglect. This implies that Germany would be playing the same role in the EMS as the US did in the Bretton Woods system, and creating a similar system with a similar ending.

When they turn to the Belgian franc depreciation they conclude that asymmetries due to differences in size cannot be remedied in an ECU-based system. 'These asymmetries will continue to exist with or without ECUs.' Does this mean that even with other intervention systems, 'size' will always create an asymmetry?

The distinction between internal and external balance is blurred by monetary union. The uncertain interpretation of these concepts reflects political tension among members as well as immediate economic issues. In the present context, external balance can be defined at the level both of the Community as a whole, and of each individual member. The relative significance of these two levels depends on the provisions for intra-Community transfers and for the financing of imbalances, and on the mechanism which is established to induce policy changes (whether national or supranational) in response to imbalance at Community level. Internal balance is equally ambiguous. Does it mean a common inflation rate at a Community natural level of unemployment which is the sum of the natural levels for each member? How will the natural rate of unemployment of the Community and of its individual members be altered by changes in the mobility of labour? What strains, political as well as economic, will result from changes in the distribution of unemployment across member states? How effective will Community-wide regional policy prove in reducing the natural rate?

The final comment concerns methodology. There is an undoubted need to consider the facts about the EMS on the lines followed by Walter. But in order to answer questions about stability, convergence, asymmetry, and internal and external balance, along with performance and success, we require a fully articulated theoretical framework, and as far as I can see none really exists. Two approaches are open: to consider some partial analytical framework for evaluating variability and convergence, on the lines of Vaubel; or to set up an econometric model and run simulations, on the lines of de Grauwe and van den Bergh. The present chapters can be considered as only a beginning.

6 European Monetary Arrangements and the International Monetary System

DAVID T. LLEWELLYN

THE CONTEXT

Following a decade of comparative stability in domestic and international monetary arrangements, the 1970s was a period of considerable turbulence. The uncertain, and at times volatile, international environment proved to be unconducive to the attainment of the ambitions of the Werner Report, and revealed a degree of disparity in economic performance among members of the EC that denied significant progress towards formal monetary integration.

Both the domestic and international monetary environment became considerably less certain and predictable over the 1970s, and early in the decade the Bretton Woods arrangements finally disintegrated after close on thirty years. The 1970s experienced a series of experiments with exchange-rate arrangements (involving varying degrees and predictability of official intervention) in the context of four major shocks to the system: (i) the inconvertibility of the US dollar and the end of the Bretton Woods system of fixed exchange rates; (ii) the general acceleration and greater international diversity of rates of inflation; (iii) substantial imbalances in the pattern of world payments associated with OPEC pricing decisions and cyclical divergencies between major industrial countries; (iv) major portfolio diversification by reserve holders at various times in the 1970s, involving sharp movements in exchange rates against the dollar. In the face of these shocks, which affected individual European countries in different degrees, predominantly national rather than European responses were made.

While the 1970s began with an air of unrealistic optimism for European monetary integration following the *Grand Design* of the Werner Report, little if any progress was made over the decade in formal European monetary arrangements. Very little materialised along the lines outlined in Werner and, far from establishing full monetary union as envisaged for 1980, the decade during which gradual moves were to be made towards this goal ended in some respects with less monetary coordination and certainty than at the beginning. Although various formal exchange rate arrangements were instituted in Europe (snake-in-the-tunnel, joint float, mini-snake and the European monetary system) and associated short- and medium-term credit facilities were created, in general less progress has been made in the monetary area in the EC than in many other major aspects. In neither the international monetary system generally nor in European monetary arrangements did the *Grand Design* concept materialise. The international monetary reform negotiations did not produce a universal coherent system to replace the Bretton Woods arrangements. Indeed, many of the strains in the global monetary system (acceleration and diversity of inflation, the structural payments imbalances in the world economy, and the volatility of the dollar) hampered formal monetary integration moves within the EC. In addition to revealing the general disparity of economic performance between members of the EC, the economic conditions of the 1970s demonstrated that the political commitment towards formal monetary integration and its implications were weak.

This chapter addresses three main issues. First, the constraints and limits imposed on national sovereignty by international and inter-regional integration and the implications for the global and European monetary systems. Second, the requirements for minimising conflict (both regionally and globally) in an interdependent world economy, and third, the issue of whether formal monetary arrangements within the EC are able to contribute to stability in the global monetary system. In the process, the links between developments in the international monetary system and moves towards monetary integration in the EC are noted. At times during the 1970s (particularly when the US dollar was under pressure in the exchange markets) European initiatives were taken in response to developments in the international monetary system. But at other times global trends hampered moves towards formal monetary integration in the EC, and in general the international monetary system developed in a way that made the ambitions of the 1969 Werner Report clearly unrealistic. The emphasis on fixed exchange rates was perhaps appropriate in the context of the Bretton Woods arrangements (there were, after all, only four parity changes in the EC between 1958 and 1971) but this proved to be against the general trend of the 1970s.

APPROACHES TO INTERDEPENDENCE

Before considering European monetary arrangements in the context of developments in the international monetary system generally, it might be useful to review the broader perspective of the implications of economic and financial integration and how they impinge upon global and regional monetary arrangements. Indeed, there are distinct parallels between the major issues within the global international monetary system and within an integrated region within the global system. These issues derive from international integration, the degree of which varies between different groups of countries. We may identify five common key issues to be resolved which are highlighted in the discussion of this paper, with respect to monetary arrangements of the international monetary system generally and the EC in particular: (i) the problem of securing compatibility of policy targets and the means by which any *ex ante* inconsistencies are resolved; (ii) the question of the distribution of power and particularly whether monetary arrangements in the system or sub-system are based upon the hegemony of one dominant partner; (iii) the extent to which members recognise and adhere to agreed rules of conduct and abide by agreed obligations mutually determined: in turn, the nature, precision and compulsion of the rules is significant; (iv) there are several specific issues related to the question of payments adjustments between members and particularly over who adjusts, under what circumstances and through what mechanisms; (v) given the overall importance of monetary aspects of integration, there is the important issue of the compatibility of monetary policy of different members of a system and how consistency is ultimately achieved.

In various ways, either explicitly or implicitly, it is these five issues that have dominated developments in the international monetary system and the debate over reform. They are equally relevant to specifically European monetary arrangements. Most of the significant issues of concern in both the international monetary system generally and within regional blocs relate to the consistency of policy targets between countries. International interdependence necessarily implies that in one way or another *ex post* compatibility is secured between countries with respect notably to the balance of payments, the exchange rate and the rate of growth of the money supply. However, these may be secured *ex post* at the expense of some *ex ante* plans not being achieved. This is obvious with respect to the balance of payments, as the sum of separate *ex ante* targets might imply an aggregate world surplus or deficit. In various ways, *ex post* these inconsistencies are eliminated. But, unless all central banks refrain from foreign exchange market intervention, the same is also true of monetary policies. The degree of conflict and potential instability in the international monetary system, or any regional component of it, is likely to increase: (i) the less consistent are *ex ante* plans for those variables influenced by international transactions, (ii) the greater is the degree of economic and financial integration, and (iii) the more governments resist the mechanisms through which *ex post* compatibility is secured. De Grauwe (1973), for instance, suggests that the Bretton Woods arrangements became unstable largely because monetary policies between countries were inconsistent, and automatic equilibrating mechanisms were impeded by incompatible sterilisation strategies.

It is of interest, therefore, to consider how conflict and potential instability within a regional or global monetary system might be minimised through various arrangements for either ensuring *ex ante* consistency or minimising the resistance to *ex post* equilibrating mechanisms. Logically, five broad mechanisms or options are identified: (i) automatic market mechanisms such as floating exchange rates or non-sterilisation of balance of payments induced changes in the money supply; (ii) the $(n-1)$ approach, whereby one country in the system agrees not to have an external target; (iii) *ex ante* policy coordination designed to ensure consistent targets and compatible means of securing them; (iv) an agreement to a precise set of policy rules which indicate what is required of policy-makers in specified circumstances; (v) a multilateral approach, whereby some supranational authority indicates (and enforces?) policy measures which have been calculated to ensure consistency and stability in the system. In practice, the mechanisms are likely to be a composite of several, including an element of the most powerful parts of an integrated system imposing their own desired targets. These apply at both the global and regional level.

At the global level, the Bretton Woods system as it developed in practice was based essentially upon the $(n-1)$ strategy, with the passive role played by the US. A similar option is also available within regional arrangements, and to some extent Germany performed a similar role in the mini-snake. It is a feasible option if there is a clearly recognised dominant power in the global or regional system (though this still presupposes that the central country agrees not to have an external target), and if partners are prepared to accept the hegemony of that country, particularly with respect to monetary policy. It was the latter that proved to be a major weakness in the final years of the Bretton Woods system but a strength of the mini-snake arrangement. The major potential weakness of this mechanism is the moral hazard confronted by the key country, which can largely determine its own policy and targets and in the process impose costs (in terms of non-attainment of targets) on partner countries. In the monetary sector, for instance, with a fixed exchange rate the rate of growth of the money supply in an integrated group as a whole can be determined by the dominant country if, like the US in the 1960s, it chooses to sterilise the monetary effects of its balance-of-payments position. On the other hand, a country might choose to be dominated in this way through a self-imposed discipline if it is in agreement with the monetary policy of the dominant country.

These alternative approaches to securing consistency apply both within regional blocs and between blocs in a global system. But in terms of the global system a major issue is whether there is advantage in creating a dual structure, whereby different solutions are adopted for countries within regional blocs and between the blocs. Clearly this is particularly apposite when considering monetary arrangements within the EC and its relationship with other areas such as the US and Japan. The case for a regional approach might be made in terms of there being less formidable problems of *ex ante* coordination between countries with a comparatively high degree of integration, and where other general political objectives might also also be served by policy coordination. Nevertheless, the requirement of securing consistency between blocs remains, though different solutions might be appropriate. Thus, fixed exchange rates with *ex ante* co-ordination might be feasible within a bloc while 'collective exchange rates' might float between regional groups.

BRETTON WOODS IN DECLINE

For close on thirty years arrangements in the international monetary system were those outlined in the Bretton Woods agreement of 1944, though the system was operated in practice very differently from the intentions at the outset. In particular, exchange rates were more rigid than originally envisaged, and the US came to dominate the system through the role of the dollar. The first and major initiatives towards formal monetary integration within the EC were made in the context of the experience of two decades of predominantly fixed but adjustable exchange rates. But at various times the fixed-exchange-rate system came under strain as the volume of funds that could move between countries and currencies grew markedly after the general moves towards convertibility in the late 1950s. Indeed, towards the end of the 1960s it became increasingly apparent that fixed exchange rates, freedom of international capital flows and independent control over the domestic money supply were incompatible. Towards the end of the 1960s an attempt was made to resolve this fundamental conflict by imposing controls on capital movements. As these were circumvented, and introduced their own unintended distortions, the conflict was later resolved by adopting floating exchange rates. The adoption of floating exchange rates in the early 1970s was associated in part with a desire on the part of governments in Europe and elsewhere to determine their monetary policy independently of the US.

The general and specific weaknesses of the Bretton Woods arrangements as they emerged through the operation of the system during the 1960s are well known. These led to the eventual breakdown at two points in the 1970s: the gold-exchange standard in August 1971 and the adjustable-peg aspect in March 1973. Increasingly over the 1960s, Europe became concerned at the dominance of the US that was implicit in the Bretton Woods arrangements. This was most marked in the monetary area, though the US argument was that this was not an inherent feature of the system but arose through the way Europe chose to operate it.

In the final analysis, most of the strains on and the eventual collapse of the Bretton Woods arrangements can be ascribed to the attempt at pursuing incompatible monetary policies. In particular, the divergent stances of monetary policy in Europe and the US proved to be a major source of conflict. American monetary policy dominated Europe partly because of the size of the US economy, but also because of the reserve currency role of the dollar and the insulation this afforded the US money supply from its balance of payments (see Llewellyn, 1980). Balance-of-payments-induced changes in the money supply were asymmetric between the US and other countries, a fact which implied that US monetary policy had a decisive impact on the world money supply.

In itself the Bretton Woods system was potentially stable, and indeed, given the $(n-1)$ constraint, had a lot to commend it. It became, in effect, a dollar standard, and this could have proved durable had Europe been prepared to accept the permanent monetary dominance of the US, or had the US pursued a monetary policy consistent with that being attempted by key European countries, notably Germany. But when the US adopted an increasingly expansionary monetary policy at the turn of the 1960s and in the early 1970s, in part associated with the method of budgetary financing in connection with the war in South-East Asia, the conflicts in Europe became acute. In effect, European governments sought control over their own money supplies, though at that time little was heard of a concerted European monetary policy. Thus the global monetary system had become a dollar standard on the basis of an unstable dollar and with a major conflict of monetary policy strategy.

EUROPE'S ATTITUDE

One of the fundamental objections of European countries to the Bretton Woods system (though this never crystallised as a concerted EC strategy either against the US or in the reform negotiations of the 1970s) concerned the central and reserve currency role of the dollar. Most of the particular objections resulted from this and specifically: (i) the lack of monetary autonomy and the dominance of US monetary policy in determining the world money supply; (ii) the inflationary bias to the world economy due to the type of monetary policy conducted by the US (a point particularly emphasised by Germany); (iii) the avoidance of balance-of-payments adjustment costs by the US; (iv) the ability of the US to conduct foreign policy without reference to any external financial constraint; (v) the general seigniorage gained by the US as the issuer of world money, though the advantage to the US was somewhat exaggerated, especially as for much of the 1960s the US was in surplus on current account. Overall, as the relative power of the US declined while that of Europe increased, the dominance of the international monetary system by the US, and the general political power this conferred, became increasingly resented. But European countries were individually not strong enough to challenge the hegemony of the US (although France registered its voice by converting dollars into gold at the FED), and at no time faced America with a united strategy.

EUROPE'S RESPONSE

This was the context in the late 1960s of the first plans towards formal monetary integration in the EC. In the second half of the decade a series of proposals, notably the Barre and Schiller plans, were made with a view to inducing a greater degree of monetary integration in the EC.[1] The Werner Report was an attempt at reconciling fundamentally conflicting approaches to monetary integration, particularly over the issue of whether fixed-exchange-rate mechanisms were to be the spur to policy co-ordination or the culmination of a general process of convergence. In December 1969 the EC Heads of State agreed to establish full economic and monetary union by 1980.

With the benefit of hindsight, the early plans for monetary integration were formulated and decided upon at a time when the Bretton Woods system was subject to insurmountable pressures and the regime of fixed exchange rates was coming to an end. While, for reasons already noted, European governments and monetary authorities had become increasingly disenchanted with many features of the operation of the Bretton Woods system (especially the role of the dollar and the US), this was not the predominant motive for monetary integration in the EC in the late 1960s. The ambition to secure greater monetary independence from the US was real enough and held more by some members than others. But, unlike a decade later when the EMS was instituted in 1979, the main impetus was internal. After the establishment of the Customs Union and Common Agricultural Policy, formal moves towards monetary integration were viewed as the obvious next stage in the broader political ambitions of the EC. The driving force was internally rather than externally generated.

But less than two years after formally agreeing to establish full monetary union within a decade, the international monetary system was subject to the first of a series of shocks that fundamentally changed the functioning of the global monetary system. In May 1971, under the influence of substantial monetary inflows, the Deutschemark and Dutch guilder were unilaterally floated after Germany had failed to persuade its EC partners to float jointly against non-EC currencies and particularly the US dollar.[2] The international monetary crisis of 1971, and President Nixon's decision finally to make the dollar officially inconvertible into gold, were the first of a series of shocks in the 1970s. There was no concerted EC response, and the international monetary turmoil of the early 1970s revealed rather than caused internal conflicts in the EC that made the achievement of full monetary union within a decade almost totally infeasible. Following the failure of the EC to adopt a concerted response to the crisis of May 1971, Raymond Barre commented:

The situation . . . derives from the dissimilarity of the situations, and consequently of the interests of the various countries within the Community, from disagreement among member countries on economic doctrine, and from differing viewpoints on the methods to be used to solve international monetary problems. So long as the Member States do not arrive at some measure of political consensus on certain major problems, we shall always have to live . . . with qualified commitments and, in difficult situations, with decisions designed mainly to safeguard what each country considers to be its own vital interests. (Bloomfield, 1973, p. 16)

Indeed, this comment could have been made at several times in the 1970s as the EC failed to make a concerted response to a series of external shocks.

While the *motive* for the plans for monetary union in the late 1960s was predominantly internal, given the change in the global monetary environment the specific actions in the early 1970s were made largely in response to developments in the international monetary system. In particular, action over exchange-rate arrangements (snake-in-the-tunnel, joint float etc.) are to be interpreted more as a response to the weakness of the dollar than to the implementation of a *Grand Design* towards economic and monetary union. It was predominantly the *weakness* of the dollar in the exchange markets that was of practical concern to Europe, rather than the general role of the dollar in the system. Thus the snake-in-the-tunnel was abandoned in 1973 in favour of a joint float following speculative pressure against the dollar in favour largely of the Deutschemark. This was true also of the Committee of Twenty reform negotiations, in which the impetus for a *Grand Design* reform was weakened after the weakness of the dollar abated. In fact, during the protracted negotiations over the reform of the international monetary system the EC did not present a concerted strategy, for reasons similar to those noted earlier by Barre (Williamson, 1977). Not only were there varying degrees of commitment to closer monetary integration within the EC, but the implications for the international monetary system generally were greatly disputed. Williamson notes, 'the Europeans were paralysed by their disagreement on almost everything except their dislike of the subordinate political status assigned them by a dollar'. The US was at one time concerned that Europe might seek to delay reform negotiations until it had established its own monetary mechanisms and negotiating position, which might weaken the bargaining position of the US, and that, given the known disagreements within the EC, this delay could be lengthy.[3]

DEVELOPMENTS IN THE 1970s

In practice very little, if any, discernible progress was made during the 1970s in the direction of formal moves towards European monetary integration. The only significant developments were the snake and mini-snake systems (with varying degrees of success), the establishment of short- and medium-term financing arrangements, and the establishment of the European Monetary Co-operation Fund. No durable common EC exchange-rate system was established, there has been no pooling of external reserves, and no monetary co-ordination or common external monetary policy emerged. The snake arrangement was established in April 1972, but three countries (UK, France and Italy) withdrew when the required policy adjustments implicit in the arrangement proved unacceptable. The diversity of economic performance (especially with respect to inflation) militated against fixed exchange rates in the Community as a whole. The basic requirements to make the Werner proposal viable would have been strict under the most propitious of circumstances. They proved to be totally infeasible in the uncertain environment of the 1970s.

Similarly, there was no *Grand Design* reform of the international monetary system generally following the demise of the Bretton Woods system in the early 1970s. The initial response to the breakdown of the Bretton Woods system was an attempt to devise a *Grand Design* reform of international monetary arrangements which would avoid the weaknesses that had developed in the previous regime. In practice, none of the major issues and weaknesses highlighted by the Committee of Twenty (the primary role of the US dollar, the liquidity of the US external position, the asymmetrical nature of the exchange-rate system, official convertibility arrangements, symmetrical incentives for balance-of-payments adjustment, control of international liquidity, the role of reserve currencies and requirements for asset settlement, together with the potential destablishing effects of volatile international capital movements) was subsequently resolved through multilateral agreement. In effect, a decision was made to live with a non-system and a set of more or less informal monetary arrangements. Throughout the 1970s, there was no common exchange-rate system, no clearly defined 'rules' of official intervention (though various attempts were made to design and implement certain guidelines), no effective control over the growth of international liquidity, and no clearly defined obligations with respect to balance of payments adjustment. Above all there were no clearly defined rights and obligations of governments in their international monetary relations. The scope for conflict was therefore substantial, particularly in the oligopolistic structure of the world monetary system that emerged. Indeed, it has been argued that one reason for the failure of the *Grand Design* concept of reform was the absence of a sufficiently dominant power or small number of powers (such as the US and UK in 1944) able to impose a system. Except for the snake and mini-snake in the decade during which it was envisaged that preparations would be made to move towards full economic and monetary union in 1980, Europe did not in practice develop a clearly defined regional approach to international monetary relations.

While no currency was left totally free of official intervention during the 1970s there were substantial differences in intervention policy between countries. The predominant strategy of the US authorities was again one of 'benign neglect', with monetary and fiscal policy framed on the basis of domestic targets, and the exchange rate allowed to reflect foreign exchange market trends (Midland Bank, 1979).

For much of the 1970s the FED reserved foreign exchange market intervention for periods when exchange markets were manifestly 'disorderly'. For this reason, until 1977 the dollar–Deutschemark rate was only slightly managed and only at times of 'disorderly' markets. At the same time other rates were managed more powerfully and persistently, though while the dollar was the major intervention currency the initiative was seldom taken by the FED. The attitude of the US authorities changed, however, towards the end of 1977 when the dollar came under sharp downward pressure. There was massive intervention in support of the dollar in the final quarter of 1977 and the first three months of 1978, when the German Bundesbank and FED intervened to an amount of over DM 17 billion. Again towards the end of the year, as pressure continued, similar intervention amounted to DM 16 billion in two and a half months. The strategy of 'benign neglect' clearly changed after 1977, and towards the end of 1978 the FED announced a support package of US $ 30 billion.

Towards the end of the decade, a certain disenchantment developed over the working of the global system, and the concept of a European approach became less remote. In fact, trends that emerged in the global monetary system were remarkably similar to those that, in the late 1960s and early 1970s, fundamentally undermined the Bretton Woods arrangements. First, there was a substantial and uncontrolled growth in the volume of international liquidity which expanded by $ 64 billion in the five years to 1971 and a further $ 200 billion by 1979. As in the previous period this was associated with liability management rather than asset settlement arrangements for balance-of-payments financing, although this time all countries (including many developing countries) were involved. Second, the US current account moved into substantial deficit ($ 28 billion in the period 1977–8 against $ 8.8 billion in the period 1971–2). In both periods sharp conflicts arose between the US on the one hand and the surplus countries on the other as to whose prime responsibility it was to adopt balance-of-payments adjustment policies to alleviate the strains in the money markets.

As in the late 1960s there was also a sharp rise in US external liabilities to official institutions and a substantial deterioration in the US net external reserves position. Indeed, the magnitude of US external liabilities is in 1980 considerably more than double that at the end of 1971 (then referred to as the dollar-overhang, which was probably more instrumental than any other single factor in bringing about the final breakdown of the Bretton Woods system and the call for a fundamentally reformed system). Finally, the dollar came under substantial pressure in the foreign exchange markets in the early and late 1970s. In effect, the potentially unstable gold-exchange standard of the 1960s had given way to a predominantly dollar standard, and yet towards the end of the decade (and for similar reasons associated with the external liquidity position of the US) the pivotal role of the dollar was again challenged. A move out of the dollar induced a $ 2.4 billion reduction in US reserve assets in 1971 (when exchange rates were fixed) and a sharp decline in the value of the dollar in the exchange markets towards the end of the decade. In both periods pressure resulted in part from structural shifts in the composition of reserves designed to secure more balanced portfolios. In both periods substantial international capital movements unsettled exchange markets, and caused a dual problem of exchange-rate management and domestic monetary control in Europe. In particular, at various times during the 1970s, weakness of the dollar in the foreign exchange markets strained intra-European exchange rates as much of the speculative and arbitrage capital flows was between the US dollar and the Deutschemark. Between 1970 and the middle of 1973 the effective exchange rate of the dollar declined steadily by close on 20 per cent, but rose by close on 10 per cent by the end of 1976, though this was subsequently reversed during a persistent downward movement through 1978.

These trends and tensions produced the environment in which in 1978 a specifically European response seemed appropriate, and which resulted in the establishment of the European Monetary System. In particular, arrangements were sought which would offer a degree of insulation to intra-European exchange rates from the weakness of the US dollar, associated both with the conduct of US monetary policy and moves towards greater portfolio diversification in external reserves.

MOTIVES FOR A NEW INITIATIVE

Given this background in the global monetary system, renewed interest in a European monetary initiative developed towards the end of the decade and the European Monetary System (EMS) was formally instituted early in 1979. According to official statements at the time several factors in the world economy and financial system prompted this move: (i) a general disillusionment with the operation of floating exchange rates; (ii) the long standing European concern at the hegemony of the US dollar in the international monetary system, and (iii) a rather imprecise view that a co-ordinated policy approach by European governments would be a more effective means of improving the general performance of the European economies, and for reducing unemployment and inflation in particular. But above all else it was the substantial pressure on the dollar in the exchange markets that was the dominant factor. As already noted, when the dollar came under pressure it was largely into the Deutschemark that speculative funds flowed. The predominant motive was to mitigate the disruptive effects on intra-EC exchange rates that resulted from this pressure. This is related, however, to the more general and long standing objective of EC countries of securing a higher degree of monetary independence from the US without having to accept the implications of floating exchange rates between themselves. The broad objective of the EMS was to create a 'zone of monetary stability' in Europe. However, such a scheme, while collectively enhancing the monetary independence of the EMS group as a whole *vis-à-vis* the US, implies even less monetary independence between members. Nevertheless, there might be a greater chance of members of the EMS being able to co-ordinate and agree upon monetary targets between themselves than with the US.

Germany viewed the EMS as a means of deflecting the upward pressure on the Deutschemark resulting from the weakness of the dollar, which in 1978 was a reflection of a major diversification move by wealth-holders whose objective was to reduce the proportion of dollars in their external reserves. Thus between September 1977 and December 1978 the Deutschemark appreciated against the dollar by 20 per cent. The German authorities had long resisted (not altogether successfully) the Deutschemark becoming a reserve currency. In an official statement in December 1979 the Bundesbank noted several reasons for resisting a reserve currency status for the Deutschemark. First, the limited capacity of the German money markets meant that substantial inflows and outflows of non-resident funds placed undue strain on domestic markets. Second, such flows complicated exchange-rate and monetary management. Third, the statement argued that the size of the US economy made the US dollar a more 'natural' reserve currency, and that it was potentially unstable to have several reserve currencies. It was also argued that, as Germany usually has a current-account surplus there would be no seigniorage gain to Germany, and that the net effect of portfolio diversification was to pass on the exchange-rate risk to the Bundesbank. Given the sharp decline of the dollar during 1978, the book-keeping losses of holders of dollars, and the extent of the 'dollar-overhang', this was more than a minor issue to the German authorities.

At this stage it is interesting to compare the motives for the two major monetary initiatives in the EC in 1969 (Werner Report) and 1979 (the EMS). In the first period, as noted earlier the predominant *motive* was internal to the EC, though the practical steps made in the early 1970s were dominated by the weakness of the dollar. In the second phase the motive was unambiguously associated with the disruptive effects of exchange market pressure on the dollar. While Mr Roy Jenkins (1978) had earlier attempted to revive interest in European monetary union, this did not feature in the ambitions of politicians and central bankers when devising the EMS. It was purely a reflection of disturbances in the foreign exchange markets. There was no serious consideration given to the wider issue of economic and monetary union at the end of the 1970s.

EMS AND GLOBAL MONETARY ARRANGEMENTS

The major elements of the EMS agreed in December 1978 relate to: (i) the exchange rate system; (ii) the role of the ECU; (iii) credit facilities resulting from exchange market intervention; and (iv) regional transfers. The members of the EC, except the UK, agreed to commence the scheme on 1 January, 1979, although this was delayed for several months due to protracted negotiations over the implications for the monetary compensation accounts associated with the CAP.

Under the exchange-rate system, each currency has an ECU-related central rate which is used to establish a grid of bilateral exchange rates. Members undertake to maintain bilateral exchange rates within a permissible margin of fluctuation of 2.25 per cent. Intervention must occur, normally in member currencies, when these limits are reached. However, an indicator system exists which suggests when earlier intervention is desirable. A 'threshold of divergence' is fixed at 75 per cent of the maximum spread for each currency, and when a currency passes this threshold a presumption in favour of policy action is established in the form of : (i) diversified intervention; (ii) domestic monetary policy adjustments; (iii) changes in central rates; and/or (iv) other measures of economic policy.

These latter details distinguish the EMS from the snake arrangements when intervention was permissible only at the margins. The 'early-warning' signals, if acted upon, should increase the durability of the scheme by encouraging economic adjustment before the mandatory margins are approached. However, the tightness of the fixity of exchange rates is reduced by other details. Actual changes of the central parity itself are envisaged, particularly in the transitional period, while wider bands of fluctuation of 6 per cent were negotiated by Italy in return for agreement to join the scheme. In addition, those EC countries that were not members of the snake system are to be allowed to use such wider bands until economic conditions permit a narrowing of margins. Finally, provision for a temporary leave of absence (*congé*) is available to any member. Clearly this is a very loose form of 'fixed'-exchange-rate system. However, complete fixity was never the aim of this particular initiative. The aim was simply to remove some of the sharp and often unjustified fluctuations in exchange rates between the members, and to establish a stable bloc of currency relationships. This is not, therefore, any return to the idealistic aims of the Werner Report.

The previous short- and medium-term credit facilities, with their existing rules of application, will be maintained for the initial phase of EMS but later consolidated into a single European Monetary Fund. As under the snake arrangement, the very short-term credit facilities will be unlimited in amount but repayable within forty-five days of the month in which they are used. The short-term facilities (ECU 14 billion) have a maturity of nine months, and the medium-term credits (ECU 11 billion) a maturity of 2–5 years. Thus a total of ECU 25 billion will be available as against ECU 15 billion previously. The newly-named EMF will be formed with 20 per cent of members' foreign exchange reserves being deposited on a revolving three-month basis (to overcome the possible political issues of a permanent transfer of reserves). The EMF, to be set up within two years, will credit each member with ECUs equivalent to the value of the funds deposited. It is envisaged that at that time ECUs (also to the value of 20 per cent of member's reserves) will be created on a fiduciary basis against the deposit of domestic currency.

The role of the ECU (equal to one European Unit of Account) is limited in the first stage to being: (i) a numeraire for exchange rates, on the basis of which the grid of bilateral exchange rates is formed; (ii) the basis of a divergence indicator as noted above, and (iii) the denominator of operations in both the intervention and the credit mechanisms. Ultimately, it is envisaged that it will become a full reserve asset and a means of settlement between central banks.

The EMS could have an important impact on the international monetary system generally, given the significant number of currencies involved and their importance in the global monetary system. Viewed in terms of the basic conditions for a stable international monetary system, the arrangements envisaged are a move in the right direction. With respect to the balance-of-payments process the most significant feature is the 'threshold of divergence' indicating the need for a policy response. The burden of adjustment is in principle directed at the country whose currency diverges from a weighted average of the partner currencies. This means that, unlike the snake arrangement which was based upon a grid of bilateral exchange rates, a country may be uniquely beyond the threshold (in either direction) indicating the need for a policy response. While admittedly the form of response is vague, this represents the first ever implementation of an objective indicator to induce balance-of-payments adjustment.

The EMS also scores well in terms of the exchange market intervention arrangement. The obligations for multi-currency intervention are clearly defined. What still remain indeterminate are the conditions under which changes in central rates will be made.

The EMS *per se* makes no explicit arrangement with respect to intervention between member currencies and currencies outside the bloc. It is not obvious that the EMS itself will reduce exchange market pressure between the Deutschemark and the dollar. In practice, the key issue is the intervention strategy between the dollar and the Deutschemark, as this is a powerful axis in the international monetary system. The FED is known to regard this as the important exchange rate, and when it intervenes in the foreign exchange market it does so predominantly against the Deutschemark. In effect, the FED focuses upon the dollar–Deutschemark relationship and leaves it to other European central banks to react to it. Whatever is the attitude of other European central banks, the FED regards the Deutschemark as the central and dominant European currency. In this respect, the Deutschemark dominates European monetary arrangements as far as the American authorities are concerned. The durability of any European arrangement therefore depends in part upon whether the decisions made by the Bundesbank and the FED about this key exchange-rate relationship are acceptable to partner central banks and governments. This also raises the issue of the extent to which the Bundesbank consults its European partners about the key dollar–Deutschemark rate. We therefore now have the elements of the dual monetary system, based upon regional blocs, that was postulated in an earlier section. An immediate conflict arises over the German authorities' current attitude, which gives a higher priority than do partner governments in the EMS to reducing the external deficit. In the absence of European acceptance of the hegemony of the Deutschemark, and its implications for the conduct of monetary policy, at times of general exchange market pressure the Bundesbank could face serious conflicts of interest in that its target for the dollar–Deutschemark rate might compromise European exchange-rate arrangements. This again reinforces the view that reasonable stability of the dollar is a prerequisite for the durability of intra-European monetary arrangements.

The contribution of the EMS to the stability of the global monetary system in other areas (international liquidity, the balance between financing and adjustment, and overall confidence) is more ambiguous. The arrangement substantially extends access to intra-EC credit arrangements and the maturity of the credits has been lengthened. The aggregate volume of world liquidity[4] is increased only to the extent of any intervention balances acquired in community currencies, though these will take the form of liquidity denominated in terms of ECU. The eventual arrangement to pool 25 per cent of members' existing external reserves will increase global liquidity only to the extent of the gold contribution being valued at market prices. In the process, however, the currency composition of liquidity will change as contributions will be valued in terms of ECU. It is envisaged that ultimately the European Monetary Fund will manage a part of members' consolidated gold and foreign exchange reserves.

The effect of the arrangement upon the members' collective demand for reserves is indeterminate, though there is a presumption that pooling reserves achieves a degree of economy and hence reduces demand. But in practice the effect upon demand is determined by a multitude of factors such as the extent to which balance-of-payments accounts are consolidated (in which case external reserves are needed only for the aggregate balance-of-payments position of the group with the rest of the world), the extent of internal credit arrangements, the proportion of members' trade that is within the group, the exchange-rate policy of the group with respect to non-members, and the extent of intervention with member currencies. In a different context these issues are exhaustively discussed by Salant (1973). On balance, the demand for external reserves is reduced to the extent that internal reserves (member currencies) are substituted for external reserves (e.g. dollars), and the total demand for reserves is reduced as intra-group financing and credit arrangements are developed.

The effect of the arrangement on the balance between adjustment and financing is particularly ambiguous. Credit facilities have been extended and to that extent the balance might appear to shift towards easier financing. But against this must be set the degree of conditionality that will be imposed. Consideration must also be given to what the alternative would be. If, in the absence of use of EMF credit, the alternative would be borrowing in the international markets (as has been the case for some members over the 1970s), the arrangement would probably impose a higher adjustment requirement to the extent that market borrowing is unconditional and with longer maturities. It remains an open question whether members in need of external finance for balance-of-payments reasons will use the EMF facilities as an alternative to market borrowing. Over the 1970s many governments (including those of the UK, France and Italy) borrowed foreign currency from the international money markets at market-related interest rates substantially higher than those charged by the IMF, in order to avoid the latter's conditionality provisions. The revealed preference of avoiding conditionality proved to be strong in the 1970s, and aggregate indebtedness to the IMF declined from SDR 14.0 billion to SDR 8.0 billion between June 1977 and December 1979. This aspect seems to have been neglected in the EMS debate.

The confidence issue, originally emphasised by Triffin, is also difficult to define. One of the key issues is the extent to which the ECU becomes an international reserve currency and the extent to which there are shifts between reserve currencies. The German authorities' resistance to the Deutschemark becoming a reserve currency has been unequivocal. And yet the Deutschemark has emerged as the second largest reserve currency, partly through central bank holdings of the currency in the Euromarkets. The recent moves toward portfolio diversification also testify to the objective of many central banks, which is to reduce the proportion of reserves held in dollars. The issue is whether this is to be done through: (i) market transactions (with resultant implications for exchange rates and monetary conditions), (ii) bilateral off-market arrangements, or (iii) supranational mechanisms such as an IMF substitution account. In the absence of the second and third, market diversification could continue on a potentially large scale.

It is an open question whether the ECU will emerge as a reserve currency for non-EC countries. ECUs could be issued to non-member central banks in one of two ways: (i) against the deposit of US dollars, or (ii) through an aggregate payments deficit in Europe, as with dollars in the Bretton Woods arrangement. In the latter case, Europe gains the advantage of seigniorage and the volume of world liquidity rises. In the former case, excess dollars are transferred to the EMF, which incurs an exchange-rate risk, and there is no net increase in the volume of international liquidity. These options are analogous to the liquidity effects in the Bretton Woods system of accepting dollars or demanding gold from the US. While the issues are complex there is advantage in meeting the demand for diversification through supranational arrangements which do not involve national currencies and money market conditions.

On balance, the EMS has the potential for lessening tensions in the global monetary system, not least because of the more orderly arrangements that could materialise between the member currencies. But the mechanisms for intra-Community exchange-rate adjustments remain unspecified, as do the arrangements for the necessary monetary co-ordination. Whether the arrangement enhances the voice of the EC in global negotiations also remains to be seen, as hitherto, and in the absence of a common external policy, the EC has not spoken with a single voice. Throughout this chapter emphasis has been placed on the common elements of global and regional monetary arrangements. Whatever mechanisms are created within the EC, there remains the issue of how the EC as a whole integrates with other regional groupings.

ALTERNATIVE APPROACHES TO FORMAL MONETARY INTEGRATION

It is clear that little progress has been made in terms of formal monetary integration in the EC. Our remarks so far have been addressed specifically to the international monetary context of European monetary arrangements. But as the issue of monetary integration in Europe remains live, and as there is still in principle an EC objective to move towards economic and monetary union, the discussion might usefully be concluded by reference to a yet broader context. This will reveal some of the more fundamental reasons (some of which are related directly to international monetary arrangements) for the comparative lack of progress in formal monetary arrangements within the EC.

Following the approach adopted earlier when considering for the international monetary system as a whole how either *ex ante* consistency can be secured or *ex post* mechanisms can operate with a minimum degree of friction, three broad alternative approaches to formal monetary integration in the EC can be identified. First, exchange rates can be fixed and institutional arrangements made to ensure compatibility of monetary conditions through: (i) a dominant currency; (ii) *ex ante* coordination of monetary policy; (iii) centralised monetary policy; or (iv) acceptance of automatic mechanisms, which implies an agreement not to sterilise the monetary effects deriving from the balance of payments.[5] A second broad approach is to establish the necessary conditions for fixed exchange rates (perhaps through policy coordination etc.) as a first stage in the move towards fixed exchange rates. A third option is to establish a new Community parallel currency.

An important issue is whether the exchange-rate arrangement should come early or late in the process of monetary integration. In the early debate this was discussed in terms of the *monetarist-versus-economist* approach. Vaubel (1978b) has recently argued strongly against fixed rates within the EC on two main grounds: (i) any foreign exchange market intervention imposes external costs on others in terms of its interference with the monetary policy of foreign countries, and (ii) the moral hazard problem when deficit countries can secure a form of seigniorage through access to balance-of-payments financing on non-market-related terms, and hence be tempted towards inflationary policies. But, as Vaubel recognises, the two arguments presuppose exchange-rate unification without *ex ante* harmonisation of monetary policies.

One option for a fixed-exchange-rate system in the EC is to base the arrangement on a single dominant currency. This has a parallel in the dollar standard in the global monetary system of the 1960s. Indeed, the reasonably successful operation of the mini-snake in Europe can be attributed in part to the dominant role of the Deutschemark, and to the fact that the smaller countries associated in the arrangement were prepared to align their monetary policy with that of Germany. In the mini-snake Germany determined its own monetary policy without reference to its partners, while the smaller members framed their monetary policy with reference to the exchange rate against the Deutschemark (Oort, 1979).

Whether such an arrangement would be feasible in the EC as a whole is open to question. First, the fact that there are three potentially dominant currencies would make such an arrangement politically difficult. Second, and recalling Europe's attitude towards American monetary policy in the late 1960s and early 1970s, would member governments be prepared to accept the monetary domination of any one partner? The smaller countries within the mini-snake seem to have been prepared to accept this, but they have also perceived advantage in being subject to the monetary discipline imposed by a low inflation centre. Lamfalussy (1979), for instance, notes that the pegging of the Belgian franc to the Deutschemark contributed to a deceleration of inflation in Belgium without adversely affecting exports. Third, the standard moral hazard faced by any dominant country might be raised as an objection, though the experience of Germany might temper this objection. Although for those countries linking their currency with the Deutschemark the hegemony of the US is replaced with that of Germany, this has been acceptable given the type of monetary policy pursued by Germany. In the final analysis, agreement has to be reached over the targets (e.g. with respect to inflation) to be arrived at.

POLICY CO-ORDINATION

In the final analysis, any durable fixed-exchange-rate arrangement requires compatible monetary trends. This is true of the global system and within regions. But the problems of *ex ante* co-ordination cannot be dismissed. First, there would inevitably be protracted negotiations over the standard to aim at resulting from a conflict of interest, at least in the short run, between high and low inflation centres. While, as argued earlier, this may be a short-run problem, it would nevertheless almost inevitably prove to be a difficult one. Second, the technical problem of calculating for each member the rate of growth of the money supply that is compatible with a fixed exchange rate would also be formidable. In addition, the experience of monetary targets suggests that, even if consistent money supply targets can be agreed, there would remain difficult problems in attaining them. Also, to the extent that credibility of fixed-exchange-rate arrangements is a necessary ingredient for their durability, an *ex ante* co-ordination strategy might prove to be an insecure basis. Effective co-ordination also requires a recognition that co-ordination is a less costly and more certain method of securing targets, which in turn presupposes the absence of attempts to impose national targets on unwilling partners. As is implied in Meade's analysis (1951), if national targets are not consistent and each country *believes* it is powerful enough to impose its will, *ex ante* co-ordination is unlikely to be adopted. Conflict can also arise over the distribution between countries of the net policy changes required.

It is largely for these reasons that the creation of a parallel currency has been proposed as an alternative route towards monetary integration in the EC. Notable among the various proposals is one for a constant purchasing power parallel currency as advocated in the All Saints' Day Manifesto (Basevi *et al.*, 1975) and by Vaubel (1978b). In principle, such an approach has the advantage of being gradual and market determined, and avoids the difficulties inherent in *ex ante* co-ordination and the hegemony of a single currency. It also has the advantage of moving towards ultimate monetary union without the prior step of exchange-rate unification. To the extent also that the constant purchasing power element remains credible, the short-run costs for high inflation countries of decelerating monetary growth (inherent in the approach of *ex ante* co-ordination of monetary policy) can in principle be avoided (Vaubel, 1978a). In this scheme currency reform rather than currency stabilisation is envisaged.

THE MONETARY DIMENSION

The traditional argument against formal moves towards regional monetary integration (particularly fixed-exchange-rate arrangements) is that members cease to have independent control over their domestic money supply and the use of the exchange rate as an instrument of policy is lost. This implies that governments can be forced away from internal balance targets. It is argued that internal balance becomes more difficult to achieve for each member of an integrated group, because of differences in both the technical relationship between unemployment and inflation and the policy preferences with respect to the trade-off. With a Community-wide exchange rate and monetary policy, low productivity members are forced to accept a higher level of unemployment than desired and/or high productivity regions must accept more inflation. These have been powerful and influential arguments and have formed the traditional basis against European monetary integration. But it is not clear that such 'regional' unemployment problems can in fact be solved by either monetary policy or exchange-rate adjustments. The power of monetary policy and the exchange rate to influence real magnitudes in the economy in the long run is questioned by *monetarist* analysis. This analysis casts some doubt over whether the apparent monetary independence gained by floating exchange rates is of long-run significance if monetary policy is unable to affect the long-run values of real income and employment. Similarly, if the exchange rate is not a powerful balance-of-payments adjustment mechanism in the long run the case for floating rates is weakened. While a floating exchange rate may enable a government to decide upon its own monetary policy, this is viewed as conferring only the ability to choose the domestic inflation rate (Parkin, 1976). While this might be of value in the short run, its longer-run significance might be questioned. In this case, a major argument against monetary union and fixed exchange rates relates to the loss of the benefits a country might secure by being able to choose its own long-run rate of inflation at given levels of output at the natural level of unemployment.

The basic theoretical background to this may be briefly summarised in terms of three basic propositions: (i) in the long run, monetary policy has no influence on the level of real income; (ii) in the long run, for a small open economy a balance-of-payments deficit with a fixed rate or a depreciating floating rate are symptoms of an excess supply of money; and (iii) exchange-rate adjustment has no long-run effect upon the balance of payments or level of real income.

The third proposition doubts the equilibrating power of floating rates on two grounds: (i) in the short run, the implied change in domestic real wages has little effect upon trade flows, as there is a lengthy time lag, and (ii) in the long run the initial effect upon real wages is offset by a higher price level due to resistance to the cut in real wages. This view argues that the exchange rate is not an effective adjustment mechanism. As economies become more open the benefits of devaluation in enhancing the competitive position of exports are lost by the upward impetus given to import prices, which eventually filters through to the prices of all goods. The gains to trade are therefore temporary. In particular, floating rates do not enable an independent monetary policy to secure a level of real income and employment above the *natural* level. Indeed, to the extent that balance-of-payments adjustments of any kind (tariffs, exchange-rate adjustments, etc.) operate via their impact on the excess supply/demand for money, they are not permanent alternatives to an appropriate domestic monetary policy.

Whatever their general merits, these arguments must have particular force within a highly integrated group of countries. Thus, while a fixed-exchange-rate arrangement within the EC would necessitate compatible rates of inflation and monetary growth, the implication of *monetarist* analysis is that no permanent loss of output or employment would necessarily follow from any mutually agreed inflation rate. In an important study Vaubel (1978b) argues persuasively that the necessity for real exchange-rate adjustments should be the criterion for defining viable currency areas. He notes that in the countries investigated, fluctuations in nominal exchange rates have been three times as great as real exchange-rate movements, and that movements in nominal exchange rates have been due predominantly to different rates of inflation, indicating a lack of monetary harmonisation.

The traditional argument against monetary union may therefore be less powerful than conventionally assumed. The loss of sovereignty may be more apparent than real in the long run. But the qualification is important. The crucial issue becomes the length of the analytical long-run. If it is in practice longer than the policy-makers' time-horizon, real sacrifices are implied by a move towards monetary union. In this case, the short-run costs (in terms of unemployment or inflation) of surrendering sovereignty over domestic monetary and exchange-rate policy become significant. It might be argued, therefore, that the case against monetary union should be based upon the time-horizon of policy-makers in relation to the period over which monetary and exchange-rate variables affect real magnitudes. The shorter is the policy-makers' time-horizon and the longer is the time-lag in monetary adjustments, the greater are the costs implied by monetary union. It also follows that if governments are able to minimise the short-run costs of monetary adjustment or shorten the short run, monetary union becomes more viable. In this case, little of substance is lost by surrendering use of the policy instrument. Resistance to this by governments may reflect a degree of 'policy-illusion' and a tendency to mistake *constitutional* for *effective* sovereignty: the illusion rather than the substance of effective policy. Individual governments' *effective* sovereignty tends to decline as integration increases, though collectively *effective* sovereignty of a group of countries may be raised through concerted and co-ordinated actions.

However, the basic propositions are not universally accepted, particularly by policy-makers whose time-horizons are seldom in terms of the monetarists' 'long run'. The debate is also complicated by different views about the efficacy of exchange-rate changes as a means of adjusting real wage differentials and the balance of payments between countries. As already noted, if exchange-rate changes have little long run impact on the balance of payments the case for fixed exchange rates is enhanced. If, on the other hand, the exchange rate is a powerful policy instrument, a real degree of sovereignty is surrendered by forgoing the use of this particular instrument of policy. The debate is complicated even further by differences of view as to: (i) the time period over which any effectiveness of the exchange-rate mechanism operates, and (ii) the time period over which monetary policy has real effects on the economy as opposed to purely price effects. The evidence seems to suggest that both have effects in the short run but little impact in the long run, and that the short run has become shorter over the 1970s. Indeed, the rational expectations hypothesis questions the plausibility of the assumption that the analytical long run may stretch into several years, though this hypothesis has itself been questioned by Llewellyn (1980).

A central issue, therefore, is the length of the short run in relation to the policy-makers' time-horizon. But the monetarist analysis implies that, if monetary policy has no long-run effect on real income, and a floating rate in response to monetary policy determines only the rate of inflation, no *effective* economic sovereignty is lost by fixed exchange rates with monetary policy conducted to secure balance-of-payments equilibrium.

CONCLUDING REMARKS

In the final analysis, any scheme of monetary integration, to be successful, requires that member governments pursue policies to produce consistent rates of inflation. In this respect it is not so much whether governments are prepared to concede sovereignty in the interests of some common good as the degree of acceptance of the limited extent of effective sovereignty. This in turn relates to the policy-makers' time-horizon. Above all, there is a requirement for some mechanism to ensure that the monetary policies of member governments are compatible and conducive to exchange-rate stability. It is to be regretted that much of the official discussion of the EMS tended to concentrate on the technical issues of 'grids' versus 'baskets' etc., rather than upon the more fundamental issue of how the required degree of convergence and policy compatibility is to be secured. The durability of any fixed exchange rate will be determined, in no small part, by the willingness of high-inflation countries to accept the short-run employment costs of the necessary monetary adjustment. In this respect past experience does not engender optimism, with governments implicitly tending to value the short-run costs more highly than longer-run benefits of adequate monetary control. Sooner or later, some mechanism will have to be found to ensure consistent monetary policies. This will require a substantial political commitment to the scheme. No amount of eloquent political rhetoric about the virtues of 'zones of monetary stability' can take the place of what is ultimately required, namely a mechanism for ensuring that economic policies in general, and monetary policies in particular, are sufficiently compatible to remove the temptation to use the exchange-rate mechanism.

In considering whether, and under what conditions, the EMS is likely to prove to be durable, it is important to note that, at present, it is only a loose form of fixed-exchange-rate system. Indeed, given the possibility of wider bands, parity changes and even leaving the system temporarily, if the EMS in its present form cannot be made to work, then any other formal monetary arrangement involving fixed rates between members will be difficult to work. The one qualification made, however, is that renewed pressure on the US dollar could increase the strains on the European arrangement, particularly if the Deutschemark is again the major recipient of the hot-money flows. Stable intra-European exchange rates require a reasonably stable dollar–Deutschemark rate. For this reason specifically European monetary arrangements can never be entirely isolated from the global monetary system and can never be an alternative to international co-operation within the global system.

NOTES

1. See Presley and Coffey (1971) for a discussion of these plans.
2. It would have been technically difficult in 1971 to implement a joint float as all foreign exchange market intervention was made in US dollars. When the snake-in-the-tunnel was instituted intervention was made also in member currencies, which made the joint float of 1973 more feasible.
3. See the papers and comments by Trezise, Fried, Bergsten, and Bowie, in Krause and Salant (1973).
4. For a general discussion of the implications of monetary integration in Europe for international liquidity see Salant (1973).
5. See, for instance, McKinnon (1974) for a discussion of the last-mentioned option.

REFERENCES

Basevi, G., M. Fratianni, H. Giersch, P. Korteweg, D. O' Mahony, M. Parkin, T. Peeters, P. Salin and N. Thygesen (1975), 'The All Saints' Day Manifesto for European Monetary Union: a Currency for Europe', *The Economist*, 1 November; reprinted in M. Fratianni and T. Peeters (eds), *One Money for Europe* (London Macmillan, 1978).

Bloomfield, A. E. (1973), 'The Historical Setting', in L. B. Krause and W. S. Salant (eds), *European Monetary Unification and its Meaning for the United States* (Washington D.C.: The Brookings Institution).

Grauwe, P. de (1973), *Monetary Interdependence and International Monetary Reform* (Farnborough, Hants.: Saxon House).

Jenkins, R. (1978), 'European Monetary Union', *Lloyds Bank Review*, no. 127. (The text of the Jean Monnet Lecture delivered at the European Institute, Florence, on 27 October 1977.)

Krause, L. B. and W. S. Salant (eds) (1973), *European Monetary Unification and its Meaning for the United States* (Washington, D.C.: The Brookings Institution).

Lamfalussy, A. (1979), 'An Overview of the Problems', in S. I. Katz (ed.), *US–European Monetary Relations* (Washington, D.C.: American Enterprise Institute for Public Policy Research).

Llewellyn, D. T. (1980), *International Financial Integration: the Limits of Sovereignty* (London: Macmillan).

—— (1980), 'Can Monetary Targets Influence Wage Bargains?', *The Banker*, January.

McKinnon, R. I. (1974), *A New Tripartite Monetary Agreement or a Limping Dollar Standard!* (Essays in International Finance, no. 106) (Princeton, N.J.: Princeton University Press).

Meade, J. (1951), *The Balance of Payments* (Oxford: Oxford University Press).

Midland Bank (1979), 'The Dollar: an End to Benign Neglect?' *Midland Bank Review*, Autumn.

Oort, C. J. (1979), 'Managed Floating in the European Community', in S. I. Katz (ed.), op. cit.

Parkin, J. M. (1976), 'Monetary Union and Stabilisation Policy in the European Community', *Banca Nazionale del Lavoro Quarterly Review*, September, vol. 76, no. 118.

Presley, J. R. and P. Coffey (1974), *European Monetary Integration* (London: Macmillan).

Salant, W. (1973), 'Implications for International Reserves', in L. B. Krause and W. S. Salant (eds), op. cit.

Vaubel, R. (1978a), 'Minimising Imbalances in Monetary Union', in M. Fratianni and T. Peeters (eds), *One Money for Europe* (London: Macmillan).

—— (1978b), *Strategies for Currency Unification: The Economics of Currency Competition and the Case for a European Parallel Currency* (Tübingen: J. C. B. Mohr).

Williamson, J. (1977), *The Failure of World Monetary Reform 1971–74* (London: Thomas Nelson).

Comments on Llewellyn

GEOFFREY I. LIPSCOMBE

The late Richard Crossman contrasted political man with a fish swimming in a stream. The fish has no way of visualising the world which lies outside the river banks, whereas man is able to make the necessary intellectual 'leap' and analyse his social, political and economic framework in the context of the world at large and not merely within narrow geographical constraints.

David Llewellyn's paper succeeds in relating the European Monetary System to the international financial framework, but it is the traditional framework of the developed countries which underpins his analysis. His is the IMF of the 1950s and the early 1960s in which the *dramatis personae* are the Group of Ten. Little is heard of the problems of the remaining nations, particularly those of the Third World, which have begun to take up an increasing proportion of the Fund's time and financial facilities. In other words, the analysis does not make that final 'leap' which Crossman hailed as the hallmark of political man.

Perhaps it is unfair to criticise a paper on this account, because the subject is so far-reaching that it is an almost impossible task to cover it within the confines of a single paper. Nevertheless, we must realise that the problems of the Third World and their political strictures on the financial and tariff arrangements of the developed world will form an ever-increasing part of the political and economic discussions of the 1980s.

A second major comment is that an analysis of the relationship between Europe and the International Monetary System must recognise distinctions among four decision-making tiers. Decisions which affect such a relationship are taken at the national level, where each nation is, by and large, homogeneous; at the regional level, e.g. the European Community, the Latin American Free Trade Association and the Economic Community of West African States, where each region is not homogeneous and whose members may not even have common frontiers or a common language; by the political groupings, e.g. OECD, Group of Ten, Group of Twenty-Four, Group of Seventy-Seven, where each group is homogeneous to the extent that it represents countries with a common economic interest, and finally at the global level, e.g. in the IMF, the World Bank and Gatt, where, by virtue of the all-embracing nature of the bodies concerned, the membership is heterogeneous.

A close scrutiny is required of the decision-making processes at each of these levels, in order to identify the various forces which act upon them. Economic factors are by no means the only ones which affect the outcome of negotiations. Thus, the comment that too much time was devoted to determining the grids and baskets for the 1979 negotiations ignores the fact that these grids and baskets cannot easily be changed once the decisions have been taken. However, 'convergence' and 'policy compatibility' are much more nebulous terms whose meanings can be altered or 'harmonised' if necessary at a later date. A cynic might term the technical discussions 'horse trading'.

A factual question is whether the members of the EMS, and the Community as a whole, are presenting a unified appearance in their relations with the remainder of the world A second, forward-looking question is whether, if EMU is achieved, its achievement will solve more problems than it creates. In particular, will the achievement of EMU facilitate the convergence of policies at the global level? An immediate response would probably be in the negative, because a number of independent countries will be replaced by a monolithic bloc with almost as much voting power in the IMF as the US. The possibility of a direct confrontation would be increased.

The next stage of the analysis would be to apply games theory and operational research techniques to the bargaining positions taken up by the various groups concerned. International organisations such as the United Nations and the World Bank would seem to be ideally suited to the application of such analysis.

Finally, stress should have been given to the fact that European Monetary Union is but a means to the end of political harmonisation, if not unification. The International Monetary System, typified by the IMF, is, to a much greater extent, an institutional framework to achieve certain limited ends, as stated in the Bretton Woods Agreement and the two Amendments.

7 The Case for Flexible Exchange Rates in 1980

DAVID LAIDLER

> Flexible exchange rates . . . are a means of permitting each country to seek for monetary stability according to its own lights, without either imposing its mistakes on its neighbors or having their mistakes imposed on it.
>
> (Milton Friedman, 1953)

INTRODUCTION

Flexible exchange rates have never commanded universal support among economists, but it is fair to say that they found more enthusiastic adherents during the 1950s and 1960s, when a (more or less) fixed-exchange-rate regime was in force, than they do now, after close to a decade of experience with them. In this chapter, I seek to contribute to the ongoing debate about flexible exchange rates in a number of ways. First, I shall review briefly the by now well-known arguments about fixed and flexible exchange rates that monetary economics in and of itself permits us to develop. Second, I shall consider what may loosely be termed the political arguments about 'discipline', or lack thereof, in the conduct of policy that alternative exchange-rate regimes are said to promote, in the light of the experience of the 1970s. I shall pay particular attention here to British experience. Finally, I shall consider the issues raised in the first two substantive sections of this paper from a more general perspective, and will argue that there still remains a powerful case to be made for flexible exchange rates as a means of organising international monetary relations. The case however is essentially political rather than economic.

TRADITIONAL ECONOMIC ARGUMENTS

I have developed many of the arguments set out in the next few pages in more detail in Laidler (1979) and this section can, therefore be relatively brief. It is conceded at the outset that there must inevitably be an element of 'second best' about any economic arguments that can be made in favour of exchange-rate flexibility. The following well-known *reductio ad absurdum* shows this clearly enough: if it is to the advantage of a group of countries to have separate currencies whose exchange rates are flexible, then why is it not equally to the advantage of the regions of any country, or of the towns of any region, or of the streets of any town, or of the inhabitants of any street? This argument forces us to face up to the essentially social nature of the monetary system, and to the role that it plays in facilitating trade and co-ordinating economic activity among individuals, streets, towns, regions and countries. Once such considerations are explicitly recognised it becomes difficult to resist the conclusion that, other things being equal, a system that uses a single money, or a group of monies whose exchange rates are fixed and are known to be fixed, will involve the consumption of fewer resources in the trading process than one which uses a series of national monies whose exchange rates are free to vary over time. If there is an economic case to be made for flexible exchange rates in the face of such an argument, it must rest upon factors buried in that dangerously vague phrase 'other things being equal'.

In the 1960s the 'Phillips curve' was frequently cited as such a factor. It was argued that the nature of the real world was such that there existed, within each national economy, a stable inflation–unemployment trade-off, and that a system of flexible exchange rates would permit each country to exploit that trade-off as its inhabitants preferred. This argument is not sustainable as Sumner (1976) showed quite clearly. Though there may be differences of opinion about why a stable inflation–unemployment trade-off no longer exists, there can be little room for disagreement about the fact that, at the end of the 1960s, the relationship vanished. Moreover, the particular explanation of why this happened that is implicit in the 'monetarist' style of macroeconomics to which I subscribe enables us to go far beyond demolishing this particular aspect of the case for flexible exchange rates, as we shall now see.

The relevant argument is straightforward, and perhaps is not the exclusive property of 'monetarists'. It asserts that economic agents understand the difference between money prices and relative prices, between money wages and real wages, and that their economic activity is informed by that understanding. This does not imply that agents never make mistakes about such matters, but it does imply that such mistakes will be recognised when they occur and will be corrected. In short 'money illusion' is asserted to be a temporary phenomenon and not a permanent feature of any economy. The implication of this for the Phillips curve is that the trade-off only exists for so long as the actual behaviour of money wages and prices departs from what agents expect, and hence that it is at best short-lived. However the 'no-money-illusion' hypothesis has implications for other aspects of the debate about flexible exchange rates as well, and indeed Laidler and Nobay (1975) have argued that the no-money-illusion hypothesis, more than anything else, distinguishes the monetary (or monetarist) approach to the analysis of international financial issues from the Keynesian alternative.

Much is sometimes made of the capacity of a flexible-exchange-rate regime to insulate the domestic economy from shocks originating abroad. If we accept the no-money-illusion hypothesis then we must also accept the proposition that such an exchange-rate regime can offer to the domestic economy only, and at best, temporary shelter from any events abroad that require the structure of relative prices, the level of real income, or any other real variables, to change. For the exchange-rate regime to provide permanent insulation from such shocks would require that variations in the exchange-rate could permanently affect the real terms of trade. Though there can be no denying that a considerable amount of balance-of-payments and exchange-rate theory has been based on just such an assumption, it is quite obviously inconsistent with the no-money-illusion postulate.

This point is of considerable practical relevance to current discussions about the effects of variations in energy prices in general, and about the activities of OPEC in particular. It implies that, unless one entertains the absurd notion that OPEC is interested in only the nominal price of oil – that is to say, suffers itself from money illusion – there is nothing that can be accomplished by way of domestic monetary policy, even in those countries that are willing to let their exchange rates fluctuate freely, to offset the effects of the price changes in question on domestic variables. (Which is not to say that domestic policies towards subsidising energy prices, or taxing particular energy sources, do not affect the way in which the real effects of OPEC's activities impinge upon different groups.) It also implies, on the other side, in the specific case of Britain, that the difficulties currently faced by manufacturing industry as it tries to compete on world markets should not be blamed on too high an exchange rate brought about by the effects of North Sea oil. The no-money-illusion postulate implies that if the exchange rate were to be lower, then domestic wages and prices would be higher, the terms of trade for manufacturing would be just what they are now, and that sector would still face the same problems.

If a flexible exchange rate offers no long-run protection against 'real shocks', it does of course offer such protection against foreign monetary disturbances. However, the phrase 'long run' is all-important here; to say that there is no money illusion in the long run does not mean that it may not be an important short-run phenomenon. If a foreign monetary disturbance has temporary effects upon real variables abroad – if for example an increase in the rate of monetary expansion drives down real interest rates and causes real income to expand for a while – then those changes will, under flexible exchange rates, impinge upon domestic variables. In the example cited, capital market activity will ensure that the exchange rate will be driven up before foreign prices have begun to respond to monetary disturbance, and the terms of trade will, therefore, be temporarily changed. In the long run, of course, when expectations abroad have adjusted to the new monetary expansion rate these effects will vanish, and the domestic economy will indeed be insulated from further effects of the foreign policy change. In short, exchange-rate flexibility does, as we all know, confer on a country the ability to choose its own-run rate of inflation independently of that ruling in the rest of the world.

At first sight, and from the narrow viewpoint of economic analysis, it is difficult to attach too much importance to the advantages conferred by a flexible exchange rate. A long-run inflation rate is, by definition, a fully anticipated inflation rate. Monetary theory tells us that the ability to select its value implies only the ability to select the yield of the 'inflation tax' and also the values of whatever real variables are influenced by 'super-non-neutrality' effects. Since the inflation tax should be looked upon as one component of an optimal tax structure, the ability to choose its value is not entirely without value. However, it is difficult to get excited about this advantage, either one way or the other, while there is ample room for disagreement about how much weight should be given to the other possible advantage that exchange-rate flexibility confers – namely some degree of temporary insulation against real shocks originating abroad, as Purvis (1979) has argued.

If the debate about flexible exchange rates was simply concerned with the issues I have discussed so far, it would be hard to understand why it generates so much heat. The consensus position would surely have to be that, from the point of view of the world economy, a fixed-rate regime, or better a single money, is to be preferred for the extra efficiency that it promotes, but that, from the point of view of any individual economy there might be something to be said for exchange-rate flexibility if there existed some compelling reason to have an inflation rate that differed from that ruling elsewhere. Since, if we stick to economic issues, such reasons would have to be grounded in arguments about the place of the inflation tax in an optimal tax structure, there would, to say the least, be a certain air of irrelevance to them. However, the contemporary opponent of flexible exchange rates sees grave dangers in the possibilities that they offer for permitting the politicians of any particular country to choose an inflation rate. Not least in Britain, he points to the experience of the 1970s as an example of the monetary indiscipline which a flexible exchange rate permits, and argues that the very fact that adherence to a fixed exchange rate takes control of the inflation rate out of the hands of domestic policy makers is its greatest advantage. I will now turn to consider the reasoning on which this position is based.

STOP–GO, DISCIPLINE AND THE EXCHANGE-RATE REGIME

In the modern world the choice of an exchange-rate regime is not made in a vacuum. That regime constitutes an important component of the institutional framework against whose background economic activity, policy included, is carried on. It is a fact of contemporary political life that the institutional framework in question is the outcome of policy choices rather than constituting an externally given constraint upon them. Thus, when exchange-rate flexibility was chosen by Britain in 1972, it was as a part of what seemed to be a coherent policy package whose design followed from particular perceptions of the way in which the British economy worked, and of how its performance could be improved. As I shall argue, that perception was flawed, but, as I shall also argue, it was the failure of the overall policy package and not of exchange-rate flexibility *per se* which generated most of the problems which Britain experienced in the 1970s.

The salient features of Britain's macroeconomic performance in the 1950s and 1960s are easily summarised. First, the economy experienced what was not fully recognised at the time to be an extraordinarily high average level of employment. Second, the growth rate of real output, though relatively slow by standards being set elsewhere, for example in West Germany or Japan, was nevertheless high in comparison with Britain's own past performance, even that achieved during the second half of the neneteenth century. Third, there was a persistent inflationary trend in prices which, mild though it may seem in retrospect, was at the time perceived as a serious problem. Fourth, there was a slow but steady secular deterioration in the balance of payments. Fifth, and finally, the behaviour of employment, output, inflation and the balance of payments was cyclical in nature, the essential characteristics of the cycle in question being captured in the phrase 'stop–go'.

In 1980, with the benefit of hindsight, the 1950s and 1960s look almost like a Golden Age, with the stop–go cycle having been a relatively minor problem. However, it did not seem like that at the time. Policy-makers and economists alike were dissatisfied, and the key question for macrocconomics became how to improve the growth, inflation and employment performance of the economy by breaking out of the stop–go cycle. Given the prevailing intellectual climate, very few economists doubted that, when the solution to this problem was discovered, it would consist of a series of activist policy measures, and there did in due course emerge a diagnosis of the problem, along with an implied set of remedies that involved specific policy actions.

The diagnosis in question, and the remedies, together make up what in Britain was (and is) sometimes called 'Keynesian economics', though their relationship to anything Keynes may have said or written is, to say the least, open to debate. The outline of the doctrine is well known. To begin with, inflation was regarded as being mainly a cost–push phenomenon. Its cause was said to lie in attempts on the part of the labour force to realise aspirations for the growth of their real incomes that the actual growth performance of the economy was inadequate to provide for. The failure of the economy to grow faster was not put down to the existence of any internal constraints such as technology or available resources, however. Rather it was supposed to result from the interaction of a fortuitously high marginal propensity to import with the 'external' balance-of-payments constraint implicit in the economy's self-imposed commitment to an exchange rate fixed at a particular level.

The stop–go cycle was viewed as the inevitable result of attempting to carry out activist policies towards aggregate demand, particularly through fiscal means against such a background. Starting at a cyclical trough, expansionary fiscal policy would set output growing, and as the resulting upswing gathered momentum, the high marginal propensity to import would begin to produce balance-of-payments problems. In short order, policy would have to be reversed to cope with these problems, and a downswing would begin. Such balance-of-payments-induced policy reversals as these were seen as keeping the economy's growth rate down in the long run, and hence as being the underlying cause of the persistent cost-push inflation that the economy experienced.

Now of course, this view of the economy did not emerge suddenly, fully developed and universally accepted at the end of the 1960s. It developed on a piecemeal basis over the preceding two decades and its acceptance among economists and policy-makers grew slowly over the same period. Hutchison (1968) provides a useful source in which the development of the ideas under discussion here is traced out. By the early 1960s, two of its components, the view that faster growth would help reduce inflation and could in turn be achieved by expansionary policies, had achieved sufficiently wide acceptance to form the basis of Mr Reginald Maudling's 'Dash for Growth' of 1963–4. In its turn, the collapse of that policy in the face of a balance-of-payments crisis played an important role in popularising the view that the balance of payments placed an intolerable constraint upon the economy's performance, and upon the ability of policy to improve that performance.

The doctrine of 'export-led growth' was one attempt to come to grips with this matter, though its origins do, of course, antedate 1964. In essence its proponents argued that, if expansion were driven by an export boom, rather than fiscal policy, the balance of payments would *ipso facto* cease to be an obstacle to sustained growth. To the extent that the pursuit of export-led growth required the maintenance of an undervalued currency, the distinction between this doctrine, and that which combined advocacy of fiscal expansion with the adoption of outright exchange-rate flexibility was blurred from the outset: both amounted to proposals not to allow balance-of-payments consider-ations to force the abandonment of expansionary policies, but rather to rely on exchange depreciation as a means of offsetting the balance-of-payments effects of Britain's (allegedly) high marginal propensity to import. Thus, when the apparent 'failure' of the 1967 devaluation cast doubt upon the capacity of exchange depreciation *per se* reliably to generate an export boom, the way was cleared for exchange-rate flexibility to become the preferred way of coping with the balance-of-payments consequences of expansion.

The diagnosis of Britain's problems that I have sketched out here finally came to be accepted among those responsible for policy in 1972. A commitment to let the exchange rate float if necessary was a key ingredient of 'Go for Growth' policy. Indeed it was the chief characteristic that differentiated Mr Anthony Barber's policy from that undertaken by Mr Maudling nine years earlier. There is no need to go into details about the events that followed the adoption of the 'Go for Growth' policy. Output expanded rapidly for a while; inflation began to increase; the exchange rate to fall; and the subsequent adoption of wage and price controls seemed to do more to exacerbate the social divisiveness implicit in the way in which the economic situation was evolving than to ameliorate that situation. For present purposes the interesting questions are, first, what went wrong in 1972, and second, what role did the adoption of flexible exchange rates play in the matter. What we might term a 'monetarist' answer to these questions is far from universally accepted, but I shall concentrate upon it here both because it is the one to which I adhere, and because it underpins the widespread scepticism about flexible exchange rates, nowadays prevalent among economists, to which I have already alluded above.

The answer in question as developed, for example, by Ball and Burns (1976) and Laidler (1976) starts from the position that the diagnosis of Britain's post-Korean-War economic performance set out earlier was erroneous. The monetarist view is that inflation, rather than being a cost–push phenomenon, was the result of three interacting forces. First, the sterling devaluation of 1949 turned out, in retrospect, to have been excessive, particularly in the light of the subsequent behaviour of world prices during the Korean War boom. Hence British prices had to 'catch-up' to those ruling in the rest of the world. Second, those world prices were themselves rising, and were putting upward pressure on the domestic prices of imports and import substitutes as well as of exportables. Third, relative to long-term trends thus determined, the domestic inflation rate fluctuated with the pressure of aggregate demand on available resources, to produce the observations that appeared during this period to make the Phillips curve such a policy-relevant relationship. The monetarist view attributes sluggish growth (if sluggish it was) to the failure of productive resources to expand any more rapidly than they did and to a relatively slow pace of technical change. It takes these propositions as data, and does not pretend to be able to explain them; however, it does draw from them the implication that expansion of aggregate demand, either export-led or promoted by fiscal policy, would never have been capable of increasing the economy's growth rate. The best that expanding demand could ever do was to enable an initially depressed economy to move up to some, not very well defined, 'full employment' ceiling as, for example, Cairncross argued at the time (see Cairncross, 1975, ch. 3; first published in 1971). As to the balance of payments, its secular behaviour is to be explained by post-1949 devaluation 'catch-up' effects, while its cyclical behaviour follows from the cyclical nature of demand management policy, in particular the monetary policy of validating fluctuations in government borrowing by variations in the rate of domestic credit expansion.

In this monetarist view then, the key role played by the balance of payments in triggering the 'stop' phase of the stop–go cycle stemmed not from a high marginal propensity to import, but from the effects of over-expansionary policy, particularly monetary policy, during the 'go' phase of the cycle. Hence the maintenance of a fixed exchange rate, rather than involving the imposition of an unnecessary constraint that inhibited economic growth, instead represented a device for ensuring that over-expansionary policy was not carried too far, as Lionel Robbins, for example had argued in his evidence to the Radcliffe Committee (1959). The abandonment of the commitment to a fixed rate marked the only essential difference between the Maudling and Barber policies, but according to the monetarist view that was a key difference. Under Maudling an over-expansionary policy produced a balance-of-payments crisis and had been abandoned long before it could generate serious inflationary consequences. Under Barber it generated an exchange depreciation which the authorities had already declared themselves willing to accept if necessary. Instead of the pay-off from policy coming in the form of sustained growth, as had been hoped, it came in terms of accelerating inflation and further exchange depreciation. In short, the adoption of exchange-rate flexibility in 1972 removed a vital factor disciplining the conduct of policy, and must be seen as a key element among the causes of Britain's subsequent problems.

It is easy to see how one can progress from the above account of aspects of recent economic history to the conclusion that high priority ought to be given to the restoration of a set of institutional arrangements that will prevent mistakes on the scale of those perpetrated in 1972–4 being repeated, and hence to the proposition that exchange-rate flexibility ought to be abandoned as soon as is feasible. However, I believe that it is a mistake to draw such a conclusion. To begin with, I conjecture that, had they known in 1972 what the inflationary effects of their policies were going to be, the authorities would not have undertaken them. Fear of inflation and its political consequences would have been a sufficient source of discipline upon their actions, and the influence of a fixed exchange rate would have been redundant. If this conjecture is true, we should explain Britain's problems as the consequences of an honestly-held belief in what turned out to be erroneous economics, rather than to an inappropriate institutional arrangement. As I have already noted, institutional arrangements such as the exchange-rate regime are nowadays objects of policy-makers' choices and not constraints upon those choices.

One can go further in defence of flexible exchange rates in the light of the evidence of the early 1970s. A British government which, in 1972, had wished to restore the domestic inflation rate to the average level prevailing, shall we say, in the decade preceding 1967, and which accepted the monetarist macroeconomics upon which the foregoing critique of the policies actually adopted is based, would hardly have decided to maintain a fixed exchange rate on the US dollar. By 1972 the US was already experiencing severe inflationary problems of its own, and the Bretton Woods system did not break down because some countries, like Britain, broke away from the dollar and inflated more rapidly than that currency. Far more important were the activities of other countries, notably Japan and West Germany, whose authorities were 'disciplined' by a combination of fear of the political consequences of inflation and an essentially correct understanding of inflation's causes. Such countries as these were forced, and with considerable reluctance, to permit their currencies to appreciate against the dollar as the price of continuing to submit to their self-imposed anti-inflation discipline. During 1972–4 a flexible exchange rate was just as necessary for those countries that wished to control inflation as for those that wished to pursue what turned out to be inflationary policies. It was a divergence of policies among countries that caused the Bretton Woods system to break down, and not its abandonment that caused policies to diverge. [Zis (1980) provides a lucid account of the evolution and breakdown of the system but draws a different moral about the fixed-versus-flexible-exchange-rate debate than do I.]

To sum up then, the general lesson to be drawn from the 1970s is that whether adherence to a fixed exchange rate is a sign of strength and anti-inflationary virtue, or of weakness and inflationary vice, depends upon what is happening to the purchasing power of those currencies against which the exchange rate is fixed. Arguments about the need to exert some exogenous discipline over the conduct of policy are quite irrelevant to the general issue of whether the exchange rate should be fixed or flexible. However, this does not mean that the choice in question is either irrelevant or unimportant. There are other issues that need to be discussed before the case for flexible exchange rates is finally made, and I shall now take up some of them.

ALTERNATIVE FIXED-RATE REGIMES

I have argued in the preceding section of this chapter that an exchange-rate regime should properly be viewed as one component of a policy package, and not as a constraint upon the selection of such a package. Thus, its desirability must be assessed with reference to the pursuit of specific policy goals. As we have seen earlier, the fundamental distinction between fixed and flexible rates is that fixed rates ensure that the behaviour of the price level is, in the long run, given exogenously from 'abroad', while flexible rates permit it to be determined by domestic policy, and specifically by domestic monetary policy. It can, I believe, be taken for granted that the behaviour of the price level is a legitimate and important matter of domestic political concern in any country. It can also be taken that contemporary opponents of flexible exchange rates regard the pursuit of low inflation rates as a matter of the highest importance, and typically base their advocacy of fixed rates on the belief that such a regime promotes that pursuit. This certainly is true of the authors of the 'All Saints' Day Manifesto' that called for the establishment of a common European currency (see Fratianni and Peeters, 1978). However, whether it will in fact do so depends upon just what currency, or commodity, it is proposed to fix the exchange rate against. In concentrating on the role of exchange-rate flexibility in our preceding discussion, we have as yet failed to raise the question as to what the practical alternatives to such a scheme might be.

It was the great advantage of the gold standard that adherence to it seemed to rule out inflation ever arising as a serious problem, and that seems to be why people seriously advocate restoring it in the 1980s, not least Mr Ronald Reagan and his supporters. The cost of producing new gold on the one hand, and its value as a commodity in alternative uses on the other, served to stabilise its price relative to goods in general and rendered the system almost inflation-proof. However, even neglecting the fact that our view of how the gold standard worked in the past often tends to gloss over its problems – new gold discoveries did lead to episodes of inflation, and at other times the failure of gold production to keep pace with demand did cause deflationary problems – the idea of returning to the gold standard in the 1980s strikes me as misconceived, to say the least. Over the last decade gold has become a speculative asset just like any other commodity. Its price has shown violent fluctuations, and it is simply not true that these fluctuations reflect no more than the instability of paper currencies. They may have been *caused* by the instability of such currencies, but the fluctuations in question have, nevertheless, been in the price of gold relative to other goods, and not just in its nominal value. Whatever may have been the case in the nineteenth century, gold is no longer a reliable and stable abode of purchasing power. It would not be a good idea to base the world's monetary system on, shall we say, cocoa futures, but given recent experience, the only reason for preferring gold to the latter asset seems to be nostalgia for the nineteenth century.

It is not sufficient to counter the above argument by noting that, in adopting a gold standard, central banks would be forced to intervene to maintain the price of gold at a stable value. The point about returning to the gold standard is supposed to be that the properties of the gold market would force central banks to bring discipline to their own activities, not that the behaviour of central banks under such a system would bring discipline to the gold market.

If policy-makers possessed the kind of discipline that they would have to exercise in order to restore stability to the gold market, there would be no need to advocate returning to the gold standard in the first place as a means of generating that discipline.

As a practical matter, a fixed-exchange-rate regime must involve rates being fixed on some currency or other. For one country to fix its exchange rate on the currency of another involves granting to that other country control over its domestic price level. In 1980 is any country or institution worthy of such trust? In the 1950s and 1960s the US seemed to be, and that was why the Bretton Woods sytem evolved into a dollar standard. They ceased to be trustworthy with the onset of the Vietnam War inflation, nor was that lapse into monetary indiscipline a temporary aberration. US monetary policy has grown systematically more erratic over the past decade, and continues to do so. No monetary authority elsewhere in the world seeking to promote domestic price stability could now base a credible policy on a fixed exchange rate *vis-à-vis* the US dollar. The experience of the last fifteen years has just as much undermined trust in the stability of the US as it has of gold. That trust is only going to be restored by a long-term change in the conduct of US monetary policy, and not by attempts to put the dollar back at the centre of the international monetary system. (The contributions of Klein and Vaubel to Fratianni and Peeters (1978) have much to say that is relevant about the difficulties involved in establishing trust in a particular money.)

The Deutschemark might make a viable alternative to the dollar, but there are well-known political problems with making so open an acknowledgement of Germany's economic leadership as making the Deutschemark a key currency would imply. Moreover, one can only wonder how stable the Deutschemark would remain if, for example, the Free Democrats were to lose their seats in the Federal Parliament and the left wing of the Social Democratic Party came to exert more influence on German policy than it now does.

What then about some other national currency, or some internationally sponsored 'currency basket' such as the ECU or the SDR? From the point of view of the individual country deciding whether or not to fix its exchange rate on such an asset there arises one basic problem that is simply expressed as a question: who or what guarantees the long-run stability of the purchasing power of the chosen asset? In the case of any national currency, the matter must hinge upon predictions about the probable course of domestic policies in the relevant country, always a hazardous thing to predict as the history of the dollar standard demonstrates so clearly. In the case of internationally sponsored assets, the matter depends both upon the conduct of policy in the individual countries whose currencies make up the baskets in question, and upon the evolution of the as yet non-existent institutions that would not only co-ordinate policies between the relevant countries, but would also ensure that the policies in question were such as to make the basket of currencies a stable store of value. In either of these cases of course, a fixed exchange rate might produce the desired result, as far as domestic inflation is concerned, but if it did so, it would be for reasons beyond the control of the domestic authorities.

Now in the case of the European Currency Unit, there do exist, within the structure of the EC, embryo institutions for the co-ordination of policy, and so far (September 1980) the European Monetary System has worked well. However, I have grave doubts about its long-run viability. It is inconceivable that the lira can maintain its current exchange rate in the system, given the behaviour of Italian inflation, and yet any attempt to devalue it will put pressure on France, pressure that will become all the more acute as the advantages that France herself gained on entering the system with an undervalued currency are dissipated. There must therefore be a good probability that the system will soon degenerate into a union of West Germany and Benelux. Even so, the point here is not that the EMS is bound to break down, but that the forces that are tending to undermine it are beyond the political control of any particular country, for example the UK, that might join it. The uncertainty thus created must be contrasted with the alternative of simultaneously adopting a flexible exchange rate and pursuing a low inflation rate with domestic monetary weapons. In the latter case the authorities would have to rely on no one but themselves to achieve their goals. The implications of the foregoing observations are easily summarised. If the issues are discussed in the abstract, then there is little to be said in favour of (and for that matter against) a regime of flexible exchange rates. However, when one asks just what, in 1980, a viable alternative to such a regime might be, given that one way or another, policy toward inflation is a matter of serious domestic concern in any country, then flexible exchange rates look a great deal more attractive for the simple reason that such a regime holds out to the policy-maker in any particular country the possibility of carrying out an anti-inflation policy, designed for local conditions, without having to rely on factors beyond his control to ensure its success.

CONCLUSION: THE CASE FOR A FLEXIBLE RATE

The arguments that I have set out in this chapter are easily summarised, and their implications are straightforward. We have seen that the only advantage of flexible exchange rates is that they permit each country that adopts them to enjoy whatever inflation rate its own domestic policies generate. That observation, however, is of far from trivial importance when it is applied to a world whose political organisation is such that the individual nation state is the highest level at which effective and responsible government exists. In such a context, whether we like it or not, it is at the level of the individual nation state that the policies determining inflation rates are going to be debated and implemented. To advocate flexible exchange rates is to do no more than argue that the institutional framework underlying the monetary system should be explicitly adapted to this fact of life.

It is here of course that the question of 'discipline' arises. What if, given the power to choose the domestic inflation rate, the authorities in a particular country opt for a destructively high one? Would it not be better for such a country to be bound by a fixed exchange rate? The answer here is that such policy-makers would not in the first place adopt a fixed exchange rate if they were not externally constrained to do so, and that in a world of independent nation states, no means of imposing such an external constraint exists. In the world we inhabit, discipline in economic policy can only be effective if it arises from domestic political pressure exerted by a general public which does not like inflation but understands its causes. Without such domestic political pressure, a fixed exchange rate will be unacceptable to the authorities, and they will not adopt it, but with such pressure a fixed exchange rate on some other currency will not be needed. Only a flexible-exchange-rate regime permits each country to choose its own degree of monetary discipline independently of the choices made by others, but in the world as it is, each country is bound to do just that because the institutions to enable them to do otherwise do not exist. A flexible-exchange-rate regime is a reflection of this state of affairs, not a cause of it, and it is on the recognition of this fact that the case for persisting with such a regime rests.

NOTE

I am grateful to Nikolaus Laüfer, Michael Sumner and George Zis for helpful discussions.

REFERENCES

Ball, R. J. and T. Burns (1976), 'The Inflationary Mechanism in the UK Economy', *American Economic Review*, vol. 66.

Cairncross, A. (1975), *Inflation, Growth and International Finance* (London: George Allen and Unwin).

Fratianni, M. and T. Peeters (ed.) (1978), *One Money for Europe* (London: Macmillan).

Friedman, M. (1953), 'The Case for Flexible Exchange Rates', in *Essays in Positive Economics* (Chicago, Ill.: University of Chicago Press).

Hutchison, T. W. (1968), *Economics and Economic Policy in Britain 1946–66* (London: George Allen and Unwin).

Klein, B. (1978), 'Competing Monies, European Monetary Union and the Dollar', in M. Fratianni and T. Peeters, op. cit.

Laidler, D. (1976), 'Inflation in Britain – a Monetarist Perspective', *American Economic Review*, vol. 66.

—— (1979), 'Concerning Currency Unions', *Zeitschrift für Wirtschafts- und Sozialwissenschaften*, vol. 1/2.

Laidler, D. and A. R. Nobay (1975), 'Some Current Issues concerning the International Aspects of Inflation', in D. Laidler (ed.), *Essays on Money and Inflation* (Manchester: University of Manchester Press; Chicago, Ill.: University of Chicago Press).

Purvis, D. (1979), 'Comment on David Laidler's "Are Wage and Exchange Rate Flexibility Substitutes?" ', *Zeitschrift für Wirtschafts- und Sozialwissenschaften*, vol. 1/2.

Radcliffe Committee (Committee on the Workings of the Monetary System) (1959), *The Principal Memoranda of Evidence* (London: HMSO).

Sumner, M. T. (1976), 'European Monetary Union and the Control of Europe's Inflation Rate', in M. Parkin and G. Zis (eds), *Inflation and the World Economy* (Manchester: University of Manchester Press).

Vaubel, R. (1978), 'Minimizing Imbalances in a Monetary Union', in M. Fratianni and T. Peeters, op. cit.

Zis, G. (1980), 'Towards a Politico-economic Analysis of Inflation', *Kredit und Kapital*, vol. 2.

8 On the Relative Bias of Flexible Exchange Rates

M. T. SUMNER and G. ZIS

INTRODUCTION

The major industrialised countries have substituted the reduction of the inflation rate for 'full' employment as their principal economic policy objective. In pursuit of a lower rate of change of prices they have allowed their unemployment rates to increase to levels that would not have been considered politically possible as recently as a decade ago. It is arguable, however, that further increases in unemployment, or even maintenance of current levels for an extended period of time, would impose costs which would be unacceptable in both economic and political terms. It may, therefore, be asked whether European Monetary Union, apart from any other advantages it may offer, can facilitate the reduction of member countries' inflation rates at a relatively lower cost in terms of both short- and long-run unemployment. The answer to this question rests on an assessment of the inflation bias of flexible relative to fixed exchange rates. In our discussion of the inflationary bias of alternative exchange rate regimes we shall consider, in contrast to other studies that have addressed this question, the impact of exchange-rate flexibility not only on policy-makers' preferences but also on the constraints that face them. That is, we shall argue that the relative inflation bias of flexible exchange rates is at least partially dependent on how the short-run trade-off between the inflation rate and unemployment, and therefore the natural rate of unemployment, is affected if exchange rates are allowed to be freely determined in the foreign exchange markets.

A brief survey of studies assessing the relative inflation bias of flexible exchange rates is followed by the exposition of the analytical framework, which is then utilised to determine the equilibrium rate of inflation under fixed exchange rates. We then proceed to consider flexible exchange rates; our basic framework is successively modified to allow for differences in tastes, shifts of preferences and changes in the constraints facing policy-makers. Finally, we present our conclusions and consider how they relate to current attempts to stimulate progress towards European Monetary Union.

A SELECTIVE SURVEY OF THE LITERATURE

The study of the relationship between the exchange-rate regime and the inflation rate has proceeded on the basis of two alternative analytical frameworks. First, it is possible to identify a group of studies whose starting point was the Bretton Woods system, and which sought to analyse the inflationary impulses emanating from the international monetary arrangements in force until March 1973. Inevitably, these studies equated fixity of exchange rates with an international monetary system involving the use of a national currency as an international asset. Monetary policies in the key currency country determine the world rate of inflation; and to the extent that this feature provides an incentive for the country in question to maintain a higher monetary growth rate than it would otherwise, the system of fixed exchange rates is judged to be inflationary. In as much as it is the key currency country that determines the world rate of inflation, especially if it dominates the world economy in terms of size, it logically follows that a system of flexible exchange rates will be less inflation-biased.

In his analysis of secular inflation under the Bretton Woods system, Johnson (1973, p. 512) argued that

[for] most of the period since World War II, aside from the immediate and common postwar inflation, the United States has maintained reasonable price stability and so provided the anchor of generally stable world prices that the rest of the world required for smooth operation of the system. But since the escalation of the war in Viet Nam in 1965, US policies have provided a dragging inflationary anchor for the rest of the world, and have injected into the world economy an inflationary trend too powerful to be comfortable for the majority of other countries' policymakers.

Emminger (1973. p. 10) shared Johnson's diagnosis and went further to argue that: '*the international monetary system has not only yielded in too permissive a way to inflationary forces which emanated from domestic inflation in important countries but has also been generating inflation on its own'* (Italics as in original).

In another study of world inflation under the Bretton Woods system Meiselman (1975, p. 71) presented empirical evidence which was interpreted to show that

> worldwide inflation has been closely associated with the rapid worldwide increase in money made possible by the Bretton Woods system and the IMF and its associated fixed exchange rate system, which turned into an engine of worldwide inflation by encouraging worldwide monetary expansion.

Indeed, Meiselman went so far as to suggest that experience under the Bretton Woods system demonstrated 'the incompatibility of fixed rates and stable prices' (p. 110).

These diagnoses provided the basis for policy prescriptions which directly or indirectly implied that the inflation bias of the Bretton Woods system could be at least reduced by greater exchange-rate flexibility. Thus Emminger insisted that 'there will always be situations where inflationary money inflows can only be stopped or limited by greater exchange rate flexibility' (p. 23). Meiselman, though accepting that it was not possible to 'preclude the return to yet another and perhaps new engine of inflation' (p. 110), welcomed the collapse of the Bretton Woods system in March 1973 as it freed 'large numbers of important countries . . . to pursue essentially independent and less expansionary monetary policies' (p. 71). He pointed out that 'they did so in the second half of 1973 . . . once they were no longer tied to the fixed-rate system', and speculated that 'we may well have passed a watershed of major significance' (p. 71). Similarly, Willett (1973, p. 52) in his comment on Johnson's study concluded that 'on anti-inflationary grounds there is an argument (which holds for both surplus and deficit countries) in favour of greater flexibility of exchange rates than has been obtained under the adjustable peg system'.

In brief, then, the studies which identified fixity of exchange rates with the existence of a key currency as under the Bretton Woods system necessarily concluded that greater exchange-rate flexibility would reduce the inflation bias of the international monetary system, at least for some countries. In contrast to these studies, some economists have analysed the relative inflation bias of flexible exchange rates without adopting the special features of the Bretton Woods system as their starting point. For example, Corden (1977a, p. 238) motivates his study by posing the abstract question: 'Are fixed or flexible rates more conducive to inflation?' Similarly, Claassen (1977) attempts to address this question by critically examining those arguments that have been advanced to suggest that flexible exchange rates imply a relative inflation bias. In an analysis which provided the framework for these studies, Fried (1973) assessed the relative inflation bias of flexible exchange rates in the context of the inflation–unemployment trade-off under alternative exchange-rate regimes.

Corden reached the conclusion that there is no unambiguous answer to the question which he posed:

> It is clear that the answers are opposite for the inflation-prone and the inflation-shy countries and that this remains true even when one allows countries to have payments imbalances in the fixed rate system. Nothing in general can be said for the world as a whole. (p. 249)

A similar conclusion was reached by Claassen, who maintained that flexible exchange rates 'can be more inflationary and they can be less inflationary' (p. 232) than fixed exchange rates. Genberg (1977, p. 237) in his comment on Claassen's study commends the author for 'putting to rest the argument that flexible exchange rates *per se* necessarily bring with them higher or lower inflation rates in the world economy'. Salant (1977) in his study of the international transmission of inflation also concluded that flexible exchange rates are not necessarily more conducive to inflation than fixed exchange rates. Fried was more definite in his assessment when he argued that 'if nations can exert some influence on the rate of growth of international liquidity, the long-run world rate of inflation will be greater under a system of fixed exchange rates than under a world system where all exchange rates float' (p. 43). In sharp contrast, fifteen months of floating rates was sufficiently long for Mundell (1976, p. 154) to argue in June 1974 that 'flexible exchange rates have not lived up to the promises attributed to them even for the least inflation-prone countries', and to proclaim his belief that 'inflation will [not] be controlled until we restore fixed exchange rates and convertibility' (p. 158). Disappointment with the inflationary implications of flexible exchange rates was expressed by the last Labour government in the statement of its position *vis-à-vis* the proposed European Monetary System (EMS) following the 1979 summit in Bremen:

> Nevertheless, there has been growing disillusion with the operation of floating rates. Their contribution to eliminating payments inbalances,

though often important, has been slower, smaller and less certain, and has been achieved at a higher cost in inflation, than was hoped. (Chancellor of the Exchequer, 1979, p. 1)

Of course, it may be objected that as the conventional wisdom, with the exception of Fried's statement, does not advance an unambiguous prediction regarding the direction of change in inflation rates following the introduction of exchange-rate flexibility, as the world did not adopt a 'clean' float in succession to the Bretton Woods system, and as greater flexibility has been accompanied by a rapid growth of international liquidity, world experience since 1973 cannot be invoked as empirical support for Mundell's conclusion that flexible exchange rates are inherently more inflationary than fixed exchange rates. We do not propose, therefore, to assess the relative inflation bias of flexible exchange rates simply by contrasting pre- and post-1973 inflation rates. Rather, we proceed to the exposition of the analytical framework which serves as the basis of our critical assessment of the conclusions reached by Fried, Corden and Claassen.

ANALYTICAL APPARATUS

The standard method of analysing the macroeconomic implications of the choice of exchange-rate regime has been to distinguish between the preferences of and the constraints facing policy-makers in inflation–unemployment space. Subject to the qualifications discussed in the remainder of this section, the same framework is adopted here. Preferences are represented by a conventional indifference map relating these two components of the social welfare function; the constraint is a Phillips trade-off.

In a world of 'ideally' flexible rates each country's short-run opportunities locus, denoted by WW in Fig. 8.1, takes the standard form found in the extensive closed-economy literature. Any point on this curve represents a feasible short-run option: any difference between the inflation rate chosen by a particular country and that of the rest of the world is matched by a change in the exchange rate of its currency, so that the equilibrium relative price structure is not disturbed by movements along WW. Under a regime of fixed rates, however, the individual 'small' country faces an externally given rate of change in the price of the tradeable good, and any departure which it makes from equilibrium in isolation will affect only the rate of change of the non-tradeable's price.

Since the inflation rate is a weighted average of these two components, the short-run trade-off is necessarily flatter under a regime of fixity, as shown by AA in Fig. 8.1.

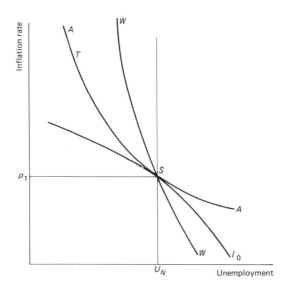

Fɪɢ. 8.1 The 'small' country under fixed exchange rates.

While the existence of a non-tradeable good permits even a small country to vary its inflation and unemployment rates, its freedom to do so is constrained by its ability to finance payment imbalances. Only one point on AA is consistent with the maintenance of equilibrium-relative prices, and therefore with balance-of-payments equilibrium; isolated departures from this point, which for simplicity is assumed to be characterised by a constant price ratio, generate equilibrating changes in the stock of exchange reserves. This mechanism also ensures that a departure from the initial equilibrium by the rest of the world will be transmitted to any country which tries to resist such general expansion or contraction: the restoration of equilibrium requires that the rate of change of the non-tradeable's price should again conform to that prevailing in the world market. Thus the position of the AA curve depends upon the externally given rate of change in the price of the tradeable good. If the rest of the world expands, the AA curve of a deviant small country will be pushed to the north-west by the pressure of reserve inflows. The relatively favourable trade-off shown by AA is therefore available only to a small country acting in isolation. When the fixed-exchange-rate world expands en bloc, its opportunities locus corresponds to the steeper curve WW.

While this framework, or a derivative, has been widely adopted, its use in the existing literature has provoked some dissatisfaction and has obscured some important issues. A primary purpose of this exercise is to clarify those obscurities and to consider explicitly assumptions which have so far remained implicit. In the remainder of this section four focal issues are identified.

The most immediate criticism of many of the standard discussions concerns the casual basis on which fixed and flexible exchange-rate regimes are compared. In particular, the initial situation under fixed rates, which serves as the reference point for the comparison, is rarely characterised precisely. The initial position in Claassen's analysis appears to be quite arbitrary, so it is scarcely surprising that he is unable to reach a definite conclusion. Corden's agnosticism stems from the same source of an under-determined starting point. As a matter of historical fact changes in the exchange-rate regime are, of course, usually associated with major disturbances, but the comparison of confusion with an equilibrium position is not a useful analytical technique. Accordingly, the initial equilibrium under fixed exchange rates is examined in some detail in the next section. It is by no means true that all previous analysts have adopted an arbitrary starting point; Fried, for instance, is careful to compare equilibrium positions, although his exposition disguises that important feature by prefacing it with a parabolic process-analysis. His contribution exemplifies the second common defect, however, of confining the analysis to the small-country case. Corden is the only author to depart from this tradition, even to the extent of a preliminary investigation. Yet, as McMahon (1979, p. 84) has observed, '[it] is not accidental that the two most striking periods of (international monetary) stability in modern times were achieved when one country held an overwhelmingly predominant position in the world'. The 'large' country case is therefore much too important to be ignored or to be treated as an afterthought.

Corden raises a third difficulty in the form of 'the instability over time of the trade-offs' (1977a, p. 242); the preference function may involve the same problem. The stability of the basic tools of analysis has not been explored at all thoroughly in the international literature, a lacuna which is particularly surprising in the light of closed-economy analyses of the vertical long-run Phillips curve. Corden himself resorts to implicit theorising with the suggestion that one should then redefine the inflation benefit curve as referring to the present value of discounted perceived utility resulting from various short-run rates of price inflation. This would take into account not only possible short-run employment gains from a high rate of inflation but also the unemployment to which it may give rise later. (p. 242)

Other writers do not even register the possibility of a problem. Claassen assumes implicitly that the curve corresponding to WW in Fig. 8.1 offers a long-run, negatively-inclined trade-off. Fried makes the same assumption explicit, and appeals for justification both to the possibility that 'a change in the rate of inflation (both expected and actual) will alter the real and/or nominal rates of interest and therefore the structure of the economy will be altered' (p. 44), and, with striking selectivity, to empirical studies of wage inflation which reported a coefficient on price changes of less than unity. These empirical foundations for the belief in a stable long-run trade-off were insecure even at the time when Fried was writing, for Vanderkamp (1966, 1972) and Turnovsky (1972) had shown that Canadian evidence, the only contemporary source of information on a floating-rate regime, was consistent with a unit price coefficient in the wage equation. What still remained of these foundations has been steadily eroded during the past decade, and conventional wisdom, embodied even in traditional large-scale macroeconometric models (Ormerod, 1979), now holds that there is no long-run trade-off. Accordingly this assumption is maintained in the following analysis: when the anticipated inflation rate changes, the WW curve, which constrains the choices of an individual country under flexible rates and the world economy under fixed rates (Duck *et al.*, 1976), shifts vertically by the same magnitude.

Once changes in expectations are recognised as shifting the WW curve, the question naturally arises of how expectations influence the AA curve, whose position has so far been determined solely by the world inflation rate. To answer this question requires a brief consideration of the consistency of expectations under a regime of fixed exchange rates. Absolute faith in fixity implies the belief that any departure from the prevailing world inflation rate will subsequently be not only reversed but actually offset by an opposite deviation from the equilibrium rate of price change. Equilibrium in the balance of payments requires each participant in an agreement which fixes exchange rates to inflate at a uniform rate only when price levels are in equilibrium, for it is relative price levels, rather than inflation rates, which govern the balance of payments. This truism, like any other, would not be worth repeating had its significance not been widely ignored. Indeed, it has been acknowledged more readily in the essentially closed-economy literature on the quality of money typified by Klein (1975), than in the open-economy analyses in which it might have been expected to occupy a central role. Claassen and Fried both recognise the role of the relative price level, though the former is terse to the point of obscurity; but neither appears to appreciate its significance for the formulation of expectations. Corden (1977b, p. 62) confuses even the basic distinction between levels and rates of change when he asserts that after a *ceteris paribus* expansion which raises its inflation rate above the world level, an individual country's optimal inflation rate 'will steadily fall, approaching the world rate . . . at which point the balance of payments deficit disappears'. The significance of complete faith in fixity is simply that its corollary, the implied belief that any deviation from the equilibrium relative price will be transitory, provides an anchor for expectations which no other system can rival. For a given rate of world inflation, therefore, the position of the AA curve will be independent of the choices made by the domestic authorities.

An increase in an individual country's inflation rate above the world level, whether planned or stochastic, implies a cost in terms of man-hours of future output sacrificed in exchange for present employment which increases with convexity of the AA curve. Faced with the unpopular prospect of restoring the equilibrium relative price by deflation, the authorities may of course choose the ostensibly cheaper policy of devaluation. This alternative will generate a disproportionate reaction in the factor markets, for, as the results reported by Eckstein and Brinner (1972), Gordon (1972), Hamermesh (1970), Sumner (1972) and Thomas (1974) all demonstrate, wages respond to prices with a threshold effect. The shock of a large discrete price increase will therefore have more extensive repercussions, which cannot readily be predicted on the basis of past and more tranquil experience, than an equivalent series of smaller adjustments. Furthermore, confidence in the fixity of exchange rates will be diminished, and the restraint on inflationary expectations which is inherent in fixity will be relaxed. Laidler (1981) notes both the role of fixed exchange rates in maintaining a stable trade-off between British inflation and unemployment down to 1967, and the disintegration of the trade-off when fixity ceased to be a rational expectation. Once confidence has been shaken, the operative constraint in subsequent periods of expansion becomes less favourable; the real effects of a given nominal injection will be correspondingly diminished, and the balance-of-payments deficit will be increased by leads and lags as well as more direct forms of speculation. It is tempting to regard *WW* as the relevant constraint when devaluation is anticipated, for *ex hypothesi* the equilibrium price ratio will be restored by adjustment of the exchange-rate peg; but it would be analytically illegitimate to equate a discrete change in the value of a currency with the continuous process of depreciation, and there is abundant, if unsystematic, evidence that anticipated devaluation is vastly more disruptive than a floating exchange rate.

It has sometimes been suggested that the conventional analysis of macroeconomic choices as a problem of constrained optimisation could not survive the demise of the negatively-sloped long-run Phillips curve: the only possible solution would be a tangency at the optimal rate of inflation and the natural unemployment rate, regardless of the exchange-rate regime. It is certainly true that the revelation of a vertical long-run Phillips curve would be expected to change preferences, as long-run consequences of decisions made in a succession of short-runs became apparent; but it is far from clear that the outcome would be as suggested above. The standard analysis remains valid, when modified appropriately to incorporate genuine rather than illusory long-run possibilities, because an inter-temporal trade-off continues to exist, and because the relevant time-horizon for macroeconomic choices is politically determined. An additional facet of the stability question is that political change may alter the structure of preferences, but there are also grounds for predicting endogenous changes in macroeconomic tastes, as the next section will demonstrate, and changing perceptions of the long-run Phillips curve provide merely one instance.

The fourth and final theme of the chapter is related to the stability problem, but in a sufficiently special sense to justify separate treatment. One of the unquestioned and usually implicit assumptions of the traditional literature is that both constraints and preferences are invariant with respect to alternative exchange-rate regimes. Despite general acceptance of this assumption its plausibility will be questioned below. Indeed, the conclusion that flexible rates exhibit an inflationary bias hinges critically on the contrary proposition that both preferences and constraints will differ systematically under the two regimes.

EQUILIBRIUM AND INSTABILITY UNDER FIXED EXCHANGE RATES

The main purpose of this section is to rectify two defects of the existing literature. The initial position under fixed exchange rates, which serves as the reference point for the comparison, has generally been in-adequately defined; and Fried's analysis, which constitutes the exception, is confined to the small-country case. This case is logically possible but historically uninteresting. The arbitrary character of the initial position in other studies reflects in part their emphasis on the diversity of tastes among the participants in a fixed-exchange-rate bloc, who are divided schematically into 'inflation-shy' and 'inflation-prone' countries, and on the compromise which results from this diversity. The centrifugal forces which periodically threatened and ultimately de-stroyed the Bretton Woods system provide an obvious justification for this emphasis; but to attribute these forces to arbitrary differences in taste merely pushes the question one stage further back. Moreover, it leaves the determinants of the initial position unspecified, and diverts attention from the centripetal tendencies which are inherent in a fixed-exchange-rate system. Fundamentally, the arbitrary element stressed by Claassen and Corden is inconsistent with their analytical framework of constrained optimisation. While this section attempts to rectify the inconsistency by making outcomes correspond to choices, differences in tastes are not ignored.

The obvious starting point is Fried's analysis of the small-country case. Each member of the group is sufficiently insignificant that it can treat the world price of the traded good as parametric; and accordingly it seeks equilibrium at the tangency of an indifference curve and the perceived constraint AA in Fig. 8.1. This position can be maintained only if each country is inflating at a rate consistent with balance-of-payments equilibrium, here assumed to be the world inflation rate p_1, so that AA must intersect WW at the point of tangency. Finally, WW will be stable only if the actual world inflation rate corresponds to the expected rate, so that the equilibrium must lie on the long-run Phillips curve through U_N. Point S satisfies all the necessary conditions for the representative small country.

What of the unrepresentative countries? National tastes may be inflation-shy or inflation-prone; since an individual country's freedom to depart from the world inflation rate varies inversely with its dependence on trade, there is no reason to suppose that the perceived constraints will be identical. If the differences are sufficiently pro-nounced they may be resolved by exchange-rate realignments, or they may precipitate the collapse of the system; but such drastic outcomes are not a necessary consequence of international diversity. Consider, for example an inflation-prone country whose indifference curve cuts AA from above at point S, and which would prefer point T in Fig. 8.1. If it chooses to indulge these preferences it will incur balance-of-payments deficits and deplete its reserves; in the process its indifference map must tilt in the direction of the representative country's as the consequences of inflation become more serious with the diminution of its capacity to withstand unfavourable shocks in the future. A commitment to maintain fixed exchange rates therefore implies that preferences among other objectives are endogenous, and must respond to changes in the conditions affecting the pursuit of the primary objective. This consequence of a lexicographic preference structure is scarcely surprising, but its role in preserving equilibrium has been overlooked in attempts to answer the broader question of whether that equilibrium is worth preserving.

The assumption of the small-country case that world prices are exogenously given to each member of the fixed-exchange-rate bloc is patently special, and distinctly implausible. Suppose, instead, that one member becomes sufficiently large that it influences the price of the tradeable good; the constraint facing the dominant country is then no longer AA, but in the limit becomes WW. Position S would no longer be an equilibrium, and the dominant country would move to a new position, D in Fig. 8.2, where its presumably unchanged indifference map yields a point of tangency with WW. The reduction in the world

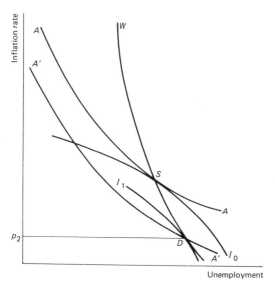

F ɪɢ. 8.2 The 'dominant' country under fixed exchange rates.

inflation rate to p_2 would drag AA, which still confronts the remaining members of the bloc, down to $A'A'$, which intersects WW at point D. The immediate consequence would be an increase in welfare for all the participants, but only the dominant country would regard the new situation as an equilibrium; the remainder would prefer to move north-west along the improved trade-off $A'A'$.

In the longer run, two further developments would occur. First, the disequilibrium confronting the small countries would induce departures from the inflation rate set by their dominant partner, reserve outflows, and a consequential rotation of their indifference maps until the confluence of preferences and perceived possibilities established a new equilibrium, in which the discrepancy between the constraints facing the dominant country and its smaller trading partners would be matched by the discrepancy between their indifference maps, those of the smaller countries now reflecting greater distaste for inflation. How far the combined effect of their deviations from point D were to influence the rate of inflation during the transition period and, through the response of the dominant country's own tastes to reserve inflows, the position of D itself, would depend on the degree of dominance exercised by the major participant in the bloc. Second, the movement from S to D involves an unemployment rate above the natural level, and hence an expectational adjustment which would push WW itself downwards. Full equilibrium would therefore lie south-west of D, on the vertical long-run Phillips curve.

The essential feature of the preceding parable is that the dominant country recognises the endogeneity of 'world' prices and inflation. Other institutional mechanisms for revealing that the individual small country faces possibilities which are not open to the world as a whole are conceivable, but to date no alternative mechanism has been observed. A further stylised fact is that dominance is not measured along a single dimension. McMahon, in a continuation of the passage quoted above, characterised the dominant country as being 'in an unchallengably strong economic and financial position, both externally and internally; maintained near price stability; was able to practice liberal trade policies even when they were not fully reciprocated; and acted as banker to the rest of the world, both lending long term and taking deposits'. It is the banking function of the dominant country which has been omitted from the foregoing analysis.

The dominant country's role in providing a key currency, like its role in exploding the fallacy of composition, is not intrinsic; but the two functions are associated. Under a fixed-rate system based on commodity reserves, as implicitly assumed so far, there is an obvious incentive to substitute a lower-cost reserve asset. The dominant country's currency is the principal candidate, because of the country's evident predisposition towards lower inflation during the period of its emergence, its balance-of-payments surpluses, and its concomitant accumulation of an increasing share of the world's commodity reserves.

The emergence of a key currency implies further changes in the fixed-rate equilibrium. Relaxation of the dominant country's balance-of-payments constraint reduces the cost of inflation, and makes it possible to pursue a policy of 'benign neglect'. Moreover, the prospect of extracting seigniorage from the rest of the world provides a positive incentive to raise the rate of monetary expansion above the level indicated by domestic considerations. While interest rates on key-currency deposits will eventually rise in compensation for higher inflation, the transitional gains remain attractive to governments elected for a limited term. The diagrammatic counterpart of these developments is a clockwise rotation of the dominant country's indifference map, a movement (which drags the *AA* curve with it) along *WW*, and an expectational adjustment. This upward spiral will be exacerbated if the rest of the world responds to payment surpluses by raising its own rate of domestic credit expansion, in preference to continuing accumulation of reserves in the decreasingly attractive form of key-currency deposits. It is highly unlikely that the relative price of the tradeable good will remain at its equilibrium level during the rise in the world inflation rate, so that the efficiency of the price mechanism will be impaired. Whether the process will converge to a new equilibrium before the fixed-rate system becomes less attractive than the alternatives is a question which lies beyond the scope of qualitative analysis.

THE ADOPTION OF FLEXIBLE EXCHANGE RATES

When exchange rates are permitted to float freely, changes in the level of economic activity no longer imply changes in the relative price of the tradeable good, since the domestic price of the latter is no longer fixed by commodity arbitrage. In diagrammatic terms, a switch of exchange-rate regime is equivalent to a switch for each individual country from *AA* to *WW* as the relevant constraint on macroeconomic policy.

In the small-country case discussed by Fried, the clockwise pivot of the constraint causes a movement away from the fixed-rate equilibrium, at *S* in Fig. 8.2 down the *WW* curve. If both the latter and macroeconomic preferences are unaffected by the change of regime, the new equilibrium under flexible rates will correspond to position *D*, with lower inflation and higher unemployment than before. The *ceteris paribus* conditions on which this prediction is based will be relaxed later, but are retained for the present.

One immediate conclusion is that the analysis is either incomplete, or the small-country case under fixed exchange rates is logically, as well as empirically, irrelevant. Faced with the options presented in the diagram, the small country would choose flexible rates to attain position *D* in preference to fixed rates and the corresponding position *S*.

Fried's own conclusion clearly does not extend to the case of the dominant country; rather, flexible rates are a substitute for the latter as a means of exposing the fallacy of composition which underlies the dubious small-country analysis. The question which naturally arises is whether there are any grounds for distinguishing between these two alternative means of attaining position *D*.

In one sense, Fried's attachment to money illusion leads him to understate the superiority of flexible rates, within the terms of his own argument. Position *D* represents only a short-run equilibrium, for the reasons discussed in the previous section; in the long run, a movement back to U_N will occur, at an inflation rate below p_2 in Fig. 8.2. Furthermore, by concentrating on the representative country, he neglects to point out that a flexible-rate system can accommodate differences in tastes without resorting to the ostensibly Procrustean mechanism of reserve changes and rotating indifference maps. On closer inspection, however, these apparent additions to the case for flexible rates entail serious drawbacks.

Even with identical tastes, under a regime of flexible rates there is no mechanism to ensure that all countries move along their constraints at the same speed in the transition from *S* to *D*, and no reason to hypothesise that expectations will adjust uniformly in the longer-term transition to the natural unemployment rate. Given differences in tastes, differences in inflation rates will be more variable in the transition, and will persist even in the longest of runs. At that stage the differentials should, in the absence of further disturbances, be constant; but in the transitional phases inflation differentials, and substantially higher-order transforms, are unlikely to be stable or, therefore, predictable. The same holds, of course, for the exchange rates which reflect those differentials.

The creation of a new and unpredictable set of relative prices among national currencies when exchange rates are permitted to float introduces a new and socially disruptive form of trade. Shifts of the money demand function in response to expectational adjustments have been investigated by Vaubel (1980b), who concluded that 'exchange-rate changes [of sterling, the Deutschemark and the Swiss franc] are to a large extent due to international shifts in the demand for money' (p. 36). The induced instability of the national money demand functions increases the variance of output within each country. In turn, and in addition to its intrinsic undesirability, a higher output variance increases both the variance and, provided the constraint is non-linear as generally assumed, the mean of the inflation rate.

In summary, even if fixed and floating exchange-rate regimes arrive at the same destination, the stability afforded by a uniform 'world' rate of inflation would make the former a more desirable means of transition between equilibria. Whether the final outcome would in fact be identical would depend, as already seen, on the form and regulation of international reserves under the fixed-rate system, and on the validity of the *ceteris paribus* assumption which is now relaxed.

The identity of the body whose preferences are represented by the indifference curves in Figs 8.1 and 8.2 is a question which has not been addressed in the literature on exchange-rate regimes. The proximate answer is evidently that only the government is able to exercise any choice in the macroeconomic sphere; but whether its tastes represent its perception of the social interest, or merely its belief about the vote-maximising strategy for future elections, is less obvious. In either case, however, its preferences will be altered by the adoption of flexible exchange rates.

Consider first an altruistic government, and suppose that the initial position is a fixed-exchange-rate regime dominated by a key currency, the issuer of which is extracting seigniorage. If the smaller participants maintain the composition of their money supply constant, they derive revenue from the inflation tax only to the extent of their domestic credit expansion. After the change of regime, however, the money supply is determined domestically, and the 'tax' base is accordingly expanded. The optimal rate of inflation tax will therefore increase, because the revenue collected by each 'small' government at any tax rate will rise. This increase in the efficiency of the inflation tax relative to other revenue sources corresponds to a clockwise rotation of the indifference map.

This argument is clearly reversed for the key-currency country, whose inflation-tax base is reduced. Its reactions are, however, unlikely to be as rapid as those of the other countries, for during the transition to a lower inflation rate it will experience adjustment costs which offset some of the subsequent gains, whereas the gains from a higher rate of inflation tax are permanent and involve no intertemporal trade-off.

The adjustment costs of moving to a lower inflation rate are higher in a trading nation on a floating exchange rate than in the traditional closed-economy setting, for, as an empirical matter, nominal exchange rates respond more rapidly than inflation rates to policy changes (Dornbusch, 1978). Conversely, the possibility of lowering the real exchange rate, albeit only temporarily, by expansionary policies provides a further reason for predicting a more pronounced inflation bias under a flexible-rate regime.

If, rather than being altruistic, the government is concerned primarily with its own survival, an additional argument may be invoked. Exchange-rate flexibility, by eliminating the balance-of-payments constraint, both reduces the penalties for inefficient economic management and enlarges the scope for the pursuit of political ends. Under fixed rates, an 'irresponsible' or merely careless government is restrained by the fear of reserve losses, which can be rectified only by deflation or devaluation; either of these would be politically unpopular, whereas exchange-rate depreciation is less dramatic and so less visible to the electorate, and its consequences are less widely appreciated. Even if mistakes were random and the increase in the amplitude of the political business cycle were equally distributed around the natural unemployment rate, higher variance of economic activity would imply a higher average inflation rate given a non-linear constraint. In addition, however, reactions to departures from equilibrium differ asymmetrically under the two systems: as Michaely (1971) confirmed, the limited scope for sterilising reserve inflows under fixed rates is less severe a constraint than limited capacity to sustain reserve outflows; while under flexible rates, appreciation incurs more immediate and more vociferous criticism than depreciation. Thus the target unemployment rate is likely to be lowered when the constraint of fixity is relaxed.

However naïve or misguided the belief may appear, politicians themselves seem to regard fixed and flexible exchange rates as significantly different. When introducing his highly expansionary 1972 budget, for example, the British Chancellor observed (Barber, 1972) that 'it is neither necessary nor desirable to distort domestic economies to an unacceptable extent in order to maintain unrealistic exchange rates. . . . I do not believe that there is any need for this country . . . to be frustrated on this score in its determination to sustain sound economic growth and to reduce unemployment.' This statement not only evinces a change in preferences, but also encourages the expectation that the monetary authorities would be more willing to accommodate inflation than under a regime of fixity. That expectation, in turn, provides an incentive for stronger cost–push pressure (Gordon, 1975) which shifts the constraint upwards. Goldstein (1980, p. 12) corroborates this diagnosis and indicates the policy response when he voices the suspicion that

> it seems more than coincidental that since the disappearance of fixed rates, there has been an active search in high-inflation countries for some type of *institutional* mechanisms that will provide discipline against inflation – be it tax-based incomes policies, pre-announced money-supply targets, IMF letters of intent, the European monetary system, or even a constitutional amendment for a balanced budget. [Italics in original]

He is surely incorrect, however, in confining this Voltairian activity to high-inflation countries. Bockelman (1977, p. 11) observes that in Germany, after the collapse of the Bretton Woods system, 'as the effectiveness of monetary policy increased, concern about the unwelcome developments that might ensue if enterprises and trade unions based their actions on a wrong assessment of monetary policy increased as well'. Significantly, Germany initiated the practice of announcing monetary targets. The repercussions of flexibility on the inflation–unemployment trade-off, through its effect on expectations of monetary accommodation, are thus not confined to countries where monetary policy has traditionally erred in the direction of laxity.

There is a further reason for expecting an unfavourable shift of the constraint when flexible rates are adopted. Opponents of flexibility have traditionally argued that it would discourage international trade because of increased exchange-rate uncertainty. Advocates have retorted that forward exchange markets would ensure that the impact of exchange-rate flexibility on trade is negligible. In turn, Lanyi (1969) has observed that advocates of exchange-rate flexibility have erroneously identified the cost of exchange risk with the cost of forward cover. He argued that, while forward cover can eliminate the exchange risk with respect to a particular transaction, it cannot eliminate the long-term risk associated with the economic activity of specialising in the international exchange of goods and services. Fixity of exchange rates, by eliminating exchange-rate uncertainty, can be regarded as a means of avoiding the dead-weight transactions tax, on international trade as an economic activity, which is inherent in exchange-rate flexibility. It follows, therefore, that exchange-rate flexibility will induce a reallocation of resources towards the production of non-tradeable goods; but since the rate of productivity growth is lower in the latter than in the tradeable good sector, such a reallocation of resources will necessarily imply that the aggregate productivity growth rate of the individual economy will decline. This is undesirable in itself, and it will additionally generate an unfavourable shift in the short-run trade-off, unless and until the expected productivity growth rate built into factor-price changes adjusts to the changed conditions. In the short run, the shift of the constraint may be reflected in a higher rate of inflation; but if price expectations adjust more rapidly than expectations of real growth, it must induce a higher rate of unemployment if accelerating inflation is to be avoided.

Exchange-rate uncertainty combined with risk aversion is thus sufficient to establish that exchange-rate flexibility will result, *ceteris paribus*, in a higher natural rate of unemployment than a system of fixed exchange rates. It is not, of course, necessary that exchange-rate flexibility and uncertainty are correlated. For example, if countries pursued money supply growth rates consistent with their respective demand for money growth rates, one would expect deviations from purchasing power parity to be both small and infrequent, so that exchange-rate flexibility would not induce greater exchange-rate uncertainty. In this case, the forward rate would be an efficient predictor of the corresponding future spot rate; but exchange rates have exhibited a degree of volatility since 1973 that has surprised even the sternest opponents of flexible exchange rates, and this volatility has been associated with greater inaccuracy in predicting future spot exchange rates. Mussa (1979, p. 18) has argued that one of the 'regularities' than can be deduced from the post-1973 experience with floating rates is the following: 'The forward exchange rate is an unbiased predictor of the corresponding future spot exchange rate, is close to the best available predictor of the corresponding future spot exchange rate, but is not a very good predictor of the corresponding future spot exchange rate.' More specifically, Aliber (1977) has utilised data on forward and spot rates to demonstrate that the forecast errors increased sharply during the period March 1973–November 1974 in comparison with the period December 1967–July 1969. This result, of course, implies that for firms which maintain an exposed position exchange-rate uncertainty has been much greater since 1973. But for firms which do hedge their foreign exchange exposure, transactions costs have risen steeply since the collapse of the Bretton Woods system. Finally, and most fundamentally,

Aliber draws attention to the fact that large and unpredictable deviations from purchasing power parity have involved firms being exposed to increased price uncertainty. In brief, then, developments since 1973 are consistent with the hypothesis that exchange-rate flexibility leads to greater exchange-rate uncertainty, and hence to a reallocation of resources which increases the natural rate of unemployment.

At a less formal level, two other developments during the 1970s are worth noting at this point. The first is the birth of the EMS and the renewed impetus towards EMU, both of which reflect a reaction against the floating-rate regime rather than the pursuit of an abstract ideal. They differ significantly from the other 'institutional mechanisms' listed by Goldstein, both in their requirement of international co-operation, albeit on a limited scale, and in their timing, after other expedients had been tried with limited success. Secondly, it has often been maintained that flexibility would foster international trade, by eliminating the need to erect tariffs or impose quotas to protect the balance of payments. If this claim were generally valid, the deleterious effects of greater exchange-rate uncertainty would be at least partially offset; but on the contrary, demands for protection have become more vociferous since the collapse of the Bretton Woods system, and governments appear to have become more sympathetic towards such demands.

To summarise, a fixed-rate regime, provided it does not involve the use of a national money as an international reserve, is preferable to floating rates, even on the *ceteris paribus* assumption, because it facilitates a smoother transition between equilibria. The other things, moreover, are unlikely to remain unchanged when the exchange-rate regime itself is changed.

CONCLUSIONS

Our analysis demonstrates that flexible exchange rates are more conducive to inflation than fixed exchange rates in that they cause an increase in the natural rate of unemployment. Second, under flexible exchange rates all countries, with the possible exception of the key-currency country, become more inflation-prone than under a system of fixed exchange rates. Allowing the exchange-rate regime to be a determinant of countries' preferences and constraints therefore leads to the conclusion that the world average rate of inflation will necessarily be higher under floating rates. More significantly, the inflation bias of a floating-rate regime applies also at the level of the individual economy, subject to the qualification concerning the divergence of interests which arises when a fixed-rate system is based on a key currency.

In the light of this analysis, the creation of the EMS and the discussion of a possible second-stage development into EMU are significant for two reasons. First, and more obviously, the movement towards fixity *per se*, although limited in both space and time by currency realignments, and subject to a variety of weaknesses (Vaubel, 1980a), indicates some degree of recognition that an externally imposed constraint offers some protection against both the domestic pressures and international uncertainties which have dominated the last decade. Second, the fact that EMU is being discussed at all raises the hope that any further development based on the EMS will be consciously planned. In particular, a deliberate choice of reserve asset will be required, or a key-currency system will reappear as a direct consequence of fixity.

Even if EMU developed on the undesirable basis of a key-currency, it is unlikely that the instability associated with the Bretton Woods system would recur. One reason is that lags in the adjustment of nominal interest rates to inflation have shortened under the impact of learning by losing, so that the potential seigniorage gains from inflation of a reserve currency have diminished. More importantly, none of the possible candidates for the role matches the US in relative size or in the political and military dominance it enjoyed during the Bretton Woods era.

If the EMS collapses instead of developing, the cost of restoring monetary stability, in terms of the extent and duration of unemployment during the adjustment process, will be higher than otherwise. One possible consequence would be that the present emphasis on the reduction of inflation as the primary objective of macroeconomic policy would be abandoned in response to pressures for policies aimed at reducing unemployment, with all the social and political implications such a reversal would entail. The case for fixed exchange rates and the survival of the EMS as a step towards that end rests, therefore, not only on economic but also on political desirability.

REFERENCES

Aliber, R. Z. (1977), 'The Firm under Pegged and Floating Exchange Rates', in J. Herin, A. Lindbeck and J. Myhrman (eds), *Flexible Exchange Rates and Stabilization Policy* (London: Macmillan).

Barber, A. (1972), 'Budget Statement', *Hansard*, vol. 833, col. 1354 (London: HMSO).

Bockelman, H. (1977), 'Quantitative Targets for Monetary Policy', *Cahiers Economiques et Monetaire*, no. 6 (Banque de France).

Chancellor of the Exchequer (1979), *The European Monetary System*, Cmnd. 7405 (London: HMSO).

Claassen, E. M. (1977), 'World Inflation under Flexible Exchange Rates', in J. Herin, A. Lindbeck and J. Myhrman (eds), op. cit.

Corden, W. M. (1977a), 'Inflation and the Exchange Rate Regime', in J. Herin, A. Lindbeck and J. Myhrman (eds), op. cit.

—— (1977b), *Inflation, Exchange Rates and the World Economy* (Oxford: Oxford University Press).

Dornbusch, R. (1978), 'Monetary Policy under Exchange-rate Flexibility', in J. R. Artus *et al.*, *Managed Exchange-rate Flexibility: The Recent Experience* (Federal Reserve Bank of Boston).

Duck, N., M. Parkin, D. Rose and G. Zis (1976), 'The Determination of the Rate of Change of Wages and Prices in the Fixed Exchange Rate World Economy, 1956–71', in M. Parkin and G. Zis (eds), *Inflation in the World Economy* (Manchester: Manchester University Press).

Eckstein, O. and R. Brinner (1972), 'The Inflation Process in the United States', study prepared for the Joint Economic Committee, 92nd Cong., 2nd sess., Washington, D.C.

Emminger, O. (1973), *Inflation and the International Monetary System* (Basel: The Per Jacobsson Foundation).

Fried, J. (1973), 'Inflation-unemployment Trade-offs under Fixed and Floating Exchange Rates', *Canadian Journal of Economics*, vol. 6.

Genberg, H. (1977), 'Comment', in J. Herin, A. Lindbeck and J. Myhrman (eds), op. cit.

Goldstein, M. (1980), *Have Flexible Exchange Rates Handicapped Macroeconomic Policy?* (Essays in International Finance, no. 14) (Princeton, N. J.: Princeton University Press).

Gordon, R. J. (1972), 'Wage-price Controls and the Shifting Phillips Curve', *Brookings Paper on Economic Activity*.

—— (1975), 'The Supply of and Demand for Inflation', *Journal of Law and Economics*, vol. 18.

Hamermesh, D. (1970), 'Wage Bargains, Threshold Effects, and the Phillips Curve', *Quarterly Journal of Economics*, vol. 84.

Johnson, H. G. (1973), 'Secular Inflation and the International Monetary System', *Journal of Money, Credit and Banking*, vol. 5.

Klein, B. (1975), 'Our New Monetary Standard: the Measurement and Effects of Price Uncertainty 1880–1973', *Economic Inquiry*, vol. 13.

Laidler, D. (1981), 'Monetarism: an Interpretation and an Assessment', *Economic Journal*, vol. 91.

Lanyi, A. (1969), *The Case for Floating Exchange Rates Reconsidered* (Essays in International Finance, no. 72) (Princeton, N. J.: Princeton University Press).

McMahon, C. (1979) 'The Long-run Implications of the European Monetary System', in P. H. Trezise (ed.), *The European Monetary System: its Promise and Prospects* (Washington, D. C.: The Brookings Institution).

Meiselman, D. I. (1975), 'Worldwide Inflation: a Monetarist View', in

D. I. Meiselman and A. B. Laffer (eds), *The Phenomenon of Worldwide Inflation* (Washington, D. C.: American Enterprise Institute for Public Policy Research).

Michaely, M. (1971), *The Responsiveness of Demand Policies to Balance of Payments: Postwar Patterns* (New York: National Bureau of Economic Research).

Mundell, R. A. (1976), 'The "New Inflation" and Flexible Exchange Rates', in M. Monti (ed.) *The 'New Inflation' and Monetary Policy* (London: Macmillan).

Mussa, M. (1979), 'Empirical Regularities in the Behaviour of Exchange Rates and theories of the Foreign Exchange Market', in K. Brunner and A. H. Meltzer (eds), *Policies for Employment, Prices, and Exchange Rates*, Carnegie-Rochester Conference Series on Public Policy, vol. 11. (Amsterdam: North-Holland).

Ormerod, P. (1979), *Economic Modelling* (London: Heinemann).

Salant, W. S. (1977), 'International Transmission of Inflation', in L. B. Krause and W. S. Salant (eds), *Worldwide Inflation* (Washington, D. C.: The Brookings Institution).

Sumner, M. T. (1972), 'Aggregate Demand, Price Expectations and the Phillips Curve', in M. Parkin and M. T. Sumner (eds), *Incomes Policy and Inflation* (Manchester: Manchester University Press).

Thomas, R. L. (1974), 'Wage Inflation in the UK: a Multi-market Approach', in D. Laidler and D. L. Purdy (eds), *Inflation and Labour Markets* (Manchester: Manchester University Press).

Turnovsky, S. J. (1972), 'The Expectations Hypothesis and the Aggregate Wage Equation: some Empirical Evidence for Canada', *Economica*, N. S., vol. 39.

Vanderkamp, J. (1966), 'Wage and Price determination: an Empirical Model for Canada', *Economica*, N.S., vol. 33.

—— (1972), 'Wage Adjustment, Productivity and Price-change Expectations', *Review of Economic Studies*, vol. 39.

Vaubel, R. (1980a), 'The Return to the New European Monetary System: Objectives, Incentives, Perspectives', in K. Brunner and A. H. Meltzer (eds), *Monetary Institution and the Policy Process*, Carnegie-Rochester Conference Series on Public Policy, vol. 13 (Amsterdam: North-Holland).

—— (1980b), 'International Shifts in the Demand for Money, their Effects on Exchange Rates and Price Levels, and their Implications for the Preannouncement of the Monetary Expansion', *Weltwirtschaftliches Archiv*, vol. 116, no. 1.

Willett, T. D. (1973), 'Comment', *Journal of Money, Credit and Banking*, vol. 5.

Comments on Laidler and Sumner and Zis

GEOFFREY E. J. DENNIS

Through the use of alternative approaches these two papers come to different conclusions on the fixed versus floating exchange rate debate in 1980. Laidler presents a pragmatic and persuasive case for floating rates without stating the positive merits of the fixed rate alternative, while Sumner and Zis present a useful survey of the theoretical literature on the relationships between exchange rates and inflation, and by rectifying certain faults of the literature conclude that floating rates exhibit an inflation bias.

Laidler rests part of his case against fixed rates on the absence of a stable, non-inflationary asset against which a national currency may peg, and on the rejection of the argument that fixed exchange rates impart a discipline to domestic monetary policy. Both these arguments are, however, incomplete.

It is valid to argue, as Laidler does, that neither gold nor the dollar is at present an adequate peg, while a currency basket such as the SDR, not being guaranteed by an individual monetary authority, is also unsuitable. Therefore, by default, floating rates are a better prospect. However, the first eighteen months of operation of the EMS demonstrated that in the restricted grouping of the EC such a satisfactory peg may be available. Technically, all member currencies of the EMS are pegged against the ECU; as a currency basket it has the same ultimate disadvantage as the SDR. However, the Deutschemark has acted as a *de facto* non-inflationary 'focus' in both the defunct snake and the EMS. Although this role for the Deutschemark is only implicit, West Germany's post-war economic performance, in particular in regard to inflation, suggests that such an arrangement is likely to retain a bias against inflation in the EMS.

An example of the role of the Deutschemark may be given. In the first twelve months of the EMS (from March 1979) Germany tightened her monetary policy progressively in response to worsening inflation, a deteriorating external balance and some early weakness of the Deutschemark in the EMS. In response, certain of the smaller EC members (notably Belgium, Denmark and the Netherlands, which had acted, in effect, as satellites of West Germany in the snake) were forced to raise their own interest rates to maintain the strength of their currencies in the EMS. Certain strains developed within the EMS as these smaller nations (Denmark excepted, perhaps) argued that there was little internal economic justification for tighter monetary policy, so that Germany was foisting on the EMS an *ex-post* harmonisation of monetary policy at the level of the lowest inflation performance.

A continuation of this behaviour pattern in the EMS – notwithstanding the objective of symmetrical adjustment so that the EMS should therefore be *a priori* more inflationary than the apparently inflation-biased yet asymmetrical Bretton Woods system – provides the non-inflationary peg required, and presages the rejection of the view that fixed rates and low inflation are incompatible *per se*.

The doubts over the durability of such a non-inflationary solution are, however, notable. First, it is possible that other economically powerful nations with a bias against such restrictive policies such as France, Italy and the UK may, in effect, combine to impose a less deflationary 'average' on the EMS – in effect that true symmetry may be approached. However the fact that certain smaller countries in the EMS have actually chosen to follow the discipline of Germany makes this development less likely. Second, and expanding the last point, it may be easier to achieve harmonisation at intermediate rates of inflation, where adjustment is shared by all member countries, rather than at the lowest rate of inflation, where the poorer performers in respect of inflation bear a particularly large adjustment burden. Third, the author argues that due to political developments in Germany, there may, in the future, be a reordering of macroeconomic objectives to convert her into a high-inflation member of the EC. While the validity of all these arguments is clear, the solution is equally obvious – at that stage the case for floating exchange rates on the basis of the lack of a non-inflationary peg would be made; until that time, on all evidence of the post-war period, in particular since the inception of the snake, it appears that membership of the EMS would provide an implicit link with the dominant country that exhibits a low inflation performance.

Laidler argues that under fixed rates any economic discipline is internally-generated, and no country would submit to long-term membership of a fixed rate arrangement if such discipline were absent. This argument is logically correct but may be expanded. A government may be tempted to relax its economic policy – and so deny its self-imposed discipline – for short-term gain such as in the run-up to a general election. Such relaxation is easier to justify and achieve under floating rates. In addition, governments may use the discipline of fixed exchange rates as an 'excuse' for tight domestic policies. It is not unusual for a country (e.g. the UK in 1976–7) to blame an outside party (in that case the IMF) for the imposition of restrictive economic policies that may involve a fixed exchange rate. In this way, such an exchange-rate arrangement may enable a government to impose economic discipline, that it is aware is urgently needed, on an unwilling electorate and yet not suffer the full political costs of so doing. Indeed, it may be argued that membership of the EMS was attractive to certain European governments in that it introduced 'an outside disciplinary force' (see above, chapter 3 by Norbert Walter).

A practical attack on the weaknesses of fixed rates in the context of the EMS may be augmented by a brief consideration – not undertaken by Laidler – of the positive argument in favour of such an arrangement. The latter are that, if the validity of the vertical, long-run Phillips relationship is accepted, there is no long-run unemployment cost of membership of a monetary union (e.g. Parkin, 1976) and that due to the increased integration of countries in Europe and the rest of the world, and the increasing invalidity of the assumption of money illusion in wage bargains, there is a powerful case in favour of the inability of exchange-rate movements to equilibrate external payments positions. The doctrines of the 'vicious' and 'virtuous' circles have gained ground during the floating-rate era in the 1970s (e.g. Bilson, 1979).

A preference for fixed exchange rates is confirmed in the summary of a complex literature by Sumner and Zis. Their conclusion that floating rates exhibit an inflation bias does not imply, however, that the *actual* inflation rate will always be higher than under a fixed-rate regime. Assuming the absence of a long-run trade-off between inflation and unemployment, it is argued that floating rates shift the short-run trade-off upwards. This need not affect the inflation rate, however, once all price changes are perfectly anticipated, as the economy will settle down at the higher natural level of unemployment and at an inflation rate that may be higher, lower or no different from that under fixed rates. The argument in favour of the inflation bias is therefore essentially a short-run one (assuming the possibility of a long-run trade-off is dismissed). In the face of an unfavourable shift in the trade-off, a government may seek to maintain a target level of unemployment and therefore accept a higher and accelerating rate of inflation. However the costs of the accelerating inflation are likely to outweigh eventually the gains from unemployment at less than the natural rate, so that in the long term equilibrium at the natural rate is achieved.

However, although the inflation bias result is a short-run conclusion it is nevertheless a crucial point. Economic policy-makers 'live in the short-run' and may consider that the political gains of lower unemployment outweigh the ultimate costs of accelerating inflation. In addition, the length of time that must elapse before inflation accelerates sufficiently to force governments to deflate and accept the natural rate of unemployment is uncertain.

Whether the argument is couched in terms of a short-term inflation bias or a long-term shift in the natural level of unemployment, the Sumner–Zis approach concludes that floating rates worsen the inflation–unemployment mix whatever the time scale considered. This is powerful support for the opinion that in 1980 fixed exchange rates are a more acceptable alternative, particularly in the context of the EC.

REFERENCES

Bilson, J. F. O. (1979) 'The Vicious Circle Hypothesis', *International Monetary Fund Staff Papers*, vol. 26.

Parkin, M. (1976) 'Monetary Union and Stabilisation Policy in the European Community', *Banca Nazionale del Lavoro Quarterly Review*, September, vol. 76, no. 118.

9 Increased Wage or Productivity Differentials in a Monetary Union

POLLY REYNOLDS ALLEN

INTRODUCTION

The economic costs of belonging to a monetary union are closely correlated with the size and the frequency of disturbances that affect the member countries differently. Such disturbances are described as 'asymmetric disturbances'.

By forming a monetary union, the members have lost one obvious means of adjusting to asymmetric disturbances – a realignment of their mutual exchange rates. The impossibility of altering exchange rates within the union may raise the costs of responses to remaining disturbances. Changes in exchange rates would allow for different ongoing rates of price inflation among the countries, and might accomplish some real wage and income changes that cannot be achieved more directly.

Several other factors can help to reduce the costs of responding to asymmetric disturbances under fixed exchange rates. A high degree of substitutability between member countries' goods, mutual trade of a large proportion of their national products, and free movement of the factors of production among the member countries have all been cited in the literature on optimum currency areas (see Tower and Willett, 1976; Ishiyama, 1975).

It is unlikely that any group of actual countries, or even any single country, can ever be described as a truly optimum currency area, in which the costs of responding to asymmetric disturbances are at the minimum.[1] Moreover, at least some asymmetric disturbances are bound to occur within any group of countries. Nations can expect that formation of a monetary union will impose some economic costs on the members. They may judge none the less that there are economic and political benefits of monetary union that outweigh these costs. Once monetary union has been formed, the question of whether or how to create such a union disappears. The member countries then need to learn how to reduce either the asymmetric disturbances or the ensuing adjustment costs, within the context of the monetary union.

Such asymmetries are particularly relevant in a monetary union, because the union is less of an aggregate economic and political unit than a nation. The union is composed of countries with their own national governments, who control national fiscal policies and respond to national electorates. By joining a monetary union, the member countries have given up independent national monetary policies, probably at some perceived cost. But because they remain sovereign nationalities in other respects, they retain the ability to withdraw from the monetary union if they feel it is working to their disadvantage.

Adjustments to asymmetric disturbances are required both among the member countries and between the union and the outside world. It is important to consider not only the reactions of the country directly affected by the disturbance, but also the spill-overs onto other members of the union. Moreover, an asymmetric disturbance is likely to affect the external balance of payments in the union. The resulting balance-of-payments adjustment impinges on all member countries, in a manner that depends on the union's choice of external exchange-rate policy.

Such responses cannot be analysed with a macroeconomic model of a single country that interacts with the large outside world, nor with a model of two interdependent countries that interact solely with each other. Single, small-country models fail to capture the diversity and the interdependence within the monetary union. Two-country models, while capturing some of this interdependence, do not allow for the union's interaction with the outside world. Consequently, many of the countries' responses are constrained to be mirror images of each other, and considerations of exchange-rate policy are necessarily eliminated.

Analysis of asymmetric disturbances in a monetary union requires a model of minimally three countries – two member countries whose economies are interdependent and who also interact with a third country representing the outside world. Peter Kenen and I have developed such a model and have analysed questions of market integration and market interdependence, and their implications for policy integration and policy interdependence (see Allen and Kenen, 1980, parts IV and V). My analysis is based on our model, which is summarised in this paper.

Kenen and I used our model to analyse, among other disturbances, asymmetric demand disturbances in a monetary union, such as a shift of demand from one country's good to another country's good within the union or an increase of demand for a single country's good. We also examined the potential uses of monetary and fiscal policies in a monetary union. We did not consider responses to asymmetric *supply-side* disturbances, which alter production conditions in only one country of the union. That is the purpose of this chapter.

Supply-side disturbances by definition involve changes in the constraints under which goods are produced. They usually generate opposite movements in prices and outputs, such as a rise in price and a decline in output. By contrast, demand management policies, monetary or fiscal, usually push both prices and outputs in the same direction in the short run, and have only limited potential for influencing output in the long run. When both price and output are regarded as policy targets, supply-side disturbances present particular problems for the effective use of demand management policies. I consider here two asymmetric supply-side disturbances: a nominal wage increase and a decline in productivity, both in one country of the union.

The monetary union we have modelled is not an optimum currency area by Mundell's standard of factor mobility (Mundell, 1961). Labour and capital are assumed to be in fixed supply in each country. There is no investment, and thus no growth of the capital stock; there is no growth of the labour force; and there is no migration of labour or physical capital, either within the union or between the union and the outside world. These assumptions are important for the behavior of the model and render the conclusions more relevant for the short and medium term than for the long run, even though the model moves to a steady state.

Two versions of the model embody alternative assumptions about labour markets. In the 'Keynesian' version, nominal wages are determined exogenously, at a level above the market-clearing wage, and demand for labour determines the level of employment. In the 'classical' version, nominal wages are assumed to be flexible, adjusting to equate the demand for labour in each country with a fixed supply. The nominal wage increase can be considered only in the Keynesian version of the model, but the decline in productivity is analysed for both versions.

The responses to the two disturbances are similar. I shall discuss in some detail the responses to both in the Keynesian version of the model, and then briefly compare the responses in the Keynesian and classical versions to a decline of productivity. I emphasise the Keynesian version, largely because of the short- and medium-term implications of the

model, and because of my belief that the classical version is appropriate
rather for the long run. Moreover, increased wage pressures from the
relatively low-wage member countries may be one result of forming a
monetary union, as workers come to identify more closely with their
counterparts in other countries of the union.[2]

In order to isolate those asymmetries in the member countries'
adjustments that are directly the results of the asymmetrical disturbance, the member economies are assumed to be symmetrical in all other
ways. I shall explain these symmetry assumptions below.

A comparison of changes in individual member countries with the
corresponding changes for the union as a whole requires aggregate
measure of prices and outputs for the union. Price and output of each
country's good are measured explicitly, and nominal income for each
country equals its output multiplied by the current price. Nominal *union*
income is the sum of the nominal incomes of the member countries. A
union price level cannot be measured explicitly, however, because the
countries produce different goods. Rather, changes in union prices are
calculated as changes in an implicit *union price index*. This index is a
weighted average of changes in national prices from levels prevailing
before the disturbances, with the weights based on the national outputs
produced before the disturbance. It follows that a change in the *union's
real product* can be calculated by deflating the change in nominal union
income by this implicit union price index. With the strong symmetry
assumptions mentioned above, the percentage change in the union price
index equals the sum of the percentage changes in the member countries'
prices, and the percentage change in the union's real product equals
the sum of the percentage changes in the member countries' outputs.

The major responses in the Keynesian version of the model to either of
the two labour-market disturbances – an exogenous rise in one
country's nominal wage rate or an exogenous decline in that country's
productivity – can be summarised:

(1) In the country with the labour-market disturbance, the price of
the country's good increases and its output declines, both immediately
and permanently; the country's current account immediately moves into
deficit. These responses dominate any responses by the partner's
economy and thus describe the responses of the aggregate union
variables – an increase in the union price index and a decline in the
union's real product, both immediately and permanently, and an
immediate worsening of the union's current account. These conclusions
apply whether the union's external exchange rate is flexible or pegged,

although the magnitudes of the changes in the steady state depend on the exchange-rate regime.

(2) The union's currency gradually depreciates under a flexible external exchange rate, with expansionary effects on the union's economy, enough to guarantee an eventual rise in the partner's output. By contrast, under a pegged external exchange rate, the union gradually loses reserves, with deflationary effects on the union's economy, with the strong possibility that the partner's price level may decline. The disturbance causes member countries' outputs to move in opposite directions under a flexible exchange rate and may cause their prices to move in opposite directions under a pegged exchange rate.

THE MODEL

The two countries of the monetary union, North and South, each produce a single good, which they export to each other and to a third country, the World; they each import a third good from the World. Each member country's government is assumed to have financed its past budget deficits by issuing bonds, which are traded within the Union. Portfolios of Union residents also include foreign-currency bonds from the World. Capital flows occur within the Union and between member countries and the World.

The Union has a single central bank, which issues the Union currency. The Union money supply changes in response to central-bank purchases and sales of foreign exchange or of Northern and Southern bonds. The Union may choose to peg the external exchange rate, in which case the central bank buys and sells foreign exchange as necessary to support the rate. Alternatively, the Union may choose a flexible exchange rate, in which case the central bank refrains from all foreign-exchange intervention. Open-market operations in Northern and Southern bond markets are assumed to be an exogenous policy decision and to be zero unless specified otherwise.

Markets for goods and assets are assumed to clear at all times. The Union is small in the markets for the World good and the World bond, each of which is available in perfectly elastic supply at the fixed World price or interest rate. The Union is none the less large enough, in the markets for its own goods and bonds, to influence the respective market-clearing prices and interest rates. The foreign-exchange market is cleared either by adjustments in the exchange rate or by movements of reserves between the Union and the World.

The Union labour markets are the only markets that do not always clear. Labour is assumed to be paid its marginal product, which diminishes with increased labour inputs. In the Keynesian version of the model, the nominal wage rate is exogenously determined at a level above the market-clearing wage, with resulting unemployment. In the classical version of the model, nominal wages are assumed to adjust to clear the labour markets, equating the demands for labour with fixed supplies.

Consumption demands for goods depend positively upon income and wealth and negatively on the interest rates and prices of other goods.[3] Demands for assets are stock demands that depend positively upon wealth and the asset's own interest rates. The exclusion of a transactions demand (no income effect on demands for assets) emphasises the portfolio approach to the balance of payments. In line with the portfolio approach, the exchange rate responds immediately to disturbances in the asset markets, but only gradually to goods–market disturbances. As current-account flows actually occur, they produce changes in wealth, which in turn disturb asset–market equilibrium and induce gradual adjustments in the exchange rate. The steady-state level of the exchange rate is that which is consistent with a balanced current account for the Union. In this manner, the exchange rate is determined in the asset markets in the short run, but by the requirements of the current accounts in the steady state. (The simplifying assumption that transfers between governments offset interest payments on foreign bonds leaves current-account balances equal to trade balances at all times.)

The two economies are symmetrical in their initial conditions, in their responses, and in the World's interactions with them. The countries are assumed to be initially the same size with the same incomes and the same levels of nominal wealth; their savings functions are identical. Moreover, their demands for goods and for assets are *symmetrical*. For example, each country has the same marginal propensity to spend on its domestic good and the same marginal propensity to spend on its partner's good; the own price elasticity of a country's demand for its own good is the same in both countries, with corresponding symmetries for other price elasticities; each country's demand for its domestic bond is affected equally by a rise in its own interest rate and equally by a rise in the partner's interest rate or by a rise in the World interest rate. World demands for each country's goods are initially identical and have the same price elasticities; and although the member countries produce different goods, the production functions are identical.[4] These symmetry assumptions serve to isolate those asymmetries of responses that result from the asymmetrical nature of the disturbances. I discuss below the implications of relaxing some of these symmetry assumptions. Current-account flows can be aggregated into balances for member countries or for the Union. Each member country has a *global balance*, which is the sum of its *bilateral balances* with its partner and with the World. The *Union global balance* is the sum of the Northern and Southern bilateral balances with the World, and is also the sum of the Northern and Southern global balances. (These two sums are equivalent, for a member country's bilateral balance with the World equals its global balance minus its bilateral balance with its partner, and the North's bilateral balance with the South is the mirror image of the South's bilateral balance with the North.) Zero global current-account balances, which must prevail in the steady state, require that the relevant bilateral balances be offsetting, but not necessarily zero.

The model is stationary, in that there is no steady-state growth; all exogenous variables are assumed to be constant, unless a disturbance is specified. In the steady state there can be no saving in either member country and no capital flows: by implication, national government budgets and current accounts must be balanced, leaving all variables constant. Government budget deficits are assumed to be a policy decision, controlled by the necessary adjustments in taxes, and to be zero unless otherwise specified. A disturbance can induce temporary saving or dissaving and corresponding current-account surpluses or deficits. The resulting movements of money or the exchange rate, along with the induced adjustments in the prices of goods and bonds, serve to bring the economies to a steady state.

When the Union's external exchange rate is pegged, a positive level of Union saving (matched by a Union global current-account surplus) implies a gradual accumulation of wealth from abroad in the form of bonds (a net capital inflow for the Union) and money (increase of Union reserves). As Union wealth increases, desired saving gradually declines to zero, bringing the economy to a steady state.

When the external exchange rate is flexible, the same Union global current-account surplus (matched by positive Union saving) implies an excess flow supply of foreign exchange at the prevailing exchange rate. Wealth is acquired solely in the form of foreign-currency bonds. The Union currency gradually appreciates, reducing the Union's current-account surplus until it is zero and the economy is in a steady state.[5] This appreciation of the Union currency, while reducing the Union global surplus, does not always help to balance *each* member's global current account, for one of the countries may have a global deficit.

Within the Union, adjustments of the difference between the Northern and Southern global current accounts is accomplished by flows of bonds and money from the member country with the greater global deficit (or smaller global surplus) to its partner. The intra-union movements of wealth, in combination with the external movements either of wealth or of the exchange rate, guarantee a gradual closing of the global current-account balance and the absolute saving level for each country.

RESPONSES TO AN ASYMMETRIC SUPPLY DISTURBANCE

Short-run effects

An exogenous rise in the Northern nominal wage rate, or a decline in Northern productivity, has the initial effect of reducing Northern output and raising the price of the Northern good.[6] Either disturbance makes the Northern real wage greater than the marginal product of labour in the North. For any given price level, Northern producers reduce their demand for labour in order to equate its marginal product with the real wage; lower output corresponds to such a reduction of labour input. The producers' response is shown in Fig. 9.1 as a leftward shift of the supply curve for the Northern good from S to S.

The demand curve, D, in Fig. 9.1 is drawn to show the influence of the good's price, both directly and through the price effect on disposable income. The disturbance directly reduces demand for the Northern good, by the fall in output times the Northern marginal propensity to consume the Northern good. This is shown in Fig. 9.1 as a shift of the demand curve from D to D'.

If the Southern price were held constant, the economy would move from a to b. Because our assumptions about demands for goods guarantee that demand for the Northern good is relatively elastic with respect to its own price, at point b in Fig. 9.1 output has declined proportionally more than the price has risen, and Northern nominal (and thus disposable) incomes have declined.[7]

The spill-overs onto the Southern and World economies are ambiguous. On the one hand, consumers switch away from the higher-priced Northern goods to Southern and World goods: positive substitution effects. On the other hand, the negative income effect on Northern consumption expenditure reduces Northern demands for imports. Whether or not the spill-overs onto the Southern economy are

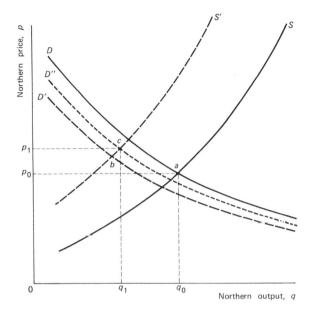

Fig. 9.1 Impact effect on Northern goods market of a wage increase or productivity decline in the North.

positive depends on whether the substitution effects dominate the income effect on demand for the Southern good; if the spill-overs are positive, Southern price and output both rise, and vice versa.

The repercussions on the Northern economy, in turn, are in the same direction as the spill-overs onto the Southern economy. Positive spill-overs produce positive repercussions, through both substitution and income effects. The shift of the demand curve from D' to D'' in Fig. 9.1 depicts the response to an induced increase in Southern price and output, a case of positive spill-over and repercussions. The labour-market disturbance does not immediately impinge upon asset markets, so there are no immediate changes in interest rates, the external exchange rate, or reserves.

All of these effects combine to move the economy immediately from a to c. The price elasticity of demand for the Northern good is sufficient to guarantee that Northern nominal and disposable incomes decline.

For all variables, the responses of the Northern economy are proportionally greater, in absolute terms, than the corresponding responses of the Southern economy. Northern price rises by more, Northern output and employment fall by more, and the Northern global current account is more in deficit. By implication, the Northern responses determine the direction of aggregate Union responses, regardless of the direction of the spill-overs onto the South. On impact, the Union price index increases, the Union's real product and employment decline, and the Union global current account moves into deficit. If the Northern and Southern goods markets were more closely integrated, the disturbance would induce a smaller price differential between the two countries and a greater output differential, but would effect the same changes in the Union price index and the Union's real product.

The immediate changes in the current accounts are depicted in Fig. 9.2. The upper points of the triangle denote the two member countries, North and South, and the lower point denotes the World. The arrows indicate changes in net bilateral current-account flows, the direction indicating which country is entitled to payment and the length indicating the size of the flows. (For simplicity, assume that the bilateral balances were all zero before the disturbances, so that a change in a balance equals its level.)

The solid arrows indicate net trade flows directly attributable to the rise in the Northern wage or decline of Northern productivity, holding prices constant. The disturbance alone, by lowering Northern nominal income, reduces Northern demands for imports; this is shown in Fig. 9.2 by the solid arrows pointing toward the North.

The broken arrows indicate the remaining changes in the trade flows, induced by the price adjustments. The higher Northern price serves to

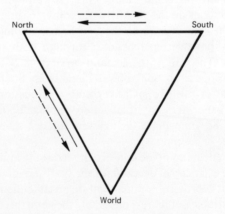

F ɪɢ. 9.2 Immediate changes in the current accounts due to a wage increase or productivity decline in the North.

worsen both Northern bilateral balances, as shown in Fig. 9.2 by the broken arrows pointing away from the North.

The sum of the arrows on any *one* side of the triangle equals the bilateral current-account balance between the two relevant countries. A country's global current-account balance is the sum of the arrows on the relevant *two* sides of the triangle. The union's global balance is the sum of the Northern and Southern global balances and is the mirror image of the World's global balance.

There are numerous possibilities for the changes in the bilateral flows, all of which are ambiguous, as is the change in the global balance for the South. The depiction in Fig.9.2 of Northern bilateral deficits with both the South and the World, a Southern bilateral balance with the World, and a Southern global surplus, is just one of many possible combinations. But there are two unambiguous outcomes:

(1) the North and the Union are each in current-account deficit, and
(2) the North has a greater deficit than the South.

These are reflected in Fig.9.2

Gradual changes through time

This information about the current accounts tells us something about the direction of adjustment of the economies through time.

First, because the Union has a global current-account deficit, the Union currency gradually depreciates, when the external exchange rate is market-determined. Alternatively, if the central bank is pegging the exchange rate, the Union gradually loses reserves. A depreciation of the Union currency has equal expansionary effects on both the Northern and Southern economies. Regardless of the nature of intra-Union adjustments, the Union price index and the Union's real product begin to rise, reinforcing the initial increase of the Union price index and offsetting the initial decline of the Union's real product. Under a pegged exchange rate, the opposite happens. The loss of Union reserves has an equal deflationary effect on each economy. The Union price index and the Union's real product begin to decline, offsetting the initial increase of the price index and reinforcing the initial fall of real product.

Second, because the North has a larger deficit than the South, money gradually moves from North to South, creating a deflationary effect on the Northern economy and an expansionary effect on the Southern economy. Prices and output in the North begin to fall relative to prices and output in the South (or begin to rise relatively less).

The price differential, initially created by the disturbance, starts to diminish. But the initial output differential, with Northern output down more than Southern output, begins to increase. This narrowing of the price differential and widening of the output differential occurs equally under either exchange-rate regime.

Steady-state outcomes

Having determined the immediate responses and the directions of gradual change for price, output, and employment in each country, what can we now say about their levels in the new steady state?

A triangular diagram, similar to Fig. 9.2, is useful in reasoning out the long-run price changes. Recall that in the steady state the global current accounts of each member country, and of the Union, must be in balance (although bilateral flows need not be balanced). Steady-state current accounts are functions of Northern and Southern prices and the exchange rate, along with the Northern wage rate, Northern labour productivity, and other exogenous factors.[8]

In Fig.9.3, the solid arrows indicate these long-run influences on current-account flows that are directly attributable to the exogenous Northern wage increase or productivity decline. As in the short run, the labour-market disturbance alone lowers Northern disposable income and Northern import expenditures, moving both Northern bilateral balances into surplus. The dotted arrows indicate changes in the current accounts under a flexible exchange rate that result from any permanent

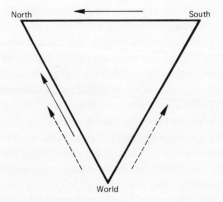

FIG. 9.3 Exogenous and exchange-rate-induced changes in steady state current accounts due to a wage increase or productivity decline in the North.

change in that rate. In this case, the Union's currency depreciates, moving toward surplus the bilateral current accounts of both the North and the South with the World.

The only other endogenous changes that affect the levels of steady-state current accounts are price changes. By looking at the current-account changes shown by the arrows in Fig. 9.3, we can determine what directions prices must change to bring the steady-state global current account of each country into balance. First, if Fig. 9.3 shows the Union to have a global current-account surplus, under the relevant exchange-rate regime, then the Union price index must rise in order to eliminate this surplus, and vice versa. Second, if Fig. 9.3 shows the North to have a greater surplus than the South, then in the new steady state the Northern price must be higher than the Southern price, and vice versa.[9]

Consider the case of a pegged exchange rate, in which case only the solid arrows in Fig. 9.3 are relevant. In the absence of any price adjustments, the Northern wage increase or productivity decline induces global current-account surpluses both for the North and for the Union, with a Southern global deficit. To balance the global current account for the Union, the Union price index must therefore be higher in the steady state. To balance the global current accounts for each member country as well, the Northern price must rise more than the Southern price.

The Northern price rises permanently under a pegged exchange rate, both absolutely and relative to the Southern price. The cumulation of deflationary pressures on the Northern economy, stemming from the gradual loss of money both to the World (in the form of reserves) and to the South, is not enough to reverse completely the initial Northern price rise. And although the Northern price fell more rapidly after its initial rise than did the Southern price, its *relative* rise on impact is never completely nullified. The change in the Southern price, ambiguous on impact and through time, remains ambiguous in the new steady state.

The long-run changes in outputs under a pegged exchange rate can be inferred from their changes initially and through time. Northern output falls more than Southern output on impact, and then declines more rapidly through time; the steady-state level of Northern output is thus reduced unambiguously. Southern output changes in the same direction as the Southern price, with the same ambiguity. The Union's real product, dominated by the decline in Northern output, is permanently lower.[10]

The changes under a pegged exchange rate in levels of steady-state prices, outputs, and nominal incomes are summarised in the upper portion of Table 9.1.

TABLE 9.1　Changes in steady state levels in response to a wage increase or decline in productivity in the North

	North	South	Union*
Pegged external exchange rate			
price	+	?	+
output (and employment)	−	?	−
nominal income	−	?	−
Flexible external exchange rate			
price	+	+	+
output (and employment)	−	+	−
nominal income	−	+	0

* For the Union, a price change refers to a change in the Union price index and a change in output, to a change in the Union's real product.

Under a flexible exchange rate, the dotted as well as the solid arrows in Fig. 9.3 are relevant. The current accounts are influenced not only by the disturbance, but also by the depreciation, which further improves the Union's global current account. The union price index must rise to eliminate this surplus; it rises more than under a pegged exchange rate, because of the inflationary effects of the currency depreciation. The depreciation improves the Northern and Southern global current accounts equally, so that their difference is the same under a flexible exchange rate as under a pegged rate. By implication, the difference in the long-run price changes must be identical for both exchange-rate regimes, the Northern price having risen more than the Southern price.

It is obvious from these responses that the Northern price rises permanently. But to determine the directions of change in Northern output, in Southern price and output, and in the Union's real product, we need one additional piece of information: under a flexible exchange rate, nominal Union income must eventually return to its original, pre-disturbance level.[11] From this we can deduce that steady-state prices must be higher in *both* countries, while steady-state output is lower in the North but higher in the South. The decline in Northern output is sufficiently large to lower Northern nominal income, just offsetting the rise in Southern nominal income.[12] Furthermore, the rise in the Union price index, combined with unchanged Union nominal income, implies a long-run decline in the Union's real product.

The changes under a flexible exchange rate in levels of steady-state prices, outputs, and nominal incomes, are summarised in the lower portion of Table 9.1.

The classical version and asymmetries

The Northern wage increase and the decline of Northern productivity have been analysed for the Keynesian version of the model, in which nominal wages are determined exogenously. The productivity decline can be analysed also in the classical version of the model, in which wages adjust to equate demands for labour to fixed supplies. The conclusions about the directions of changes in both countries' prices, in Northern output, and in the Union price index and real product are the same for both versions. But other differences are worth noting.

In the classical version, full employment always prevails. Because Northern employment does not decline when Northern productivity falls (which it did in the Keynesian version), Northern output does not fall as much, nor do Northern prices rise as much, as in the Keynesian version. Instead, the Northern real wage falls more. In the Southern economy, neither employment nor output changes, for the spill-overs are all changes of demand for Southern goods. The response is left to Southern prices, which change in the same (ambiguous) direction as in the Keynesian version. These similarities and differences between the two versions hold both on impact and in the steady state, and under both exchange-rate regimes.

The unambiguous directions of many of the responses depend heavily on the assumptions of perfect symmetry between the member countries of the Union. If such symmetry did not exist, a Northern wage increase or decline in Northern productivity would still induce both a rise in the Northern price level and a decline in Northern output. Moreover, as shown here, Southern price and output would move together and their direction would still be ambiguous. For the Union as a whole, one would expect the responses of the Northern economy usually to dominate, as they do unambiguously under the symmetry assumptions, producing an increase in the Union price index and a decline in the Union's real product. None the less, with certain kinds of asymmetries the spill-overs could produce responses in the South that were larger than the responses in the North, with unpredictable outcomes for the Union price index and real product. Furthermore, when the countries' responses are asymmetrical, there is no guarantee that the price and output differentials between the member countries will be the same for both exchange-rate regimes. And there is no basis for predicting the direction of their bias without knowing the types of asymmetries and disturbances.

POLICY OPTIONS

The disturbances examined here, a wage increase and decline in productivity in the North, raised the Union's prices and reduced its real product, both on impact and in the steady state. They also raised the Northern price and reduced Northern output, more than the corresponding changes in the South. To what extent can the central bank and the member governments use the standard macroeconomic stabilisation tools, monetary policy and fiscal policy, to offset these changes in prices and outputs?[13]

Monetary and fiscal policies work primarily through their influences on aggregate demand, moving prices and outputs together, in the same direction as the change in demand. In the Keynesian version of the model, the policy authorities can use monetary and fiscal policies to offset the decline in the Union's real product, but in so doing they will also add to the increase of prices. Alternatively, they can direct their policies to prevent or reverse the rise in the Union price index, but the fall in the Union's real product will be reinforced. Demand management policies cannot simultaneously offset both the rise in the Union price index and the decline in the Union's real product. This is the analogue of the familiar trade-off between inflation and unemployment. The authorities must decide between a price target and an output target. I consider here the case in which they choose to offset the changes in outputs induced by the labour-market disturbance. The output target is, of course, relevant only for the Keynesian version of the model.

We turn first to the use of Union monetary policy. Can the Union central bank use monetary policy, not only to raise the Union's real product, but also to reverse the *differences* in the member countries' outputs that were created by the disturbance to the Northern labour market? Since the disturbance caused Northern output to fall more than Southern output, the task of monetary policy is to raise output more in the North than in the South, and this requires raising the Northern price more than the Southern price. In order to do this, the monetary authority must be able to play upon three differential responses:

(1) It must be able to lower the Northern interest rate more than the Southern interest rate by purchasing Northern bonds. This requires imperfect substitutability between Northern and Southern bonds. If the bonds were perfect substitutes, both interest rates would fall equally, regardless of which country's bond was purchased.

(2) Demand for Northern goods must be influenced more strongly by a change in the Northern than in the Southern interest rate. This

outcome is guaranteed in the model by the assumptions that a country's desired saving is influenced more strongly by the interest rate on its own bonds than on the partner's bonds, and that each country's marginal propensity to consume its own goods exceeds the marginal propensity to import the partner's good.

(3) Increased demand for Northern goods must raise the Northern price more than the Southern price. This possibility depends upon less than perfect substitutability between the partners' goods.

As the national economies of the monetary union become more closely integrated, a probable trend in a monetary union, the likelihood is diminished that the Union will meet all three conditions for monetary policy to influence national outputs differentially.

Even if the conditions are met, the central bank can control the incidence of its policy on national prices and outputs only in the short run. With a pegged external exchange rate, there can be no effective long-run monetary policy, whether the target is aggregate or national, because the change in the money supply is gradually lost to the World through changes in the Union's reserves. With a flexible external exchange rate, which the Union may adopt in order to retain some long-run monetary independence, monetary control is limited to Union aggregates. Differences in national current-account balances are adjusted by a redistribution of assets within the Union. The long-run requirements of balanced global current accounts imply specific intra-Union relative prices and a specific distribution of the Union's money supply. These requirements cannot be altered by monetary policy, and monetary policy cannot permanently affect relative prices between the countries. This limitation on monetary policy comes, not because the authority is centralised at the Union level, but because there is no possibility of changing exchange rates within the Union. Monetary policy is best left as an instrument to control Union aggregates.

Any long-run ability to influence national outputs independently through the use of standard stabilisation policies must depend on fiscal policies. Here there are some possibilities, as long as the countries' goods are not perfect substitutes.

Fiscal policies that directly affect the *difference* between the member countries' global current accounts, given the price level, will induce a price differential, and thus an output differential, in the steady state. The price differential will be necessary in order to bring each member's global current account into balance. Examples of national fiscal policies that will induce a long-run increase in Northern output relative to Southern output are if either member government were to shift its spending from Southern to Northern goods, if the Northern government were to raise its level of balanced-budget spending for Northern goods, or if the Southern government were to lower its balanced-budget spending for the Southern good. (A balanced-budget change directly affects the country's current account through its direct effects on the country's disposable income, and hence on the country's demands for imports.)

The steady-state requirement of a balanced budget for each member government places limitations on national fiscal policies. (Member governments may run budget deficits or surpluses, but not indefinitely, if the economy is to reach a steady state.) Moreover, it is probably unrealistic to suppose that a national government would be willing to shift its expenditures from its own to the partner's good, in order to help stimulate the partner's economy relative to its own; the reverse policy may not be possible if government expenditures for the partner's imports are small. The fiscal changes that are required to create the desired national output differential may be so large as to be politically infeasible.

The policy options would be greater if the fiscal authority were centralised at the Union level, with a Union budget. The Union budget would have to be balanced in the steady state, but there would no longer be the constraint of balancing each national budget. The Union fiscal authority could raise output in the North relative to the South by reducing its expenditure for the Southern good and increasing its expenditure for the Northern good. An aggregate increase of the Union's real product, in addition to the relative increase of Northern output, could be accomplished either by an expansionary Union fiscal policy – such as more spending in the North or a smaller cutback in the South – or, under a flexible exchange rate, by an expansionary Union monetary policy.

Another problem arises in a monetary union where fiscal policies are the prerogative of national governments. If the Union central bank uses monetary policy to influence the Union's real product and the national governments use fiscal policies to influence their respective national output levels, then there are more policies, and more independent policy authorities, than there are independent targets. Only two targets are independent, for the Union's real product is made up of the national outputs. Union monetary policy and national fiscal policies must be co-ordinated if these policies are not to be in conflict and to work at cross purposes. Independent policies, formulated by separate authorities at different levels, Union and national, and in different countries, are difficult to co-ordinate. The need for such co-ordination is perhaps the strongest argument for fiscal unification along with monetary unification, if the member countries want to maximize the effectiveness of their stabilisation policies.

NOTES

1. Vaubel (1978), using the variance of real exchange rates as a measure of the actual or potential costs of a currency area or monetary union, examines the real exchange-rate variability among the countries of the European Community and among cities or regions of three existing monetary unions – Germany, Italy and the US. All were found to have experienced real exchange-rate changes, the group of European countries more than the three individual countries.
2. The countries of the European Community have emphasised the problems of regional disparities within countries more than disparities between countries in their discussions of monetary union. Balassa (1975, p. 264) pointed out that the income disparities between some of the EC countries exceeded the regional disparities within these countries. Much of the discussion of regional problems in the EC has been concerned with movements of resources out of the problem areas and with the need for structural policies, neither of which are considered here.
3. Demand for a particular good depends upon prices of all goods and on total consumption expenditure, which in turn is a function of disposable income, interest rates, and wealth. The further assumptions – that total consumption expenditure is homogeneous of degree one in income and wealth, that demand for a particular good is homogeneous of degree zero in prices and nominal consumption expenditure and has a consumption elasticity of unity, and that goods are gross substitutes – guarantee that there are no 'perverse' responses, such as the existence of inferior goods or insufficient price elasticities for the Marshall–Lerner conditions. These assumptions also eliminate the need to define 'real' income or wealth, for demands can be expressed in nominal terms without implying money illusion. (The measure of the Union's 'real' product defines Union income in terms of a weighted average of the member countries' outputs; this does not refer to perceptions of consumers of their 'real' incomes.)
4. The symmetries assumed here are the extreme case of 'full goods–market symmetry', discussed in Allen and Kenen (1980, pp. 325–33).
5. The implied depreciation of the value of the foreign-currency bond, in terms of Union currency, exactly offsets the purchases of these bonds (capital outflow), leaving the nominal value of Union wealth unchanging through time. This must be so to maintain equilibrium in the asset markets. Increases in Union wealth affect demands for both money and bonds positively, while increases in average Union interest rates affect aggregate demands for members' bonds positively and demands for money negatively. As long as stocks of members' bonds and Union currency are unchanged, there is only one combination of nominal Union wealth and average Union interest rates

that will clear the asset markets. In order to maintain this level of Union wealth, the appreciation of the Union currency must equal the rate of capital outflow. This characteristic of the model is discussed for the case of a single country in Allen and Kenen (1980, pp. 168–9).

6. For the explicit algebraic solutions, see Allen and Kenen (1980, ch. 13). Although neither a Northern nominal wage increase nor a decline of Northern productivity is among the disturbances considered there, the outcomes from either disturbance are proportional to the outcomes in Allen and Kenen from a balanced-budget increase of Northern government spending for the Northern good, dG_1. The direct correspondence holds for all variables except nominal incomes, outputs, and employment. In the case of a Northern wage increase or fall in productivity, a nominal income change always equals the change in disposable income. The change in output can be derived by subtracting the percentage change in price from the percentage change in disposable income. The change in employment is in the same direction as the change in output.

7. The assumption that consumption demands for specific goods are homogeneous of degree zero in prices and in nominal consumption expenditure guarantees that the sum of the elasticities with respect to prices and nominal consumption must equal zero. The additional assumptions that the goods are gross substitutes, guaranteeing positive cross-price elasticities, and that the consumption elasticity is unity guarantee that the own-price elasticity is greater than unity in absolute terms.

8. In the steady state, because saving must be zero, consumption expenditure in each country equals that country's disposable income, which is a function of the domestic price level. The interest-rate and wealth factors influence consumption only insofar as they affect saving, and thus effectively fall out of the steady-state consumption functions.

9. Although this discussion focusses on the current-account and goods–market adjustments, the steady state described here presumes the necessary adjustments of the asset markets. Without the gradual flows of wealth through the capital and reserve accounts, saving levels and current accounts would not move to zero. The gradual loss of Union reserves and the net capital inflow to the Union under a pegged exchange rate produce a decline in Union wealth and a rise in the average interest rate, these effects being even more pronounced in the North, because it loses money to the South. The depreciation under a flexible exchange rate offsets the net capital inflow, leaving nominal Union wealth and average Union interest rates unchanged. But the flow of money from North to South means that Northern wealth declines and the Northern interest rate rises, with exactly offsetting movements in Southern wealth and interest rate. For a more detailed discussion of similar changes in interest rates and wealth, in response to a Northern balanced-budget increase of government spending, see Allen and Kenen (1980, pp. 486–91 and 517–19).

10. Changes in the asset markets show why the Union's real product must decline. In the steady state, the average Union interest rate is higher and nominal Union wealth is lower, as described in note 9. The higher interest rate and lower wealth would induce positive nominal saving for the Union, unless nominal Union income fell; nominal Union income must fall,

therefore, in order to achieve zero nominal saving for the Union in the steady state. The fall in nominal Union income combined with a rise in the Union price index implies a decline in the Union's real product.

11. Responses in the asset markets show why nominal Union income must return to its original level. The Union's nominal wealth and average interest rate remain unchanged, as described in note 9. The gradual sale of foreign-currency bonds is exactly offset by the appreciation of their value in terms of Union currency. With the Union's nominal wealth and average interest rate unchanged, the only way to guarantee zero Union saving is for nominal Union income to return to its original level. For a discussion of a similar response, in this case to an increase of balanced-budget spending in the North, see Allen and Kenen (1980, pp. 517–8).

12. The reasoning is as follows: (i) With nominal Union income unchanged, the sum of Northern and Southern nominal income changes equals zero. (ii) Because Northern nominal income initially fell by more than Southern nominal income, and subsequently rose at a slower rate, Northern nominal income must be lower than Southern nominal income in the new steady state. (iii) From (i) and (ii), Northern nominal income must have fallen and Southern nominal income must have risen by equal amounts. (iv) Southern output and price move in the same direction. Because Southern nominal income rises, Southern price and output both rise also. (v) The Northern price is higher than the Southern price, as deduced from Fig. 9.3, and, from (iii) above, Northern nominal income has fallen. Northern output must have declined, and proportionally more than the rise in the Northern price.

13. These issues, summarised here, are analysed in detail in Allen and Kenen (1980, Part v). The policy issues are also examined in Allen (1980), in the same graphical and summary approach that was used in this paper to discuss the effects of a labour-market disturbance.

REFERENCES

Allen, P. R. (1980), 'Controlling National Incomes in a Monetary Union' (mimeo).

Allen, P. R. and P. B. Kenen (1980), *Asset Markets, Exchange Rates, and Economic Integration* (Cambridge: Cambridge University Press).

Balassa, B. (1975), 'Structural Policies in the European Common Market', in B. Balassa (ed.), *European Economic Integration* (Amsterdam: North Holland).

Ishiyama, Y. (1975), 'The Theory of Optimum Currency Areas: a Survey', *International Monetary Fund Staff Papers*, vol. 22 (July) pp. 344–83.

Mundell, R. A. (1961), 'A Theory of Optimum Currency Areas', *American Economic Review*, vol. 51 (Dec) pp. 657–65.

Tower, E. and T. D. Willett (1976), *The Theory of Optimum Currency Areas and Exchange Rate Flexibility* (Essay in International Finance, no. 11) (Princeton, N. J. : Princeton University Press).

Vaubel, R. (1978), 'Real Exchange-rate Changes in the European Community', *Journal of International Economics*, vol. 8 (May) pp. 319–39.

Comments on Allen

M. J. ARTIS

Polly Allen's paper reports the results of an interesting exercise. It explores the consequences of asymmetrical supply-side shocks on the output, income and price levels of the members of a monetary union, within a carefully specified analytical framework. In detail, the results of course must necessarily reflect the very precise assumptions of the model from which they are derived. Nevertheless, the spirit of the exercise must be that the experiment and its results speak to realistic concerns. Indeed, the particular choice of disturbance for examination is a good one. The comparative absence of such shocks has been suggested as a criterion for an optimal currency area whilst, closer to home, some observers have foreseen particular dangers for a country like the UK, prone to nominal wage disturbances, in joining the EMU and particular benefits for countries like West Germany, which are not so prone. Subject to a qualification, this paper speaks to those concerns. The qualification is that what most observers have had in mind in speaking of the British and German interests in EMU is, actually, not so much disturbances around the trends of nominal variables themselves as divergencies between the trends. At the level of direct analogy, the disturbance examined here is more akin to the famous 'événetments de 1968'.

The most pertinent of the cases examined is perhaps that of the nominal wage push, when the union as a whole is floating against the rest of the world. This is the Keynesian case (or the 'case of Keynes' as we must now say), where the supply schedule for output is derived, for a given nominal wage, from an assumption of diminishing returns to variable labour inputs, capital being fixed. This case is distinct from the market-failure version of Keynesianism in that employers are always on their demand for labour schedule. The scope for fiscal policy is correspondingly smaller; in particular, demand management policies can only raise output by raising prices. The assumption is also made, however, that the union members are not so small in the markets for

216

their goods, or that their goods are sufficiently differentiated, as to permit them some exercise of market power in determining prices. This amendment to the conventional small open-economy assumption that prices are determined by world markets independently of the country's own supply is capable of restoring some power to fiscal policy, in the sense that prices *can* rise to permit output increases whereas in the conventional small open-economy case prices are set at world levels. Balance-of-payments equilibrium, given that capital flows respond to stock adjustment forces, requires current or trade account balance. (Possible hysteresis effects arising from cumulative departures of the current account from the trade account due to a change in interest income flows as a result of preceding wealth adjustment processes are blocked off here by assumption.) Wealth adjustment considerations, in turn, then require balanced budgets in equilibrium.

The stationary steady state solutions consulted exclude consideration of possible equilibria in which budget deficits are matched by continuous nominal depreciation, inflation, and inflation tax 'receipts' just sufficient to offset the wealth-augmenting effects of deficit financing.

These features indicate the steady state results reported in Table 9.1 of the paper, in which the nominal wage increase in country North winds up having depreciated the Union currency, shifting output and employment from North to South, raising the income of the Union as a whole, and depressing its output. The difference between output and income results is due to the assumption that the Union members have some market power over the prices of their exports. For North, it seems that membership of the Union results in part of the adjustment being taken by income and output, instead of by the exchange rate. South, on the other hand – at the cost of a higher price level – increases its output and employment. (This is the analogy one is tempted to draw with the British–German tension over EMU I cited earlier. South manages to keep a 'competitive' exchange rate here, but North does not.)

North has a case for asking for corrective aid, Union fiscal or regional policy. However, in the model (though not greatly distanced perhaps from EMU reality), fiscal policy is limited in nature and in being available only at national level. The only kind of policy compatible with balance-of-payments equilibrium is balanced budget policy. There is no non-tradeables sector for fiscal policy to get a grip on, and the best that can be done is to differentiate the import–domestic content of government expenditure from that of the private sector; added output can only be tempted forth by raising prices further. Even this scope would not exist were the Union members lacking in market power in their export markets.

The nominal wage push could, though, reasonably be interpreted as an attempt to secure real wage gains. In this case, North could not roll back the employment and output effects even if it were isolated enough to employ an exchange-rate policy of its own. The result would be either perpetual inflation (if it tried to) or a perpetually higher level of unemployment. If South interprets the wage shock in this light, it will not be very happy about relieving the seeming unemployment consequences of North's membership of the Union, because this is the consequence for North in any case. The scenario is not at all a happy one. Regional policy within a nation can cause many conflicts, but basic feelings of national identity help diffuse them. In a newly formed Union such feelings of identity are not well-formed, and the situation is not amenable to regional policy solutions even if these *are* the most appropriate ones. It seems idle to think up smart fiscal devices for doing the work of exchange rates (e.g. a 'regional' – i.e. Union member – employment premium) when the basic agreement for their necessity may not be forthcoming.

10 Fiscal Policy under EMU

T. M. RYBCZYNSKI

My first reaction to writing this chapter was to add a short sub-title 'In search of principles'. But I decided against the idea because the search for basic principles has been going on for some time. It has been going on both within the EC in the form of numerous memoranda and notes sent by the Commission to the Council; in the form of various studies commissioned by the Commission, among which the MacDougall Report (1977) was an outstanding piece of work likely to be referred to for many years to come; and, finally, in the now growing number of papers dealing with this topic as well as articles in serious journals throughout the world.

The title of my chapter enjoins me to discuss the principles and problems of fiscal policy under a fully-fledged and fully-consummated monetary union, that is when the size and growth of what may be described as a sort of *monetary base* is determined by a single authority, and monetary authorities of the constituent parts have no power to create money or reduce its rate of expansion.

A fully-fledged monetary union implies that its individual members will have to accept the stance of monetary policy, that is to say, the degree of availability of finance and its cost, as determined by the central monetary authority; they will have no powers of creating money either to cover deficits incurred by their governments or intended to stimulate demand; that individual members will have no powers to alter the external value of their currencies; but that they will retain the power of taxation and borrowing in domestic, union, overseas and international markets. The extent to which they will retain this power of taxation without sharing the proceeds with the central authority will be important in determining the thrust, character and impact of the fiscal policy; likewise the extent to which individual member-governments will be free to borrow funds and whether or not such borrowing will be formally guaranteed by the central authority or deemed to be guaranteed, are very important.

While the economic implications of sharing taxation and spending powers in unitary and federal states are discussed in the MacDougall Report and also numerous other publications, relatively little practical work is available as regards the borrowing powers of the central authority and the individual members of the monetary union.

If the problems of borrowing powers are disregarded, fiscal policy under a fully-fledged monetary union in essence becomes – as far as individual members are concerned – a regional policy. This subject raises important issues and it might be more beneficial and useful if I first examined how fiscal policy has developed in the European Community until now; secondly, the principles which have emerged and which appear to have been accepted explicitly and implicitly by the Community and its members; and, finally, the present position, and the prospects ahead, as far as the intellectual underpinnings are concerned.

Looking back I think it is fair to say that the Community's fiscal policy as it has evolved since its inception has been essentially of a functional type. In other words, the Community has been given financial resources to discharge certain specific functions arising from the well-defined activities it was required to undertake either in the original Treaty or as subsequently agreed by the Council of Ministers.

While the functional character of the Community's fiscal policy is characteristic of its development, one can distinguish two distinct phases of its evolution. The first covered the period until the beginning of the seventies and the second covered the period from the seventies to the eighties. During the first period, when membership covered the original six countries, the Community's fiscal policy was related almost entirely to agricultural policy and the Social Fund. The finance required for these purposes was obtained originally from contributions related to GNP and subsequently from agricultural levies and customs duties. It is useful to remember that this period covered the transitional years during which tariffs (and other obstacles) to the free movement of goods were being dismantled, and when the common external tariff was in the process of being gradually put in place. It is worth pointing out that even during that period a small proportion of funds spent on agriculture was explicitly devoted toward structural improvement in the weakest sections of this industry and, consequently, designed to improve the relative position of the regions in which they were situated; likewise, spending by the Social Fund was intended in accordance with the Treaty of Rome to increase the availability of employment and the geographical and occupational mobility of workers within the Community', and thus was not of a strictly functional type.

Thus fiscal policy during that period can be said to have comprised three elements: the strictly functional incomes policy in the agricultural sector; structural policy in the agricultural sector, and structural employment remedies in other sectors. This policy involved some members being net payers or net beneficiaries as far as the budgetary aspects were concerned. The budgetary consequences were then not questioned, presumably because member countries must have considered that non-fiscal benefits, economic and political, were sufficiently worthwhile and at least equal to the transparent budgetary cost for net contributors.

The second period of development of the Community's fiscal policy, beginning around 1970, was characterised by four main features. The first, which essentially is a semi-technical one but has also monetary, economic and political aspects, is the transition to 'own-resources' financing on the part of the Community. The second is the growing attention paid by the Community towards the disparities between total receipts and payments by the individual members and the adoption in 1976 of the so-called 'financial mechanism' intended to correct any disproportionate burden a member might be bearing in financing the Community. The third was an increasing emphasis given by the Community to the regional aspects of its financing reflected in the creation of the Regional Fund, and increasing attention attached to the spending on structural adjustment within existing function spending procedures and its regional aspects. The final feature was growing discussion – stimulated by the estimates produced by the Commission that its own resources would be insufficient to meet its spending if existing programmes continued unchanged – about the size, character and role of fiscal policy in the process of economic integration.

The transition to 'own-resources' financing was not completed until the beginning of 1980, even though originally it was intended to be fully in force in 1979. It marks an important point in the evolution of the Community in relation to both the functional character of public finance and its extension to non-functional areas. The functional character of receipts attaching to Customs duties and agricultural levies, emphasised by the Commission and agreed by the Council, derives from the Community's responsibility for trade and agricultural policies.

However, these sources of finance were and continue to be inadequate to cover spending on agriculture and had to be supplemented by members' agreeing to contribute up to 1 per cent of VAT – used also to finance spending on the Social Fund and the Regional Fund. This can be seen from examining the income and expenditure of the Community. On the spending side some 85 per cent of the budget, excluding the administrative cost of running the Community, represented in 1979 agricultural supports, some 5 per cent Regional Fund and 5 per cent Social Fund; on the income side about 50 per cent comes from agricultural levies and customs duties, the remaining 50 per cent from VAT. Thus receipts from VAT cover a substantial part of the functional expenditure incurred by the Community; in other words non-functional income now pays for a substantial part of functional expenditure.

This change in the functional character of finance has been accompanied by the disparity in net receipts or net payments of the individual members. Recognising that such a development can result in growing tensions, on equity grounds, the Community introduced a special financial mechanism intended to reduce such disparities. In doing so it acknowledged that changes in net balances involve consideration of ability to pay, determined by real per-capita income; and that should disparity become too great, a corrective mechanism should be set in force to remedy the situation. This mechanism, whose use was advocated by the Commission in 1980 to redress the position of the UK, was first put into operation by the decisions of the Council in May 1979 to reduce the UK's contribution in the three-year period ending 1982.

The adoption of the financial mechanism in the second phase of the development of fiscal policy in the Community has implied that in addition to the functional principles, and own-resources principle, full recognition is also given to the ability to pay by individual members, assessed in essence by reference to per-capita income, rate of growth in per-capita income and the balance-of-payments position.

Accompanying this development during the second phase was the emphasis on the regional aspect of the Community's policy. The regional aspect of the Community's activities was specifically mentioned in the preamble to the Treaty of Rome in the phrase 'desirous of strengthening the unity of their economies and of ensuring their harmonious development by diminishing both the disparities between the various regions and the backwardness of the less favoured regions'. Specially allocated regional spending programmes – as distinct from the regional elements of functional spending on agriculture and by way of the Social Fund – had not been translated into a fiscal programme until March 1975 when the Regional Fund was set up. The working of the Fund, which was originally governed by a quota system, was altered in 1978 by the introduction of a small 'non-quota' section, capable of being used outside the assisted areas at national level and enabling the Community to use fiscal policy in connection with other policies and, above all, in relation to structural adjustment.

By creating the Regional Fund the Community accepted and introduced specifically a regional dimension into its fiscal policy which, in addition to working within its framework and together with the national regional policies, gives some scope for the Community to initiate such policies itself with primary emphasis on structural adjustments. The increasing emphasis on regional policy and on the structural adjustment aspects of functional policies is an important development bearing directly on the conceptual approach towards fiscal policy under fully-fledged EMU and its evolution in the transitional period.

In brief, the development of fiscal policy in the second phase of its evolution has altered its character. This has happened in three main respects. First, on the receipts side, there has been a move away from contributions by members towards own-resources financing and, on the expenditure side, a limited move away from the almost entirely functional type of expenditure towards a greater emphasis on spending devoted to some structural adjustments, both in the functional area or the agricultural sectors as well as other areas. Second, the Community has accepted the principle that functional spending, in addition to being financed by revenues under the direct control of the Community, is also to be financed by members' surrendering unconditionally a small fraction of their tax receipts from a single source (VAT) calculated on the same basis. Third, the Community accepted the principle that net financial contributions by member states should have some relation to equity, or more precisely to their ability to pay, and that the disproportionate net payments which would otherwise occur should be corrected by recourse to a special mechanism.

The way fiscal policy developed in the second phase of its evolution has brought to the fore two basic questions as regards its role in the process of economic integration. These two issues, which have been examined and debated by students of fiscal policy, of economic unions and by policy makers, comprise, first, what should be the size of gross receipts (and payments) of the Community and their composition, and, second, what the net position of the individual members should be. The first issue came to the fore following the Commission's estimates that the Community's present source of revenue, i.e. own resources, would be inadequate to meet its expenditures if existing functional and other types of spending continued on the present basis, and that, if the Community is to remain financially solvent, existing sources of income must be supplemented and enlarged or the expenditures must be contained by altering the basis on which they are undertaken, or both. The second issue is that of the net position of individual members *vis-à-vis* the Community as regards fiscal transfer, that is to say the net balance of payments and receipts.

Analytically these two issues are separate and distinct, even though the character of gross payments and receipts will inevitably affect the net position of individual members. This is so because in the ultimate analysis, as in the case of tariffs, quotas and other obstacles to international trade, there is no type of revenue or spending which would have the same effect on all members so long as the production and consumption in member countries of a region are different – which is true of the members of the Community.

To comment briefly on the second problem first, which is bound to take priority in one version or another under fully-fledged EMU, there now appears to be strong and growing support for the view that fiscal policy in the Community, and indeed any Federation or Confederation, cannot be based on the principle of '*juste retour*', i.e. that no member or region should be a net loser or net gainer as far as fiscal transfers, as distinct from non-budgetary consequences of an advance towards economic integration, are concerned. The case against the principle of '*juste retour*' is that it would contradict one of the aims of the Community stated in the Treaty of Rome of 'strengthening the unity of the members' economies and of ensuring their harmonious development by diminishing both the disparities between the various regions and the backwardness of the less favoured regions'. This aim places upon the Community the task of so arranging its fiscal efforts as to favour poorer and less rapidly growing countries. The justification for this is that rich countries are better able to bear such burdens and that there is reason to believe that richer countries and regions with well-established, advanced and competitive industrial structure will, at least in the first instance, probably obtain greater non-budgetary benefits from free movements of goods and services than poorer countries which, by definition, have less competitive and less developed industrial and economic structures. Indeed, their resource, including human and physical capital, will probably be such as not to result in capital inflow into them, and it is questionable to what extent freedom of movement of labour, in the conditions as they exist now, is likely to result in workers moving to more prosperous areas. Thus, unless offset by special fiscal transfers undertaken by central authorities, the present characteristics of relatively poor countries and relatively poor regions can be expected to persist, and indeed possibly grow as a result of the introduction of the free movement of goods and services and of factors of production.

If it is accepted that public finance under monetary union should be so arranged as to place the poorer members in the position of being net receivers of fiscal transfers to offset the disadvantages to which they may be subjected outside the budgetary calculus, the question arises as to what the size and composition of such net transfers should be so that they would help to reduce the disparities not only in per-capita income but also in relative rates of growth.

Neither economic theory nor any applied studies give any firm guidance about the relative size or make-up of an optimum transfer that would be most effective in reducing the disparities in per-capita income and the rates of growth. All that can be said as regards the size of such net fiscal transfers is that it will be governed above all by the willingness of the richer countries to make contributions to such transfers, and that there would also be a maximum disparity beyond which net fiscal transfers become inescapable. The composition of net fiscal transfers raises difficult and indeed formidable questions as regards the relative importance attaching to differences in per-capita income and to differences in the relative rates of growth, and the impact such different types of transfer will have on the rate of growth in per-capita income.

Perhaps I should say here that, while there is a strong case for reducing the differences in both absolute levels and rates of growth in per-capita income, their close approximation as an aim is neither desirable nor practicable. Evidence available – as shown in the MacDougall Report, various studies produced by the Community since then, and published data for the US and Canada – indicates that there are considerable disparities among various regions in per-capita income and its growth, notwithstanding fiscal transfers within various countries, and that the process of economic growth does not as a rule lead to the elimination of such differences.

The optimum rate of economic growth is reached not under the balanced growth approach but under unbalanced growth – provided the imbalances are not too great. What appears to be desirable on economic grounds and practicable, whatever form the monetary union assumes, is that net fiscal transfers should be decided upon by reference to the minimum attainable differences in per-capita income and their rates of growth. The brutal truth is that, despite large advances made by economic science, economists – and for that matter politicians – do not know how to accelerate growth in developed countries.

What form should such net transfers assume? The MacDougall Report, which was mainly concerned with problems of reducing such disparities by way of built-in equalising and stabilising mechanisms, pointed to using public finance channelled to the Community that would work similarly to public finance in unitary and federal states. This mechanism is well known and described in the MacDougall Report, and I will not cover it here. However, it should be stressed that stabilisation and reduction in regional disparities of income through public finance, important though they are, by themselves do not appear to contribute to reducing the disparities in rates of growth in per-capita income, nor are they intended to do so. This is the task which tends to be entrusted to a large extent in national states to regional and similar policies. This appears to be the approach also advocated and employed by the Community.

Thus, fiscal policy under EMU should involve net fiscal transfer to poorer countries. The size of such transfers cannot be determined easily. In addition to comprising transfer of funds associated with specific function, they should also include a certain proportion of funds devoted specifically to the process of structural adjustment, especially in the context of regional policies as well as the structural elements of the functional policies. In addition to helping reduce disparities in the rate of growth in per-capita income, such an approach to net regional transfers would set in motion the forces of self-sustaining growth, reducing and eliminating the need for such net transfers once the minimum economically, socially and politically acceptable difference is attained.

So far I have commented on the net transfer to various regions within the monetary union, trying to emphasise the importance of a development-oriented element of spending by central authority forming a part of regional policy. This is not to dismiss the need for the income-stabilising and income-equalising functions which must inevitably form part of fiscal policy. But this raises the question of the relationship between gross and net transfers to various regions, and also the size and composition of gross revenues and expenditures.

The MacDougall Report (1977) shows that within both the unitary and federal states up to 40 per cent of regional disparities in per-capita income are eliminated by fiscal transfers involving in one way or another the principle of ability to pay on the one hand and needs on the other. The Report also brings out the re-distributive effects of the ratio of net transfers to gross transfers, and shows that even with a relatively small total central budget the income-equalising and stabilising effects can be quite large if the ratio of net transfers to gross transfers is large.

To what extent the net/gross ratio should be composed of regional policy elements designed to reduce the disparities in the rates of *growth* in per-capita income and of elements reducing the disparities in per-capita income is something about which we know very little. This of course comes out clearly in the appraisals of the effectiveness of regional policies over the past twenty-five years in the UK, which indicate that the impact of large net transfer of resources to poorer regions by way of specific grants and income-equalising transfers on relative rates of growth in per-capita income have been very modest indeed.

Thus we must admit that while we know how disparities in per-capita income can be reduced under EMU, we know relatively little about how to reduce disparities in the growth of per-capita income. Should the Community place greater emphasis on regional policies and, if so, what should it be? How important a role should be allocated to re-structuring parts of functional policies which are now growing, as shown by the adoption of an energy policy? These are questions requiring answers which at present cannot be given.

At the beginning of this chapter I said I thought that I should give it a subtitle 'In search of principles', but that I decided against it because the search is on. Let me conclude by saying that while the search for principles is on, it must be reinforced, reinvigorated and given additional momentum.

It is by clarifying the issues involved that the economics profession can make a contribution to solving the problems which face us now and will continue to face us before the EMU is consummated, and by doing so help policymakers to make faster progress towards the achievement of the aims of the Community.

REFERENCES

MacDougall D. *et al.* (1977) *Report of the Study Group on the Role of Public Finance in European Integration* (Brussels: Commission of the European Communities).

Comments on Rybczynski

A. M. EL-AGRAA

Let me start my discussion by making two subsidiary points. First, I would turn round what Mr Rybczynski says about large interregional transfers having made little difference to growth rates; it was because the structurally-determined components of the growth-rates already differed that the transfers were required, and one could argue that in relation to their size they were pretty effective. Second, I do think Mr Rybczynski is technically wrong in regarding the 'up to 1 per cent of the yield of a uniform VAT' as not an 'own resource', but this is metaphysics!

Mr Rybczynski's chapter makes a very useful contribution to this volume in three important respects. First, in discussing the historical evolution of the EC budget he has clearly demonstrated its functional nature, particularly on the expenditure side. Second, the chapter is very illuminating in highlighting the 'regional problem' as the basic consequence of the adoption of EMU. Finally, the chapter is correct to stress that 'while the search for principles is on, it must be reinforced, reinvigorated and given additional momentum'.

However, the chapter fails to satisfy its own aims. Mr Rybczynski assumes a fully-fledged monetary union and sets himself the task of discussing its full implications, yet the major part of the paper is about the historical evolution of EC fiscal policy. It would have been more appropriate to pursue the 'search for principles'. It seems to me that the only sensible way to highlight the main points of the chapter is by reminding ourselves of the meaning of a fully-fledged monetary union (his basic premise and starting point), the meaning of fiscal policy, and the implications of a fully-fledged monetary union for such policy.

Monetary integration has two essential components: an exchange-rate union and capital market integration. An exchange-rate union is established when member countries have what is *de facto* one currency. The actual existence of one currency is not necessary, however (though one could of course argue that the adoption of a single currency would guarantee the irreversibility of undertaking membership of a monetary union, which would have vast repercussions for the discussion of EMU as an actual union), because if member countries have permanently fixed exchange rates amongst themselves, the result is effectively the same.

Convertibility refers to the permanent absence of all exchange controls for both current and capital transactions, including interest and dividend payments (and the harmonisation of all relevant taxes and measures affecting the capital market) within the union. It is of course absolutely necessary to have complete convertibility for trade transactions, otherwise an important requirement of the customs union aspect of the EC would be threatened, namely the promotion of free trade between members of the union. Convertibility for capital transactions is related to free factor mobility and is therefore an important aspect of capital market integration, which is necessary for the common market element of the EC.

Monetary union, therefore, takes place when an exchange-rate union is accompanied by capital market integration. The definition implies an explicit harmonisation of monetary policies, a common pool of foreign exchange reserves and a single central bank. Due to space limitations one cannot go into reasons for the inclusion of these elements; those interested should consult Corden (1972, 1977) and El-Agraa (1980). One only needs to stress that these elements hint at the advantages of adopting a single currency.

Let me now turn to fiscal policy. Very widely interpreted, fiscal policy comprises a whole corpus of 'public finance' issues: the relative size of the public sector, taxation and expenditure, and the allocation of public sector responsibilities between different tiers of government. Hence fiscal policy is concerned with a far wider area than that commonly associated with it, namely, the aggregate management of the economy in terms of controlling inflation, employment levels, and sustaining or boosting economic growth. When considering EC fiscal policy, there are certain elements of the international dimension that need spelling out and there are also interregional (intra-EC) elements that have to be introduced.

Internationally, it has always been recognised that taxes (and equivalent instruments) have similar effects to tariffs on the international flow of goods and services. Other devices have also been recognised as imposing similar distortions on the international flow of factors of production.

In the particular context of the EC it should be remembered that its formation, at least from the economic viewpoint, was meant to facilitate the free and unimpeded flow of goods, services and factors between the member nations. Since tariffs are not the only distorting factor in this respect, the proper establishment of intra-EC free trade necessitates the removal of all non-tariff distortions that have an equivalent effect. Hence, the removal of tariffs may give the impression of establishing free trade inside the EC, but this is by no means automatically guaranteed since the existence of sales taxes, excise duties, corporation taxes, income taxes, etc., may impede this freedom. The moral is that not only tariffs but *all* equivalent distortions must be eliminated or harmonised.

Having defined a fully-fledged monetary union and EC fiscal policy it should be quite plain that these cannot be separated: a common central bank which possesses the common pool of foreign exchange reserves and is responsible for the co-ordination of the monetary policies of the members necessarily influences, and is in turn influenced by, fiscal policy. For instance, a fiscal decision regarding regional distribution in any particular area will have its clear guidelines for the EC central bank operations.

However, these are very broad considerations. Let me be more specific. If one stood nearer to the pure economic end and asked how one would organise a European Community from first principles, the answer would be: free movement of goods, services and factors of production, central control of public finance (uniform, progressive taxation except in so far as special variations are introduced on regional policy grounds – congestion taxes etc.), expenditure in accordance with criteria of personal needs for public goods, for example, education, retraining, environmental services. This is the long view to which I subscribe, but some would argue that it is so long that its value at compound discount is rather low! Mr Rybczynski starts from where we are now and takes some account of political constraints, but the limitation of this is that it does not throw much light either on the long-term objective or on the path taken to the Promised Land.

There is an awkward middle ground which corresponds to the reality of most federations and unitary states (with local government authorities). Local (and federal state) governments do not want to be mere agents of the central government, providing the amounts of public goods that are prescribed by central policy; they want some revenue sources which they can vary themselves, even if they do rely mainly on central government grants. The division of the fisc therefore becomes of paramount importance. This is partly inconsistent with free movement and possibly also with optimum progressiveness, but it has to exist so long as there are local as opposed to either individual or central allegiances. It all stems from people being imperfectly mobile by inclination. How then does this help in a clear assessment of Mr Rybczynski's main points? If one concentrates on the longer-term objective, one realises that the basic problem discussed in the paper regarding the distinction between per capita income and growth in per capita income is a non-problem, since in a fully-fledged monetary union the monetary and fiscal authorites will be constantly and jointly engaged in pursuing the set aims. Also, given this long-term perspective, one should emphasise that *'juste retour'* as discussed in the paper is actually misconceived, since the main manifestation of adopting EMU is the 'regional problem' in the dynamic sense: the principle would implicitly allow member countries complete freedom to pursue their own fiscal policies without regard to their Community-wide monetary implications (Corden, 1972, 1977); but this does not follow if the central authority is given the task of managing the EC economy. If one adopts the shorter term nationalistic-indulgence perspective, it is clear that the EC is following the wrong path.

REFERENCES

Corden, W. M. (1972), *Monetary Integration* (Essays in International Finance, no. 93) (Princeton, N. J.: Princeton University Press).
——(1977), *Inflation, Exchange Rates and the World Economy* (Oxford: Oxford University Press).
El-Agraa, A. M. (1980), *The Economics of the European Community* (Oxford: Philip Allan).

11 EMU: the Political Implications

DAVID MARQUAND

Monetary union has twice been a live issue in the politics of the European Community – first, in the late sixties and early seventies, when the Werner Group proposed a phased plan for the achievement of monetary union by stages, and when member governments rashly committed themselves to full-scale monetary union by 1980; and, second, in the late seventies, when Mr Roy Jenkin's Florence speech 're-launching' the concept in October 1977 was followed not more than a year later by the decision to set up the European Monetary System. Both in the first, 'Werner', phase and in the second, 'Jenkins', phase, the most enthusiastic advocates of monetary union clearly appreciated that it had immense political and institutional implications. The final report of the Werner Group explicitly said that in the final stage there would have to be a 'centre of decision for economic policy' and a 'Community system for the central banks' (Commission of the European Communities, 1970, pp. 12–13). Jenkins (1978a) did not go quite as far as this, but in his Florence speech he said that monetary union 'would imply a major new authority to manage the exchange rate, external reserves and the main lines of internal monetary policy'; and in a speech to the European Parliament a few weeks later, he declared that in a monetary union 'two of what are generally regarded as the more important functions of a modern government – control over the exchange rate and control over the money supply – would be exercised by a central Community institution instead of by governments' (Jenkins, 1978b). Unofficial bodies were equally aware of the political implications. The Commission of the European Communities (1975) went furthest. In a monetary union, it declared, 'national governments put at the disposal of the common institutions the use of all the instruments of monetary policy and of economic policy whose action should be exercised for the

232

Community as a whole'; this implied a 'European political authority, an important Community budget and an integrated system of central banks'. The MacDougall Group of economists, which reported on the role of public finance in European integration in April 1977, did not itself say much about the political implications. In a working paper on the budgetary powers of the European Parliament, however, O'Donoghue argued that, if the Community Budget were increased in the way that the Group thought necessary, a political authority of some kind would have to be created to determine how the money should be spent (Commission of the European Communities, 1977, vol. ii, pp. 564–72).

Yet, by a revealing paradox, both in the comings and goings which followed the publication of the Werner Report, and in the more recent transactions which culminated in the establishment of the EMS, the authorities involved kept the political and institutional implications firmly in the background. The Commission's Communication to the Council following the Werner Report made no reference to political union, and said nothing about the need for a 'centre of decision'; by the same token, the Council's decision of March 1971, expressing the Community's political will to establish monetary union by the end of the decade, did not provide for any institutional expression of that will. Much the same was true of the second 'Jenkins' phase of the monetary union debate. The EMS fell far short of monetary union; in striking contrast to what had happened during the 'Werner' phase, the governments which set it up did not even commit themselves to full-scale monetary union at any stage in the future. In these circumstances, it is not surprising that they said nothing about the institutional and political implications of a move towards full-scale monetary union, should the EMS eventually develop in that direction. The Commission's attitude was more surprising. The central premise of Mr Jenkins's Florence speech was that monetary union had to be taken neat or not at all: that there was no point in trying to construct a half-way house since it would sooner or later collapse. The EMS was a half-way house; on Mr Jenkins's logic, therefore, such value as it had lay in its capacity to develop into full-scale monetary union at a later stage. Yet in the discussions between the Florence speech in October 1977 and the decision to set up the EMS in December 1978, the Commission carefully refrained from drawing attention to institutional aspects of the question. Moreover, though Werner and Jenkins both explicitly recognised that monetary union would involve a major political step, and, as such represent, in Mr Jenkins's words 'a formidable challenge to our institutional inventiveness', neither devoted much time or energy to exploring the nature of that political step, or to discussing what sort of institutional arrangements would be necessary either during the transition stage towards monetary union or in the final stage of full-scale union when it finally came to pass. The Werner Group suggested that its 'centre' of economic decision-making should be made responsible to a directly-elected European Parliament. In his speech to the European Parliament in January 1978, Mr Jenkins saw 'a wide range of possibilities: at one end, a body under the continuing and permanent surveillance of finance ministries; at the other something like a Federal Reserve Board which, I add in passing, is responsible to Congress rather than to the Executive of the United States'. The Werner group's suggestions, however, amounted to little more than hints and Mr Jenkins's to little more than an aside. On the official level, in other words, even among those who were prepared explicitly to recognise that monetary union had a significant political and institutional dimension, discussion of these political and institutional aspects did not go beyond generalities.

Almost certainly, the reason was two-fold. In the early seventies, France was in favour of monetary union itself but was unwilling to accept the supranational implications of the Werner Report. The Commission and the other member states feared that if they insisted on an explicit commitment to the institutional changes advocated in the Report, the French would take fright and the whole project would have to be abandoned. By the late seventies, supranationalists were, if anything, thinner on the ground than at the beginning of the decade, and opponents of supranationalism thicker. Not only the French, but the British and perhaps even the Danes could be expected to oppose institutional changes on Werner lines; and it was far from clear that even the Germans would support them. It must have seemed to the Commission that it was better to settle for the EMS, which was at least a modest step in the right direction, than to insist on the qualitative leap which Mr Jenkins had advocated at Florence, and risk getting nowhere; in these circumstances, it could plausibly be argued that discussion of the political and institutional implications of full-scale monetary union would be, at best, premature and, at worst, damaging.

But that is only part of the explanation. Where the federalists of the late forties had thought in terms of mobilising political forces and creating political structures, the 'neofunctionalist' conception of integration, on which the Community's founding fathers operated for most of the time, was, in an important sense, anti-, or at any rate, apolitical. The architects of the Coal and Steel Community of the early fifties and the Economic Community of the late fifties were trying to set in motion an irreversible process, with an irresistible dynamic, through which national governments and national parliaments would be more and more tightly constrained. Once integration had been achieved in one field, they imagined, it would 'spill over' into neighbouring fields. As it spilled, national Governments would find themselves unable to take decisions, or at any rate to make their decisions stick, in an ever-expanding cluster of policy areas. In respect of policy area after policy area, they would sooner or later be forced to conclude that effective decisions could be taken only on the European level. Integration was rather like tobogganing. Once the toboggan had been given an initial push, the governments, parliaments and peoples perched on it would be carried along willy-nilly, by the momentum of the integration process itself. Arguments about the political and institutional implications of the process were to be avoided, since they could only slow the toboggan down. The important thing was to get it moving, and that could best be done by patiently removing the technical obstacles to its descent, not by engaging in time-wasting theoretical disputes about its goal or direction.

Hence the Community's institutional structure, in which the role of 'motor of integration' was assigned to an appointed Commission, whose authority was derived partly from the text of the treaty establishing it and partly from the technical skills of its members and staff rather than from popular election. Hence, too, the Commission's increasingly bureaucratic and diminishingly political conception of its own task (Coombes, 1970). For although it attempted to play a political role in the early years of the Community, when Dr Hallstein was President, it was soon brought to heel by President de Gaulle. Since the mid-sixties it has shrunk from political conflicts with member governments, and has made few attempts to mobilise political forces in support of its policies. Its essentially technocratic and apolitical approach to the issues raised by the Werner Report and later by Mr Jenkins's Florence speech was thus all of a piece with its approach to almost all the policy areas with which it deals, and for that matter all of a piece with the logic underlying its own creation.

The central contention of this paper is that that logic and that approach – however appropriate they may have been to the problems of 'negative' integration, which were uppermost in the early years of the Community – are profoundly inappropriate to the enormously more difficult measures of 'positive' integration implied by a commitment to monetary union. The Werner group may have drawn exaggerated conclusions from its analysis, but it is hard to quarrel with its judgement that monetary union must, at any rate, entail 'the total and irreversible convertibility of currencies, the elimination of margins of fluctuations in exchange rates, the irrevocable fixing of parity rates and the complete liberation of movements of capital'. The key words in that sentence are, of course, 'irreversible' and 'irrevocable'. Both imply big reductions in the freedom of action of member governments, rules to ensure that they do not recover their freedom at a later date and – most important of all – an authority or authorities to ensure that the rules are obeyed. Though this is more controversial, it seems fairly clear that both also imply an authority or authorities to discharge at least some of the functions which will no longer be discharged at the national level. The net effect must be a big transfer of power – and therefore of political activity – from the national to the supranational level. That, in turn, implies far-reaching changes in the Community's present institutional structure.

Monetary union, it is worth remembering, is not as novel an idea as is sometimes imagined. The nineteenth century saw three attempts at monetary union in Europe – a short-lived monetary union between Austria and the German *zollverein*; a rather more durable 'Latin' union between France, Belgium, Switzerland and Italy; and a Scandinavian union which lasted for a generation. The Austro-German union was destroyed by the war between its members. The other two fell apart because the members retained the freedom to follow independent policies, and in the end used it in a way that made continuation of the union impossible. It is true, of course, that conditions have changed since the nineteenth century. But it is hard to see why the changes should have made it any less likely that the parties to a monetary union will sooner or later behave in ways which are incompatible with its survival if they have retained the freedom to do so. For there is an ominous, but instructive, parallel between monetary union and disarmament. If governments did not want arms, disarmament would be easy, but it would also be unnecessary: it is necessary because it is difficult. If the parties to a monetary union knew that there would never be any question of their changing their exchange rates against each other, they would not need to establish a union. It is because they know that they are likely to be under pressure either to change their exchange rates or to allow the rates to change that it is worth their while to agree to make such changes impossible. The trouble is that the pressures which lead to exchange-rate changes in the absence of such an agreement will still be in existence after the agreement has been made. Indeed, the value of the agreement is proportionate to the strength of the pressures: monetary union, it is worth remembering, became an issue in Community politics only when the Bretton Woods system was beginning to break down and when the consequential monetary disturbances began to call the existing *acquis communautaire* into question. By the same token, one of the main arguments for the EMS was that some dramatic step was needed to create a zone of stability in a continent where stability would otherwise be lacking. If the pressures are not to prevail in the future as they have prevailed in the past, the governments concerned will have to behave differently. To assume that they will behave differently merely because they have promised to do so is to assume that their unwillingness to break their words will be a strong enough constraint on their behaviour to outweigh the pressures. To put it at its lowest, that assumption does not square well with the experience of the last 15 years.

It is sometimes said that the freedom of action which the parties to a monetary union would have to surrender is nowadays illusory: that, in Western Europe at any rate, governments no longer enjoy real, as opposed to formal, sovereignty over their exchange rates, or even over their monetary policies, in any case. Clearly, there is something to be said for that view. As the last British Labour Government discovered, control over the exchange rate is very far from conferring complete freedom of action on its possessor, and it is not possible to follow a loose money-supply policy for very long if the rest of the world is following a tight one. But it would be a mistake to push that argument very far. As Laidler shows elsewhere in this book, a country with a floating exchange rate can at least choose its own rate of inflation. This is not the place for a long discussion of the social and political forces which lead different societies to opt for different inflation rates, and a non-economist would in any case be unwise to venture into such contentious territory. To put it at its lowest, however, it seems clear that the forces at work are both complex and powerful; and that if Laidler is right in thinking that entering a monetary union entails giving up the right to determine one's own rate of inflation, it follows that these forces will sooner or later impinge on the authority or authorities to which that right has been transferred. If the UK joined a monetary union, the authorities of which had a 'German' view of what the rate of inflation ought to be, the forces which have hitherto produced a 'British' rate of inflation in the UK would not suddenly disappear. They would make themselves felt in the union, just as they used to make themselves felt outside it. They would either prevail, or not prevail. If they prevailed, the Germans would not find themselves moving in a 'British' direction against their will. If they did not, a good many people in the UK would presumably find themselves subject to disciplines which they did not wish to accept.

Governments, moreover, do not at present behave as though they had no effective sovereignty over these matters: if they did, stability would have arrived already, and there would be no need for special measures to establish it. It can, of course, be argued that governments behave in the way that they do merely because they are too stupid or too short-sighted to recognise how limited their real freedom of action is. But even if that is true, there is no reason to believe that they will suddenly cease being stupid and short-sighted merely because they have promised to behave more wisely in future. In fact, the statement is only half true. Thanks to the monetary instability of the seventies, to the growing interdependence of the economies of the EC and perhaps also to the growing ability of wage bargainers to see through the 'money illusion', member governments of the Community have less freedom to do what they want in the exchange-rate and monetary fields than they once had. But it does not follow that they have no freedom at all. Both on the money supply and on the exchange rate, after all, the Thatcher Government's policy differs markedly from its predecessor's; even in government, the latter's policy was by no means identical with that being followed at present. Their policies differ because they have different constituencies and different ideologies, and because, as a result, they have made different trade-offs between various objectives of economic policy. The Government may find it convenient to suggest that it has no alternative but to act as it is doing: governments frequently find it convenient to make such suggestions, and the last Government said much the same about its (different) policies. The suggestion is nevertheless misleading. It is Sir Geoffrey Howe, not God, or even the Market, who is keeping interest rates and the exchange rate up. He could lower interest rates if he wanted to, and if he did the exchange rate would probably fall as well. If the Opposition came to power it might discover that the changes it is currently advocating yielded fewer benefits than expected, and imposed more costs. But it would still be free to make them. In a monetary union, such questions would not be decided on the national level at all.

This example shows, moreover, not just that the powers which the parties to a monetary union would have to surrender are real, though limited, but that their exercise (or non-exercise) is inherently controversial. In Federal Germany there seems to be a fair degree of political consensus, not perhaps on the details of exchange-rate and monetary policy but at any rate on the assumptions underlying them. That consensus may perhaps be fortified by the constitutional position of the German Bundesbank, as an independent authority free of government control, but it is unlikely to have been caused by it. There is no such consensus in France, Italy or the UK, and no reason to believe that the ideological divisions which prevent consensus at present would suddenly disappear if the governments of those countries joined a monetary union. There, decisions on the exchange rate and the money supply will be vulnerable to controversy, and the decision-makers subject to attack, no matter where the decisions are taken. The notion that monetary policy can somehow be 'taken out of politics' has obvious attractions for the authorities charged with its management, and may well have wider advantages as well. But it is hard to see how that notion can be anything more than an academic fancy in a society with a Communist Party as powerful as those of Italy and France, or a trade-union movement with the political and economic attitudes of the British. At present, the controversies are settled on the national level. In a monetary union, they would be settled on a supranational level. It would be as unreasonable for a British citizen to blame the London Government for the rate of interest in the UK as it is for a Mancunian to blame the Greater Manchester Council for the rate of interest in Manchester. But one of the reasons why the Greater Manchester Council is not blamed is that aggrieved Mancunians have someone else to blame instead; that there is an identifiable Government in London which is known to be responsible for decisions of this kind, whose right to take them is accepted even by those who disagree with them and which can be thrown out at the next election. If there were no identifiable Government in London, but only an anonymous committee of borough treasurers, the Greater Manchester Council almost certainly would be blamed; and if members of the Greater Manchester Council found that they were being blamed for the borough treasurers' decisions they would be forced, in self-defence, to claw back the power which they had transferred to the borough treasurers. If controversies over the exchange rate and the money supply are to be settled on the supranational level, there must be a supranational institution or institutions capable of settling them – capable, that is to say, of making its decisions stick in the face of opposition from those who are disadvantaged by or disagree with them.

Budgetary considerations point in the same direction. As the MacDougall Group pointed out, in most modern nation states – and, for that matter, in developed federal states – the weaker regions or states are shielded from the adverse balance-of-payments effects of monetary union with the stronger ones by substantial flows of public finance. No

European Monetary Union would survive for long unless it created a similar shield. The MacDougall Group estimated that resources could be redistributed on a sufficient scale from the stronger economies to the weaker ones if the Community budget were made deliberately redistributive and if it were expanded so as to account for between five and seven per cent of total Community GDP (Commission for the European Communities, 1977, vol. I). That figure is, of course, very much smaller than the equivalent in any existing national or federal state. Nevertheless, the 'MacDougall' budget would still be more than five times as big as the existing Community budget, and would require a substantial development of new Community policies. That, too, implies institutions to decide what the policies should be and how the money should be spent. These institutions, too, would have to make controversial decisions, benefiting some regions and groups at the expense of others; their decisions would not stick unless the decision-makers could defend themselves against attack, and unless their right to make them were accepted by those affected.

The Community's existing structure must be examined against this background. The founding fathers seem to have imagined that the integrationist toboggan which they hoped to set in motion would lead, sooner or later, if not to outright federation then at least to something not far short of it. After a transition stage, most Council decisions were to be taken by a complicated system of weighted majority voting. Since Commission proposals could be amended by the Council only if the Council were unanimous, this would enhance the Commission's influence and authority, and, *a fortiori*, the influence and authority of the Assembly, to which it was accountable. At some unspecified, but presumably fairly early, stage in the process, the Assembly was to be directly elected. Majority voting would change the whole character of the Council of Ministers. It would cease to be a kind of standing intergovernmental conference, and become something much more akin to a legislative body – to an embryo upper house or Chamber of States, in President Hallstein's words, on the model of the early US Senate or perhaps of the German Bundesrat (Hallstein, 1972, p. 68). Direct elections, meanwhile, would turn the Assembly into an embryo lower house or House of Representatives. The Commission would presumably be the embryo Government, accountable to its directly-elected Parliament as real governments are accountable to theirs. Thanks to the 1966 'Luxembourg compromise', however, the Treaty provisions on majority voting were never properly implemented. The Council of Ministers did not change in character, and the Commission did not gain the extra influence and authority which majority voting in the Council would have given it. It still retained its Treaty-conferred monopoly of the right of initiative. Increasingly, however, it eschewed the role of embryo government. More and more, the Council of Ministers became the real centre of power in the Community; more and more, the Council became a forum for intergovernmental negotiations of the traditional kind rather than a Community institution, with a coherent view of the Community interest. Increasingly, too, real decision-making took place on the margins of the Community structure, or even outside it altogether. Increasingly, it is by the European Council, rather than by the Commission or even by the Council of Ministers, that really important initiatives have been taken – not least, the decision to set up the EMS. Yet the European Council is unknown to the Treaty, and does not answer to any Community institution.

Clearly, then, the Community is not a federal state, or even a quasi-federation. There is no government, even in embryo. The Council of Ministers consists of a floating population of national ministers, with different ministers attending different specialist Councils, most of whom are concerned with Community affairs only spasmodically. In practice, the Council often takes decisions by a majority, but even when it does so, its proceedings are almost always conducted in the shadow of a possible veto. The Commission exercises some governmental functions, but only some. In any case, it is not elected, and therefore lacks the authority which is one of the essential attributes of a government. Although the Commission is accountable to and removable by the European Parliament, Commissioners are more anxious to keep on good terms with the governments which appointed them and which have the power to re-appoint them (or to appoint them to other positions), than to win or hold the confidence of a Parliament with only a negligible influence on their personal careers. Still less is there a clear dividing line between the Community sphere and the national sphere, as there would be in a federal state. The Treaty no longer provides much guidance. It committed its signatories to sweeping measures of 'negative' integration and to a few measures of 'positive' integration. Most, though not all, of its 'negative' commitments have been carried out, but so far the only important measure of 'positive' integration is the Common Agricultural Policy. In spite of the Treaty, the Community still lacks a common transport policy and has hardly begun to co-ordinate national economic policies.

Nor, however, is the Community a coalition of states. Community laws take precedence over national laws, and the Community Court over national courts. The *acquis* of the last twenty-two years is now, in effect, entrenched law in the member states, and cannot be altered by national legislation (House of Lords, 1973). Since 1975, the Community has been financially independent of the member states, its revenues being derived, not (as the present British Government has sometimes appeared to imagine) from national contributions, but from its own resources. None of this has a parallel in any other international organisation. Nor does the 'supranational' element in the Community's institutional structure and decision-making. With all its weaknesses, the Commission exists, and plays a central part in the Community's legislative process. It also plays crucial parts in other aspects of Community life – for example, in trade negotiations with extra-Community countries or in deciding whether or not to bring infraction proceedings against a member state in breach of its obligations under Community law. On a different and more intangible level, moreover, the old functionalist dynamic still has considerable constraining force. The fact that the Community *is* a Community – that virtually all Community officials and a great many national officials share the same '*communautaire*' ideology; that the Permanent Representatives and their delegations live and work cheek by jowl with the Commission, in the same, small Eurovillage; that some interests in all members states are now articulated at the Community as well as the national level; that Community business flows on, covering a wide range of subjects, and that member governments therefore know that if they are to have their way tomorrow they have to make concessions today and that if they have had their way today they will probably have debts to pay tomorrow – exerts a constant, hidden pressure on member governments, countervailing the centrifugal pressures which make themselves felt in national capitals.

Community decision-making, then, is neither national nor supranational, but a baffling amalgam of, or perhaps half-way house between, the two. Three consequences follow. The first is that it is only dubiously and fitfully accountable either to the public, in whose names decisions are taken, or to their parliamentary representatives. The second is that it is not likely to become accountable unless the whole institutional structure is changed. The third is that, in the absence of such changes, it is equally unlikely to be able to cope with the political strains which monetary union would generate.

The community's parliamentary institutions operate either on the national or on the supranational level, and are ill-equipped to venture into the intervening no-man's-land, where most Community business is transacted. The European Parliament can call the Commission to account through questions, debates and the threat of a vote of censure. Through its committees, and still more through informal contacts between its staff and the Commission staff, it probably has more influence on the 'pre-legislative' phase of Community policy-making than Westminster MPs have on the UK equivalent (Marquand, 1979, ch. 3). Yet even in its relations with the Commission, the European Parliament operates within fairly narrow limits, some formal and others informal. In the first place, the Commission is collectively accountable, not individually. Parliament can censure only the whole Commission, not individual Commissioners. There is no equivalent to the Westminster motion to reduce an individual Minister's salary. Thus, lazy or incompetent Commissioners – and, what is much more important, lazy or incompetent Directorates-General – can shelter behind their hardworking and competent colleagues. In any case, censure motions require a two-thirds majority of the total membership to pass – a larger majority than any post-war British Government has had at Westminster. More significant than these formal limits, however, is the fact that, from the earliest days of the Coal and Steel Community, the High Authority and later the Commission, on the one hand, and the Assembly, on the other, have seen each other as allies, not as adversaries or antagonists. Most MEPs have wanted to support the Commission, not to embarrass it; to prod it into taking further action, not to criticise the actions it has already taken. The result is that Parliament's attempts to hold the Commission to account contain a large element of shadow boxing.

In any case, the European Parliament's ability to hold the Commission to account is nothing like as valuable as it would have been had the founding fathers' toboggan proceeded as planned. What matters now is influence over the Council and, even more perhaps, influence over the strange, bureaucratic limbo between the Council and the Commission. The European Parliament faces formidable obstacles in its search for this. To be sure, it does have some power over the Community budget. As became clear in December 1979, this enables it to throw the Community process into considerable confusion, and so to force member governments to negotiate with it, even if not to do what it wants. Given skill and determination, moreover, its budgetary powers might be used to extract changes of policy – not necessarily in big, set-piece battles, but in small guerrilla skirmishes unreported by the press. By the same token, Parliament could use its power to censure the Commission as a lever to acquire a say in the appointment of the

Commission President, or perhaps even of all Commissioners. A really determined Parliament might use the same weapon to force the Commission to give it a share in the right of initiative. Treaty amendment would be needed to give Parliament a formal right of initiative of its own, but there is nothing in the Treaties to stop the Commission from adopting Parliament's initiatives as its own, or from putting them to the Council thereafter. Thus the *simpliste* notion that the European Parliament has no worthwhile powers at all, and that its role in Community decision-making cannot be enhanced without a fundamental change in the Treaties, is wide of the mark.

But all this is in the future conditional, not in the present. It would be absurd to pretend that Community decision makers are accountable to the European Parliament at this moment. Indeed, it is difficult to see how the Council of Ministers ever could be, for the obvious reason that it consists of national Ministers, who are separately accountable to their own national parliaments. Even if the Council evolved into a Community 'upper house', on the lines hinted at by President Hallstein, it would not be *accountable* to the European Parliament, any more than the US Senate is accountable to the house of Representatives. The future conditional can be turned into the present, moreover, only if a majority (or, more probably, a series of majorities) in the Parliament wish it to do so. Such majorities may emerge; it was because such a majority emerged during the arguments over the 1980 Community Budget that Parliament voted as it did in December 1979. But, as that example itself suggests, such majorities are likely to be evanescent. The MEPs who then voted overwhelmingly for rejection later accepted a Budget differing only marginally from the one they rejected seven months before. Almost certainly, the reason is that the December majority reflected only the institutional ambitions of the MEPs who composed it, rather than pressures from their parties or constituents. It would be wrong to suggest that rebellious parliamentary majorities will always crumble in that way. But if they do not, it will be because the pressures which have brought them into existence have also made themselves felt at the national level. If the pressures are felt at the national level, the Council will itself be affected by them sooner or later, and will presumably modify its policy without any great battle with Parliament.

There is, in short, no automatic toboggan slide to accountability on the Community level. What of the national level? National parliaments have responded to Community membership in a wide variety of ways. In France and Luxembourg, parliament has, for all practical purposes, no special machinery to deal with Community affairs. In Denmark, a special committee of the Folketing has been set up, which has to approve the negotiating briefs which Danish ministers take to the Council, and to give its approval if a change in the Commission proposal makes it necessary to change the brief. The British House of Commons has set up a kind of parliamentary sieve, designed to ensure that all important Commission proposals are debated on the floor of the House before the Council takes a decision on them. In the German Bundestag, the Dutch Second Chamber and the Italian Chamber of Deputies, Community business is scrutinised by ordinary committees. The House of Lords, the Belgian House of Representatives, the Italian Senate and the German Bundesrat have set up special committees on Community affairs, with varying terms of reference. In Ireland, a joint committee of both Houses operates in much the same way as the special committee in the British House of Lords (House of Lords, 1978).

On closer inspection, however, it emerges that a national parliament faced with the problems posed by Community membership has four options (not, of course, mutually exclusive) from which to choose. It can fail to differentiate between Community issues and 'normal' issues, and rely on its customary procedures. It can try to tie its ministers down in advance of Council meetings, as the Folketing does. It can try, as the House of Lords does, to influence its government at an early stage in the community's legislative process, before firm proposals have gone to the Council, and leave it to the government to decide what to do when the Council meets. Or it can try to bring influence to bear on the government at a later stage, when a decision is more or less imminent. It also emerges, however, that none of these options is particularly satisfactory. The first is unsatisfactory because Community issues are not 'normal'. The second is unsatisfactory because, in practice, it merely substitutes one unaccountable body for another. The Market Relations Committee of the Folketing undoubtedly exerts tight control over Danish ministers. But in order to do this, it has to meet in secret; otherwise ministers could not divulge their negotiating tactics to it. The system works because its members are leading figures in their respective parties, and can therefore 'deliver' the Folketing at large (Fitzmaurice, 1976). It is less a mechanism for ensuring parliamentary accountability than a kind of mini-coalition government concerned with only one aspect of politics.

The last two options are less unsatisfactory than the first two, but neither goes to the heart of the matter, and both suffer from the same built-in contradiction. The purpose of both is to bring influence to bear on government, either early or late, while leaving it to government to decide what to do once the influence has been brought. But influencing someone does not make him accountable. In any case, if the government can be trusted to pursue the national interest as it thinks best during Council meetings, why not trust it to decide for itself what the national interest is before the meeting has begun? And if it cannot be trusted to decide what the national interest is before the Council assembles, why should it be trusted to defend that interest thereafter? This contradiction springs, of course, from the very nature of the Community; and that, in turn, suggests not only that it is impossible to make a Community process accountable to a national parliament, but that it will remain impossible so long as the Community retains its present form. Accountability depends on clarity. If decision-makers are to be accountable, someone must always be in a position to use Harry Truman's motto, 'the buck stops here'. In the Community, such clarity is lacking. No one is unambiguously answerable for anything. The buck is never seen to stop: it is hidden from view in an endless scrimmage of consultation and bargaining. National parliaments are no more able to penetrate the confusion than is the European Parliament, and no more likely to acquire the ability to do so.

As the Common Agricultural Policy shows, opaque and unaccountable decision-making is singularly ill-adapted to the problems of resource allocation. Agricultural prices are fixed in a secret, and effectively unaccountable, cabal of agriculture ministers, all of them subject to intense pressure from their respective farm lobbies. Each knows that if prices are kept down, he will be blamed by his farmers. Each also knows that if prices are increased someone else will have to find the money to pay for the consequent surpluses; and that, whereas the farmers' indignation with low prices will be particular and precisely focused, the consumers' indignation with high prices will be generalised and diffuse. From the point of view of the Community as a whole, it would be rational to lower farm prices so as to reduce the surpluses. From the point of view of each single agriculture minister it is rational to vote for higher prices so as to avoid rows with the farmers. The results are well known; and it is hard to resist the conclusion that in the absence of changes in the decision-making process, an enlargement of the Community Budget on MacDougall lines would produce similar results in other fields. Yet, as we have seen, an enlargement of the Community Budget on MacDougall lines is a prerequisite of monetary union. Somewhat different considerations apply to decisions on the money supply and the exchange rate, but – as I tried to suggest in my imaginary example of the likely relationship between the Greater Manchester Council and a committee of borough treasurers – they point to the same conclusion. At present, member governments are rightly blamed (or praised) for what happens to the money supply and the exchange rate. They would still be blamed or praised in a monetary union, unless it had an identifiable political authority which could be blamed or praised instead. But in a monetary union they would no longer be free to take decisions on these matters and would therefore have to take the blame for things which they had not done, or for failing to do things which they could not do. Since no one willingly puts himself in such a position for very long, the union would be unlikely to last.

The implication is clear. The founding fathers of the Community assumed that politics would follow economics. In fact, the reverse is the case. Economic union requires monetary union, but monetary union requires political union. And political union requires a different institutional structure, not merely when it has been achieved but as a condition of achieving it.

REFERENCES

Commission of the European Communities (1970), 'Report to the Council and the Commission on the Realisation by Stages of Economic and Monetary Union in the Community' (Werner Report), *Bulletin of the European Communities*, vol. 3, no. 11 (supplement).

Commission for the European Communities (1975), 'Report of the Study Group on Economic and Monetary Union, 1980' (Marjolin Report), *Bulletin of the European Communities*.

Commission for the European Communities (1977), 'Report of the Study Group on the Role of Public Finance in European Integration, April 1977' (MacDougal Report), *Bulletin of the European Communities*.

Coombes, D. (1970), *Politics and Bureaucracy in the European Community*, (London: George Allen and Unwin).

Fitzmaurice, J. (1976), 'National Parliaments and European Policy Making: the Case of Denmark', *Parliamentary Affairs*, vol. 29.

Hallstein, W. (1972), *Europe in the Making* (London: George Allen and Unwin).

House of Lords (1973), *Second Report by the Select Committee on Procedures for Scrutiny of Proposals for European Instruments* (Maybury–King Report) (London: HMSO).

House of Lords (1978), *Relations Between the United Kingdom Parliament and the European Parliament After Direct Elections* (44th Report of the Select Committee on the European Communities) (London: HMSO).

Jenkins, R. (1978a), 'European Monetary Union', *Lloyds Bank Review*, no. 127. (The text of the Jean Monnet Lecture delivered at the European Institute, Florence, on 27 October 1977.)

Jenkins, R. (1978b), Speech to the European Parliament, Official Journal of the European Communities, *Debates of the European Parliament*, no. 225.

Marquand, D. (1979), *Parliament for Europe* (London: Jonathan Cape).

12 European–American Relations: the Political Context

WILLIAM WALLACE

A united Europe is likely to insist on a specifically European view of world affairs – which is another way of saying that it will challenge American hegemony in Atlantic policy. This may well be a price worth paying for European unity; but American policy has suffered from an unwillingness to recognise that there is a price to be paid.

(Henry Kissinger, 1965, p. 40)

Monetary policy – as some within the British Government are again discovering – does not exist in isolation. It interacts with a wide range of other areas of policy: economic, industrial, commercial, foreign policy. So it is with monetary co-operation. The relationship between the dollar and the major European currencies may rest in the first instance on the technical expertise of central banks, consulting and co-operating closely with each other within a tight and relatively closed network. But the context within which those central bankers operate is shaped by much wider economic, political and security factors.

John Connally, justifying the brutal manner in which the suspension of dollar convertibility in August 1971 was presented to European governments, called in aid the disproportionate share of European defence provided by the US, and the reluctance of European governments to assume a larger share; and he took the decision in the midst of a sharp dispute over transatlantic trade, over textiles, agriculture, shoes, chemicals and so on, with the threat of a protectionist bill in Congress at his back. The impetus which carried the EMS from proposal to operation was partly provided by German and French misgivings about the quality and consistency of American foreign policy, of which their

248

dislike of the Federal Reserve's dollar policy was only a part: disagreements over both civil and military nuclear matters and over the way in which the US Administration presented its initiatives to its partners, hesitations over the handling of SALT, concern about the capability of the American political élite to understand and respond to European interests, all influenced the atmosphere in which the decision was taken (Statler, 1981; Ludlow, 1981).

This chapter, therefore, aims to discuss the atmosphere of Atlantic relations, as seen in 1980, to allow the reader to draw his own conclusions on how this may affect the future evolution of the EMS. 'Atmosphere' is a very elusive concept in international relations – but important none the less. Those in Britain who, for example, dismiss current tensions in German – American relations as 'just atmospherics' fail to consider the interrelationship between the management of specific issues – or, the reconciliation of distinctive interests – and the predispositions of those who manage them, towards agreement or disagreement, towards accepting or distrusting the goodwill of the other party and their ability to carry through whatever agreement is reached. When the atmosphere is good, disagreements over particular issues are more easily handled; conversely, when suspicion, mistrust, irritation or incomprehension lie in the background, such disagreements are likely to prove far more intractable, and the risk that specific disagreements will escalate into confrontation will be far higher.

The overall atmosphere of transatlantic relations will of course be affected, in its turn, by the divergence or convergence of interests among the major governments, and by the wide or narrow spread of issues over which differences emerge. Its deterioration or improvement over time will also reflect not only the amount of attention paid by the major actors to understanding each other and to maintaining and promoting good relations, but also the effectiveness or ineffectiveness of the mechanisms through which they consult and bargain.

In what follows, the discussion therefore moves from the contextual factors which shape the atmosphere of Atlantic relations, through the range of interests which have to be managed, to the mechanisms through which the US and its European partners attempt to manage them. Two preliminary remarks should however be added. First, the Atlantic relationship has become more complicated to handle over the past twenty years not only because the range of issues in play among governments has steadily widened – to include, for example, foreign investment on both sides of the Atlantic, the balance of transatlantic trade in armaments, and the intricacies of the nuclear fuel cycle – but also because its boundaries have become less easy to define. On many issues Japan is a necessary participant in discussions, if agreement is to be reached: a point more clearly grasped by the American government, for obvious reasons, than by most European governments. On some issues the major oil-producers must be regarded as fringe participants; on others the most dynamic of the newly industrialising countries.

Second, the unavoidable shorthand term 'Europe' thinly disguises significant differences of opinion and outlook among the major European governments, most of all between Britain and the close partnership of France and Federal Germany. The more 'Atlanticist' assumptions of Labour ministers and senior civil servants – which is to say, their greater willingness to put a favourable interpretation on American actions and to listen sympathetically to American requests – were not uninfluential in disposing them not to join with the French and German governments in developing the EMS and putting it into operation. The change of government in 1979 did little to alter this; and developments since then – in particular the divergence between Britain and its continental partners over the implications of the Afghan invasion for détente, and the misunderstandings and mistrust which built up over East – West relations in the early months of 1980, as well as over the negotiations on the Community budget – have reinforced this divergence. Throughout what follows, the relative incoherence of the European response, and the central divide between the British response and that of France and Germany, must therefore be borne in mind.

THE DECLINE OF THE ATLANTIC COMMUNITY

The intensity of the Atlantic relationship at its strongest, in the 1950s, reflected a number of interrelated factors. First, there was no reason to question the US leadership, given its pre-eminent economic and military power, nor the depth of its commitment to Europe, given its evident centrality in the global power balance and the strategic invulnerability of the US. Second, American foreign policy was – and for many years remained – the province of an East Coast élite, who had been 'Europe-firsters' during the Second World War, most of whom had spent time in Europe before the war or during it, had worked closely during the war with European allies or had been involved in the reconstruction of European democracy and the European economy in its aftermath. Third, the post-war European élites accepted American leadership the more readily because of their acceptance of the benevolent influence of

American policy both during the war and in the effort to rebuild the European economy in its aftermath; some of them – such as Adenauer – had reached their positions under American tutelage, others – such as Monnet – had worked closely with American officials during the war. Fourth, the European–American relationship was without question the central factor in re-establishing a stable world. All those within the Atlantic community accepted the reality and the severity of the Soviet threat. China was part of the Soviet camp, Japan an American protectorate, the Third World with only a few exceptions an appendage of the Atlantic powers. The psychological hold which the concept of an Atlantic community established is described by Louis Halle (1967) as extending beyond the political to the social and even the scientific: he notes that American ornithologists reclassified some species of American bird in the light of their 'discovery' that species previously thought specific to North America were closely related to their cousins in Europe.

Of course, the transatlantic relationship had never been easy. There have been recurrent crises, threats of 'agonising reappraisal', demands for definition and redefinition of the Atlantic relationship and of the European identity within it, European complaints at American dominance and American complaints at European reluctance to share the burdens of power, from the early 1950s to the present day. The French Assembly's rejection of the European Defence Community treaty, in August 1954, provoked John Foster Dulles to threaten a reappraisal of the US 'foreign policies, particularly those in relation to Europe' (Fursdon, 1980, p. 304). The independent action of France and Britain in their Suez intervention of 1956, and the American refusal to support them, marked an acute crisis in Atlantic relations. The Kennedy Administration's complicated scheme for a 'Multilateral Force' (MLF) equipped with nuclear weapons, jointly manned and jointly controlled, created tensions between and within national governments as sharp as those created by the Carter Administration's proposals for the control of trade in nuclear fuels, fifteen years later. Until the mid-1960s, however, these tensions were contained by the general acceptance, on both sides of the Atlantic, of the unavoidable reality of American predominance and American leadership, both in containing the Soviet threat and in managing the international economy. They were further limited by the existence of an underlying commitment, again on both sides of the Atlantic, to the preservation and strengthening of the political, economic and personal links which had been forged during and after the Second World War.

Looking back, one can trace the decline of the Atlantic community as an underlying assumption in transatlantic relations from the end of the 1950s, when a number of developments began to undermine the coincidence of interests and attitudes on which it rested: the loss of American strategic invulnerability, complicating the American gurantee to defend Western Europe at all costs, the relaxation of the Cold War and the emergence of distinct European and American perceptions of East–West relations, the unavoidable conflict of interests and priorities which followed from the revival of European economies, and the gradual emergence of the Third World as a focus for collaboration and competition. But – with the exception of President de Gaulle's explicit challenge – the atmosphere remained positive for much of the 1960s; indeed, the influence of the Atlanticists within successive German governments severely limited the effects of the Gaullist challenge. The underlying assumptions of the Kennedy Administration's 'Atlantic Partnership' proposals of 1962, themselves an attempt to redefine the basis of the Atlantic community under the benevolent leadership of the US, were shared by all the major governments in Europe except the French.

The divergence of interests, which became steadily more evident during the 1960s, will be dealt with further below: the growth of European fears about American technological hegemony and multinational penetration, the hesitations over the European defence guarantee, the gradual build-up of American demands for a more equal share in the burdens of world power. The change in the underlying atmosphere was a parallel development, perhaps only dimly understood at the time. The American preoccupation with Vietnam, from 1964–5 onwards, was a not insignificant factor, both in focussing American attention away from Europe and in bringing home to European élites the difference between their perception of world priorities and those of their American allies. The European allies had accepted – and in some cases shared – America's responsibilities in the Korean War, because they shared the American analysis of that war: as a test of Western willingness to resist Soviet expansion, the lessons of which would be applied in the central European theatre. As its involvement in Vietnam deepened, so the American administration put increasing pressure on the European allies for support – finding instead a widespread scepticism, and an unwillingness to take on additional burdens of European defence to relieve the pressure on American forces and equipment. But the shift in the US away from an Atlantic towards a Pacific perspective, a long-term trend which has continued through and after the involvement in Vietnam, reflects many other developments. In 1968 America's transpacific trade exceeded its transatlantic trade for the first time; the importance, and the visibility, of Japan, Korea, Taiwan and potentially China as America's economic partners and competitors has grown rapidly since then. The population – and the industrial base – of the US has been shifting steadily south and west for many years, to a point where California has replaced New York as the largest state and where the 'sunshine states', from South Carolina through Texas to southern California, represent the most dynamic elements in the American economy. This reorientation towards the Pacific is to some extent counterbalanced by an increasing preoccupation with America's neighbours, as sources of instability, of immigrants and of resources. In several American states, and many American cities, the Hispanic vote is now an important factor, and Spanish the established second language.

It is therefore hardly surprising that the influence of the north-eastern élite over American foreign policy should have declined. The generation which dominated American foreign policy for the twenty years after the Second World War has of course retired; though there remain in Boston, New York and Washington many still of like mind who feel an instinctive attachment to the link with Europe and who maintain an extensive network of transatlantic contacts. But their influence in Congress and on the Administration is counterbalanced by southerners and westerners who bring their own perceptions of foreign policy priorities with them. The choice of President in November 1980, after all, lay between a southerner and a Californian, neither of them renowned for their understanding of the Atlantic relationship.

In parallel with this, European studies (and studies of the northern European languages) have precipitately declined in American schools and universities since the early 1960s. The flood of academic research on European–Atlantic relations, on the European Community, and on comparative European politics which marked the 1950s and early 1960s has declined to a trickle. Coverage of European news and developments in the American press and on American television has declined in parallel.

It is not only that the major American foundations and the government itself have moved away from their former preoccupation with Europe towards a concentration on Asia, the Middle East and the Third World; it is also that the US has been distracted from foreign policy as such by the need to adjust simultaneously to the loss of global predominance and of plentiful energy, to recession, unemployment, inflation and – as those who travel abroad are acutely aware – a shrunken dollar. The strains which these adjustments exert on American politics and society are compounded by the crisis of the US political institutions – the sharp decline in the authority and prestige of the Presidency, the resurgence of Congressional initiative, the heightened suspicion of executive activity, which followed from the Vietnam experience and from Watergate. The sense of grievance in the US over the failings of the European allies, the sense of heightened insecurity over the perceived decline in American strength *vis-à-vis* the USSR, are of course to an extent justified and rational; but their depth and occasional virulence reflect in addition domestic uncertainties. Henry Kissinger notes in his Memoirs (1979, p. 382) that the Nixon Administration came into office with the illusion that problems in the Alliance were due to uncertain American leadership, and that a reassertion of America's traditional role would restore health and harmony to the relationship. Governor Reagan and Congressman Anderson have echoed the same theme, accusing the Carter Administration – not without some justification – of uncertainty and incoherence in handling relations with the US's main allies, and calling for the assertion of more positive leadership. But their language does not display any recognition of the changed balance of the Atlantic relationship, in which the Europeans need to be treated as equal partners rather than loyal subordinates. The democratic openness of the American political system does not help in this regard. With the exception of Henry Kissinger, there have been very few within the last two Administrations – and fewer still in recent Congresses – who have any knowledge of the history of transatlantic relations with which a good many of their European counterparts are familiar. At a recent German – American conference in Bonn, Chancellor Schmidt demolished an American congressman who criticised the European reluctance to accept American leadership on matters of theatre nuclear weapons and arms control by referring to the MLF proposals of 1962 –4, about which he had been lobbied hard by a previous generation of enthusiastic American officials.

On the European side – particularly in Germany, the most influential Community member for many purposes – the atmosphere has changed as well. The generation which came to influence under American tutelage, and accepted the American view of the world, has also passed on. Emotional ties to the Atlantic relationship are weaker, except among the British élite. The rediscovery of Eastern Europe has made the Atlantic relationship appear less exclusive and less central, even as its central importance to the security of Western Europe is reasserted. The experience of détente, in the decade since the Soviet–German Treaty of 1970, has been sharply divergent. For most Americans the effort to pursue more open and more intense relations with the USSR and Eastern Europe has been an evident failure, masking the steady build-up of Soviet weaponry and the extension of Soviet power into the Middle East and Africa. For most Europeans – and above all for the Germans – it has brought evident political, economic and human benefits, in spite of all the disappointments: re-establishing links between Eastern and Western Europe, changing attitudes and expectations in Eastern Europe as in the West. The realisation of how different perceptions and interests are between the two sides of the Atlantic over a wide range of issues has clearly affected assumptions about the nature of the Atlantic relationship.

The European view of the world is unavoidably different from that of the US, now that the simple divisions of the Cold War have disappeared. Kissinger's assertion that the US was a global power and the Europeans purely regional was in many ways accurate; again with the partial exception of Britain, the European countries have been reluctant either to view world politics in terms of global strategy or to assume the responsibility of contributing to global security and the management of the global economy which the US would wish them to share. But the differences between the two sides of the Atlantic also reflect the unavoidable differences of their geographical positions, which force the US to be more interested in the Far East and in the Caribbean, and which dispose the Europeans far more towards Eastern Europe and the Mediterranean.

The basis for Atlantic co-operation is thus a good deal less secure than it was twenty years ago. Disputes can still be managed, interests reconciled. The foundations for such reconciliation, in mutual trust and understanding, in an underlying sense of common purpose and shared community, are however a good deal weaker than they were. It is a sign of the times that senior officials within the German Government have recently been discussing a number of proposals to raise the level of European studies in the US and the degree of attention paid to European attitudes and concerns in the American media.

EUROPEAN AND AMERICAN INTERESTS

It was always something of an illusion that European and American interests were ultimately reconcilable. The reality, from the outset, was that in a large number of fields the US and Western Europe shared some interests and diverged on others. In the international monetary system, the US and the major European governments and central banks share a common concern with the stability of the international monetary system and the management of crisis. But they differ over the way in which that system should be managed, the interaction between domestic economic and monetary policy and international developments, and in the precise policy priorities – and implicit national advantages – which international co-operation should promote. Similarly with most other fields of interaction, it is possible for reasonable observers to argue either that common interests are overriding or that the differences are more important than the shared concerns; a great deal depends upon the assumptions within which a particular negotiation is approached, the presence or absence of a willingness to seek agreement and to sink differences.

Two particular developments have affected the perception of common and divergent interests on either side of the Atlantic: the widening spread of issues in play, and the gradual shift in the balance of influence and economic weight. In the security field the management of détente and the pursuit of arms control was bound to prove more difficult than the maintenance of containment, as the alliance shifted from standing firmly together to attempting to synchronise its forward movement. The recovery of the European armaments industry, reinforced by European concern over support for high technology, have cut across American concern with promoting exports to make military procurement and the 'two-way street' important issues under continuing negotiation across the Atlantic. The dispersal of security concerns from Europe to the Far East, to the Middle East and Africa, have widened the need for consultation among the allies and increased the scope for differences in interpretation. The continuing imbalance between the American strategic guarantee and its conventional commitment to Europe and the European contribution to global security is a source of repeated controversy within the alliance.

In the economic field the onset of international recession has heightened traditional tensions over industrial and agricultural trade, over the 'fairness' of the rules for trade among the advanced industrial countries, and over the interaction between Atlantic trade and the economic influence of other regions and countries – most of all of Japan. The shift in the balance of economic weight has brought controversy over foreign investment across the Atlantic from Europe to the US. The international reach of American domestic economic regulations, acceptable when the American economy was predominant, is far less acceptable to America's partners when it appears as an attempt to regain advantages which have been lost in the international market. Differences of interest, and differences of perception, in the energy field reflect the speed at which the US has grown into a substantial importer, competing with Europeans for scarce supplies of oil to support a far higher level of consumption. American insistence on the strategic importance of the Straits of Hormuz has emphasised, in bringing pressure to bear on the European allies, that it is Europe's resource life-lines which the Americans are defending; Europeans have responded by noting that the US is now a larger importer of Gulf oil than any single European country.

THE MANAGEMENT OF ATLANTIC RELATIONS

The central problem of managing the unavoidable tensions of Atlantic relations in recent years is that both sides have had justifiable grounds for criticising each other, but have been unwilling to admit the real difficulties their own failings cause their partners. It has been easy for American officials, from the Johnson Administration onwards, to decry the incoherence of European diplomacy: the impossibility of achieving a co-ordinated response to American initiatives, the unwillingness to take initiatives of their own rather than to indulge in the luxury of criticising American proposals, the underlying ambivalence about bilateral relations with the US as compared with a concerted Atlantic dialogue. It is as easy for European critics to point in return to the many-headed structure of American diplomacy, the repeated failure to consult before demands for European co-operation are made, the geopolitical over-simplifications of White House strategists, the easy confusion of American economic interests with those of the international economic order, the rapid twists and turns of American intellectual fashion and domestic politics, the complications which American legislation and litigation make for American foreign policy. The decline in understanding of the domestic constraints under which other governments operate has contributed to an atmosphere of impatience and irritation.

A great deal of useful technical co-operation is conducted among the major Atlantic governments through bilateral channels, through the structures of the OECD and NATO, and through such wider inter-national forums as the IMF. This framework of intergovernmental organisations has its inadequacies and inconsistencies, but by and large it still serves the major governments well. At the political level, the increase in multilateral consultation has had more questionable benefits. Robert Schaetzel and Herald Malmgren (1980) argue that Atlantic summitry has damaged international co-operation, and that the partial replacement of regular and extensive consultation among experts by personalised and public meetings of political leaders has complicated the task of co-operation and on occasion threatened mutual understanding. The illusion that personal contact can resolve complex problems and bring together the attitudes of politicians whose international experience and whose understanding of each other's domestic contexts is limited is appealing – but it remains an illusion. For politicians with long experience of international negotiations and long acquaintance with their partners – such as Schmidt and Giscard d'Estaing, or Denis Healey – such meetings can be a useful addition to the more regular channels of intergovernmental co-operation; for politicians without much international experience or contacts, the possibilities for misunderstanding are large.

There is always a certain tendency for responses to crises in relationships to be posed in institutional terms. Thus in 1973 the US proposed a redefinition of the Atlantic relationship and a closer American link with the framework of European Political Co-operation (Wallace and Allen, 1977). The Japanese response to American pressure over Iran and Afghanistan, interestingly enough, was similarly to request a closer relationship with the machinery of European Political Co-operation. Since the interconnected crises of 1973–4 the machinery of transatlantic co-operation has been extended in a number of respects: most notably in the institutionalisation of Atlantic summitry, less publicly in closer collaboration among finance ministers and senior finance officials. By and large, the established machinery for co-operation works well, drawing up agendas, preparing for summits, exchanging information, discussing common concerns; the problems arise from the preoccupations and preconceptions of those who are involved in it, most of all at the political level, and the divergent domestic contexts within which they all operate.

CONCLUSIONS

Where does this leave consideration of the American factor in the further development of the EMS? Clearly, if the system is to move forward, a more defined dollar policy – a common attitude towards the relationship between the dollar and the EMS currencies, expressed when necessary in co-ordinated activities in the exchange markets – must be a priority. This chapter argues that the context within which that policy will be defined is likely to be one in which the willingness to subordinate immediate European interests to American concerns, to listen sympathetically to American representations, will be low. Whatever the hopes of the Reagan administration, however frequently expressed its determination to revitalise the Atlantic relationship, probable developments in Eastern Europe, continuing uncertainties in the Middle East, the predictable strains on European–American relations which will follow from the negotiations on the admission of Spain, are likely to divide Europeans and Americans and to maintain the potential for misunderstanding.

How coherent the Europeans will prove to be, as these disputes develop, is hard to predict. The closeness of the Franco-German relationship disguises differences in their underlying attitudes both to the US and the USSR, and disguises further contradictions and ambivalence within both governments which the aftermath of the Afghanistan invasion, the unresolved crisis in Poland, and the uncertainties in the Persian Gulf have only worsened. Within the British Government, the contradictions are more acute. In a number of industrial and economic matters, British industry and trade unions now see their interests closely aligned with those of their European partners in resisting American competition and lobbying American policy-makers – in steel, in textiles and in chemicals, for example. In their perception of the evolution of East–West relations, British ministers and officials inclined for most of 1980 rather more towards the American position than towards that of their continental partners. The temporary settlement of the budget dispute in the summer of 1980 removed the most immediate sense of grievance between Britain and its Community partners; but ministers remain aware that they are operating within a climate of domestic hostility towards the European Community which is largely absent in Britain's dealings with the US. The decision on whether or not to associate sterling more closely with the EMS will be taken explicitly on economic grounds; but the balance of opinion within the Cabinet, and the reception given to such a decision outside, will be very much influenced by the wider context of British perceptions of its Atlantic and European ties. The future of EMS itself, in turn, will depend in part on how far the participating governments – and above all the French and German Governments – see the need for closer European collaboration in the face of transatlantic misunderstanding and mistrust, and feel that need sufficiently strongly to make the further sacrifices of economic sovereignty necessary to build an effective European currency system.

REFERENCES

Fursdon, E. (1980), *The European Defence Community: a History* (London: Macmillan).

Halle, L. J. (1967), *The Cold War as History* (London: Chatto & Windus).

Kissinger, H. (1965), *The Troubled Partnership: a Reappraisal of the Atlantic Alliance* (New York: McGraw-Hill).

Kissinger, H. (1979), *The White House Years* (London: Weidenfeld & Nicolson).

Ludlow, P. (1981, forthcoming), *The Making of the European Monetary System* (London: Butterworth).

Schaetzel, R. and H. Malmgren (1980), 'Talking heads', *Foreign Policy*, pp. 130–42.

Statler, J. (1981), 'EMS: Cul-de-sac or Signpost on the Road to EMU?', in M. Hodges and W. Wallace (eds), *Economic Divergence in the European Community* (London: George Allen & Unwin).

Wallace, W. and D. Allen (1977), 'Political Co-operation: Procedure as Substitute for Policy', in H. Wallace, W. Wallace and C. Webb (eds), *Policy-Making in the European Communities* (London: John Wiley).

Comments on Marquand and Wallace

MICHAEL STEED

I respond to the chapters by David Marquand and William Wallace as a student of politics and particularly of the phenomenon of supranational integration. I will also be making one remark as a participant in the political process later on.

Most of my points relate more to Marquand's Chapter rather than Wallace's because it is in Western Europe, rather than across the Atlantic, that integration has taken place. Wallace analyses an important context for what has occurred and may develop in our continent; my relative neglect of his contribution is simply a mark of how fully he has done this; however, I would like to add a couple of footnote points to his paper.

I fully agree with his emphasis on the importance of atmosphere in transatlantic relations, something that social scientists are liable to neglect because of its lack of measurability. It is useful to apply the same concept to the political implications of a European Monetary Union. Atmosphere is compounded of the differing climates of national public opinion, including their perceptions of national interests, their varying attitudes towards inflation, unemployment and economic growth and their markedly different understandings of the point of European unification, with the outlooks and personal experiences of national and supranational political leaders. The interplay of objectively definable national interest and of the European Community's political structure probably tell us most of how decisions have been and will be taken. But I would have to add atmosphere to explain, for example, Italy's last minute decision to join EMS in December 1978.

Next, I am struck by Wallace's emphasis on the personal background, especially geographical, of the US's political leaders, and find an interesting comparison with Europe. The European Community's leaders may indeed be a more integrated team than those of the US. Constant participation in the Council of Ministers means that the majority of heads of government, when they meet in the European Council, have a considerable experience of working transnationally. With all the mechanisms of rotating chairmanships, recruitment of the Commission President from amongst leading national politicians and the growth of summitry cutting across treaty-based bodies, may the Community be developing a simple concept out of an institutional morass – that of a collective leadership, nationally and geographically balanced and continuously changing? The US, on the other hand, can see the arrival in Washington of a state governor, backed by a team of personal supporters from his state, grappling with complex machinery of government and the task of becoming a national leader. Which will prove the more integrated, and better trained, form of leadership?

Turning to the political implications of monetary integration in Europe, I would like to throw five points into the discussion. First, let us not underestimate the importance of money for political authority. Marquand has fully demonstrated the practical importance of the relationship between monetary and political union. But it is not just practical; it is immensely symbolic. Not for nothing, throughout the ages, have monarchs, the symbols of sovereignty, had their heads on coins. Next only to the monopoly control of the use of coercion, the right to control the issue of money comes closest to the essence of national sovereignty. I would take further Marquand's conclusion that monetary union requires political union. It points to a form of political authority that is recognised as fulfilling the role to the national governments that the London Government does now to the Greater Manchester Council. I do not see, incidentally, the European Parliament as currently set up easily performing this role – whatever the impetus it may give to integration elsewhere.

Second, I would like to challenge the concepts of the toboggan ride to which Marquand refers, or the long-jump metaphor of Roy Jenkins, which Peeters quoted. They are both fundamentally misleading. Both imply that, once movement is under way, its direction is determined – by the slope of the mountainside, or the compass point to which the athlete starts running. The athlete may stumble and the toboggan overturn; or each may proceed successfully. But the outcome is posed as simply further progress, or getting stuck. Such imagery, developed naturally from the functionalist or spill-over school of thinking, does not reflect reality.

Spill-back, or the reversal of already achieved integration, has to be recognised as another outcome to spill-over. The achievement of integration in sector A may promote pressures for integration in sector B. But if integration in sector B is in fact inherently more difficult, the outcome may be that failure in sector B undermines what has happened in sector A. In 1969, when Pompidou's devaluation of the franc upset assumptions that the Common Agricultural Policy had virtually brought about immutably-fixed exchange rates, it was not just that the process from agricultural to monetary integration was halted. Encumbered by monetary compensation accounts and funny green money, the CAP has ever since been wounded and on the defensive.

We have a degree of economic integration. That requires monetary integration, and most political scientists would agree that monetary union requires political union. That does not mean we are on a journey, by toboggan or running feet, from the economic to the monetary and so to the political. We may be seriously endangering the economic by the necessary fact of trying to move forward.

Third, there are yet more sectors involved. The movement is not just stay-put, forward or backward. It is multi-directional. MacDougallism, or the integration at Community level of resource allocation between richer and poorer regions has been aired, and is covered by Marquand. I would have given it more emphasis since free flow of capital presents such a threat to the development of so many peripheral regions and the present budgetary flows of the Community are, perversely, working to worsen the disparities within it. Then we have enlargement – as far as Greece at any rate is concerned – now determined. We are, I believe, moving towards a crisis in which the attempt to integrate three more peripheral, poor, agricultural countries and the requirements of monetary union in the political and regional resource allocation spheres will cumulatively put overwhelming pressures on the present system. Integration has to spill over in several directions at about the same time, or it will spill back. Or, to use another metaphor, we are busily overloading the present fragile and cumbersome Community structure. It has to be strenghtened or it may break and even collapse totally.

That brings me to my fourth point. There is an impression given, whenever one describes a system as it is currently functioning, that one is looking at some sort of stability. In fact it is often more like the camera freezing artificially a fleeting moment. I do not think either necessarily intends to, but both Marquand and Wallace imply this. Wallace looks back to a high point of close Atlantic relations, in the 1950s. In fact, this period contained the seeds of decline whilst it was still approaching its zenith – evident not just in the 1956 Anglo-French attack on Egypt, but also the fundamental disagreement over policy towards China from 1949. Similarly, the political system of the European Community has been in constant change and under challenge; what Marquand well describes as a baffling amalgam of the national and the supranational is in no way a stable state of play. He rightly points to the problems of accountability quite independent of the probable inability to cope with the strains which monetary union would generate. I think there are others. To continue the play with metaphors, perhaps we are in the exploratory voyage of a Wellsian 'Time Machine'. We may go forward or back, and at various speeds; we might go sideways into a time-warp (we do not know whether they exist), or the machine may explode. Monetary union is a button on the control board.

Finally, that metaphor overplays the problem of unpredictability. Machine-design may be critical and the performance of a design can be tested and assessed. An important part of monetary union must be the form and extent of automaticity, and here both political scientists and politicians need to be informed by economists. My own personal experience may suffice as illustration.

In the European election manifesto of the European Liberals and Democrats in 1979, there was a detailed proposal for monetary integration in the form of the development of a parallel currency rather than the locking together of exchange rates. I was the British member of the working party which put this forward. It came from the Italian member (a former Minister of Finance), based on the All Saints' Day Manifesto. We discussed it, as politicians, and I was persuaded that the mix of automaticity and flexibility in this proposal was the best route to monetary integration. The proposal went through several stages – via consideration in member parties to final adoption at a Congress. It was never, as far as I know, queried, let alone amended.

Such can be the innocence and amateurism of politics, and such the inertia, that once something is in the first draft, it stays there. I do not know whether our detailed proposal was for the best. We have to look to the experts for the precise design, and in all the uncertainties of the looming crisis of over-load in the European Community System, it might even be that a smoothly working monetary union or a badly designed one would make the difference between success or failure for the whole system. For loss of a nail . . . the kingdom was lost. I hope that monetary integration can be well designed and constructed.

Author Index

Ahnefeld, A. 67
Allen, D. 258
Allen, P. R. 196–7, 213–15
Aliber, R. J. 186–7

Balassa, B. 213
Ball, R. J. 159
Baseri, G. M. 13, 36, 144
Bergh, P. van den 113–14
Bergsten, F. 148
Bilson, J. F. O. 193
Bloomfield, A. E. 131
Bockelman, H. 185
Bomhoff, J. 93
Bowie, R. R. 148
Brinner, R. 176
Burns, T. 159

Cairncross, A. 160
Claassen, E. M. 171–8
Coffey, P. 148
Commission of the European Communities (MacDougall Report) 219, 225–6, 233, 239–40
Commission of the European Communities (Marjolin Report) 232
Commission of the European Communities (Werner Report) 6–7, 35–6, 42, 130, 136–7, 232–6
Coombes, D. 235
Corden, W. M. 37, 170–8, 229, 231

Deutsche Bundesbank 50
Dornbusch, R. 184
Duck, N. W. 175

Eckstein, O. 176
El-Agraa, A. M. 229
Emminger, O. 169–70

Fellner, W. 39
Fitzmaurice, J. 245
Fratianni, M. 162
Fried, J. 148, 171–8, 181–2
Friedman, M. 152
Fursdon, E. 251

Genberg, H. 171
Goldstein, M. 185, 187
Gordon, R. J. 176, 185
Grauwe, P. de 93, 113–14, 126

Halle, L. J. 251
Hallstein, W. 240
Hamermesh, D. 176
Harrison, R. J. 34, 38
Hayek, F. A. 12
Heathcote, N. 34, 38
Heller, H. R. 93
Hub, H.-J. 67
Hutchison, T. W. 158

Ishiyama, Y. 195

Jenkins, R. 16, 18, 34–5, 40, 136, 232–5
Johnson, H. G. 169

Kenen, P. B. 196–7, 213–15
Khan, M. S. 93
Kissinger, H. 248, 254–5
Klein, B. 12, 38, 163, 176
Korteweg, P. 93
Krause, L. B. 148

Laidler, D. 36, 42, 93, 153–4, 159, 176, 237
Lamfalussy, A. 143
Lanyi, A. 185

Llewellyn, D. T. 147
Ludlow, P. 249

Malmgren, H. 258
Marquand, D. 38, 243
Marris, S. 69
McKinnon, R. I. 148
McMahon, C. 18, 174, 180
Meade, J. E. 2, 144
Meiselman, D. I. 170
Michaely, M. 184
Midland Bank 133
Mundell, R. A. 171–2, 197
Mussa, M. 186

Nobay, A. R. 154

O'Donoghue, M. 233
OECD 39, 47, 60–1
O'Mahoney, D. 38
Oort, C. J. 143
Oppenheimer, P. M. 2
Ormerod, P. 175

Parkin, J. M. 145, 175, 193
Peeters, T. 42, 93, 162
Presley, J. R. 148
Purvis, D. 155

Reading, B. 40
Robbins, L. 160
Rose, D. 175

Salant, W. S. 140, 147, 171, 176
Schaetzel, R. 258
Scitovsky, T. 2
Statler, J. 249
Sumner, M. T. 153, 176

Thomas, R. L. 176
Thygesen, N. 60
Tower, E. 195
Trezise, P. H. 148
Tsoukalis, L. 1–2, 5
Turnovsky, S. J. 175

Vanderkamp, J. 175
Vaubel, R. 8, 34–8, 41–3, 53, 92–4,
   142, 144, 146, 163, 183, 188, 213

Wallace, W. 258
Walter, N. 42, 193
Willett, T. D. 170, 195
Williamson, J. 131

Zis, G. 38, 161, 175